Advance Praise for *My Sister, My Self*

Tender, touching, funny, painful and poetic . . . Vikki Stark's study of sibling relationships will take you to new depths of understanding of yourself, your sister, and the myriad ways you shaped each others' lives. Best of all, you'll find a wealth of workable suggestions for getting past old, hurtful, self-defeating patterns to a healthier, happier relationship with the one woman who shares your genes and your history.

—Adele Faber, coauthor of *Siblings Without Rivalry*

My Sister, My Self is a must-read for anyone who wants to understand the vital role that sisters play in developing and influencing each other's lives. It's an important addition to the growing body of "sister" literature as well as a valuable handbook for women trying to navigate this deep and complex relationship.

—Carol Saline, coauthor of *Sisters*

A warm and practical discussion of the sisterly relationship that—perhaps because it is between woman and woman—has never been given the attention it deserves. A scrupulous work that will be useful to a great many women.

—Nuala O'Faolain, author of *Are You Somebody?*

My Sister, My Self captures the sister bond in all of its intensity and dimensions: the delight, the need, the love, the resentments, and the deep, abiding comfort. If you are a sister, you will find yourself—and your sister—in this intimate and revealing book.

—Marian Sandmaier, author of *Original Kin*

Stark covers sisterhood in all of its glory. By the end of the book, I longed to have had a sister. While examining this wondrous bond, she also explores your birth order role you had with your sister and how it affects you today. An excellent writer, Stark is also a seasoned therapist who knows that all is not rosy in the sisterhood. She explores the 10 percent of sister relationships that are thorny. She wisely offers some techniques, not for fixing the relationship but for resolving your feelings about it.

—Cathy McClure Gildiner, psychologist and author of
Too Close to the Falls and *Seduction*

My
Sister,
My Self

Understanding the Sibling Relationship
That Shapes Our Lives, Our Loves, and Ourselves

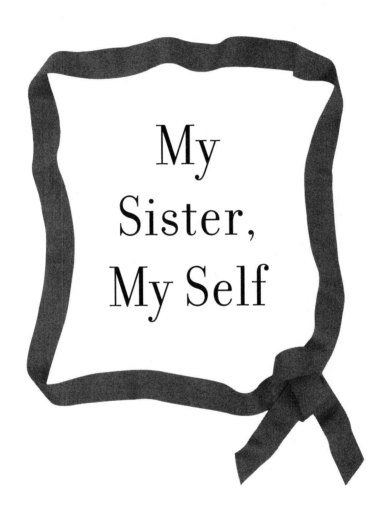

My Sister, My Self

VIKKI STARK

New York Chicago San Francisco Lisbon London Madrid Mexico City
Milan New Delhi San Juan Seoul Singapore Sydney Toronto

Library of Congress Cataloging-in-Publication Data

Stark, Vikki.
    My sister, my self : understanding the sibling relationship that shapes our lives, our loves, and ourselves / by Vikki Stark.
        p.   cm.
    Includes bibliographical references.
    ISBN 0-07-147879-5
    1. Sisters.   2. Sisters Project.   I. Sisters Project.   II. Title.

    BF723.S43S73   2006
    306.875'4—dc22   2006016648

1 2 3 4 5 6 7 8 9 10 11 12 13 14 15 16 17 18 19 20   FGR/FGR   0 9 8 7 6

ISBN-13: 978-0-07-147879-3
ISBN-10:   0-07-147879-5

McGraw-Hill books are available at special quantity discounts to use as premiums and sales promotions, or for use in corporate training programs. For more information, please write to the Director of Special Sales, Professional Publishing, McGraw-Hill, Two Penn Plaza, New York, NY 10121-2298. Or contact your local bookstore.

This book is printed on acid-free paper.

For Dan

Contents

Acknowledgments

This book is a tribute to the women, teens, and girls who opened their hearts to tell me their sister stories. One hundred sixty-five Sisters Project participants agreed to be interviewed face-to-face, welcoming me into their homes and offices or making the trek to mine. Two hundred thirty-five participated by e-mail or mail, taking the time and thought required to complete a detailed questionnaire and send it to me, a perfect stranger, somewhere in cyberspace. The existence of this book is thanks to all of you.

I am deeply grateful to my friends, Andrea McElhone, Sandra Grossman (whose glint in her eye when she talked about her sisters tipped me off, early on, that I was onto something), Nili Baider, Catherine Mauger, C. K. Williams, Chantal Sarrazin, Ole Gjerstad, Eddy Goldman, Mary Mason, Jon Kalina, Fabie Duhamel, Jay Schaefer, Ida Cook, Lillian Wachtel, and Eileen Ramos (who came up with the first five names of women to interview). Jeanette Limondjian, my partner in crime when we were teens, guided me throughout with enthusiasm and savvy. These friends and others buoyed me up with their suggestions and encouragement. My research assistant, Anne-Marie D'Aoust, contributed her meticulous attention along with her *joie de vivre*. My aunt, Sarah Ullman, and cousins, Andrea Gruber and Karen Katz, cheered me on from the sidelines. My mother-in-law and sister-in-law in South Africa, Audrey O'Meara and Maureen O'Meara, who also provided names of their friends for The Sisters Project, were always ready to give me a boost from afar.

I appreciate the interest and support of my colleagues at the Argyle Institute of Human Relations in Montreal, some of whom were interviewed about their insights on sisters gleaned from their professional lives, others of whom shared their personal stories.

Warmest thanks go to my agent, Chris Tomasino, who believed in this book from day one and worked diligently to get it launched, and to Judith McCarthy, my editor, who was committed to making sure that, once launched, the book would fly. Thank you also to Deborah Brody, my pinch-hit editor.

If it takes a village to raise a child, then it takes a family to write a book, particularly when the book is about family; I could never have enjoyed the process to the extent that I did without the patience and unwavering support of my own. I was always aware that my stepdaughter, Keri O'Meara, although out of town, was rooting for me. My daughters, Lauren Goldman and Michele Goldman, were remarkably cheerful about putting up with three years of endless conversations about sisters. Both were on call to help me think things through, contributing keen observations and advice, which I always took to heart. A special *merci* to Michele for her help with some of the grunt work—transcribing tapes, manning the printer, and endlessly photographing me for my author photo. My husband, Dan O'Meara, the world's best in-house editor, struck the perfect balance between being deeply involved and convincingly certain that I could produce this book and that it would be of value. Thank you for being the kind of man whose eyes can fill with tears reading sister stories.

Finally, a word of thanks goes to my sister, Nikki Stark, who wanted this book to be written and gave me carte blanche to speak my version of the truth about us.

Introduction

The Sisters Project

The Sisters Project started quite unexpectedly. One evening, at a family dinner, my twenty-four-year-old younger daughter, Lauren, broke off a discussion about her friends with an exasperated sigh, "No matter whom I'm with, I always feel like a little sister." Her remark flicked on a 100-watt lightbulb in my mind: "Me, too! When I look in the mirror, I see 'little sister' written across my forehead; I always feel like a little sister, too!" I thought about all of the times when I've been in a room full of women younger than me, even in situations when I've been their teacher or supervisor; I usually still feel like the ingenue. Perhaps, like Lauren, my always feeling like "little Vikki" comes from my role as the younger sister. I started devoting some serious thought to the issue.

My growing awareness of the importance of a sister's influence didn't come completely out of the blue. In the twenty years that I have been working as a family therapist, I have frequently been struck by the intensity of the sister bond. My clients have talked about their sisters with love, longing, sadness, guilt, and bitterness. As a therapist, I've explored this subject with them, often trying to help them come to terms with resentment or regret. Sometimes they were trying to sort out for themselves if "blood is thicker than water" and whether they should continue to fight for that sister connection when all it brings them is pain.

The conversation with Lauren at our dinner table suddenly made me able to see the proverbial "rhinoceros in the living room." If sister relationships were so important for my clients, for Lauren, and for me, they must play a major role in the development of identity for women in general. I mentioned this speculation to a friend and watched her eyes light up as she shared memories of her own childhood with her two younger sisters. I had never seen her so animated. I began to have some informal conversations with other friends about their sisters and was surprised when I saw that same intensity as they told their sister stories.

The next thing I knew, the phone started ringing. Having heard through word of mouth of my interest in sisters, women were calling, offering to be interviewed. The response was astounding! Pretty soon, I was doing eight or ten interviews a week. One woman told me that her sister in another city wanted to put her two cents in, so I drew up an e-mail questionnaire, posted notices on the Internet, and, within weeks, started receiving e-mail from other cities in the United States and Canada, as well as from Great Britain, Australia, India, the Middle East, and South Africa. The Sisters Project was off and running, and I was chasing after it, trying to keep up!

The Interviews

In *My Sister, My Self*, I'll be sharing with you what I learned from interviews and e-mail questionnaires contributed from hundreds of women, teens, and girls all over the world. The Sisters Project explored every aspect of the participants' relationships with their sisters, both as children and as adults. The youngest participant was four-year-old Kelly, who vividly, if briefly, described the different shades of being a sister: "I play with my sisters a lot and then I hit them . . . and then I hug them." The oldest women interviewed for the project were Heather and Anna—ninety-five-year-old identical twins! As well as explaining how your sister role imprinted your identity, we will hold the sister relationship up to the light and examine all of its facets. We will look at the special traits that come with being younger, older, middle, or twin; we will discover the hidden dynamics in conflicted, bonded, and caretaker relationships; and we will scrutinize the expectations society has for sisters in general.

The experience of interviewing participants for The Sisters Project was fascinating and often moving. Wishing to make the process as pleasant and convenient as possible, I visited most women in their homes, where I found that they opened not only their homes but their hearts to me. There was an excitement about the interviews—many women said how happy they were that someone was interested in hearing about a relationship that was so important to them. I drove all over the place and visited women in all stages of life, but the intensity with which the stories were told was everywhere the same.

I met with many women who had only one sister and learned about the dynamics of those duos. I also met with women who had several sisters—I visited the different homes of a set of five sisters, I interviewed six sisters on a native reserve, I received e-mail questionnaires from all seven sisters of a family who grew up in California, I interviewed three generations of sisters from the same family, and I heard from a seventy-six-year-old woman who is the youngest of ten sisters. I spoke to one older sister who said she still sees the younger ones as her children—even though the baby of the family is seventy-two! Whenever possible, I met with all of the sisters in each family, wanting to get the picture from all sides, but I would do the actual interviews separately so that each woman could be free to say what was really in her heart. With so many participants, I heard dozens of intriguing stories and learned about many different realities. I felt privileged that all of those women, teens, and girls let me into their lives, entrusting me with their sister stories and permitting me to share them with you.

Early on, I had a crucial decision to make about how I would handle women having brothers as well as sisters. I decided that, although brothers certainly are important in girls' lives, it is the sisters who usually have the most influence on their identity. Many women said that although they have a brother, it's not the same, and one even went so far as to quip that the closest brothers are more distant than the most distant sisters. Therefore, in the interest of simplicity, this book will exclude the contribution of brothers, although I hope to explore that topic at a later date.

My Magic Touch

It was a crystal clear winter day when I drove out to the Northeast Kingdom in Vermont to interview Sally. Her red brick house looked absolutely perfect, still festooned with garlands of fresh pine and gigantic red bows, even though it was already a month after Christmas. The house was situated on a hill in a grove of tall trees, and everything was covered in thick silent snow. The house smelled of baking, and I secretly hoped that it was for me (which it wasn't—Sally had made two chocolate cakes for a family party). We sat in her glassed-in breakfast room overlooking the back lawn and shared a pot of tea.

Sally reminisced about a time when she was a young teen and was skating with her older sister, Jeanette, in a pairs competition. They had taken their pose to begin their performance. The spotlight came on them . . . and Jeanette started giggling. Ditching the routine, she began skating in exuberant circles all over the ice. Completely bewildered, Sally raced to keep up, trying to make it look like it was planned. By the time the music stopped, the two sisters were laughing so hard that it didn't matter that they were disqualified. That memory was over fifty years old and, boy, Sally sure enjoyed telling it.

Doing interview after interview, I sometimes felt like I had a magic touch. I would sit with a woman listening to her story and by the end of it, she would say something like, "I realize I never tell my sister I love her. I'd better call her." *Bling!* I'd leave and something would change between that woman and her sister. Then I'd talk with someone else. *Bling!* She'd realize something just by talking about it and want to make some other change with her sister. I pictured myself with a magic wand like the fairy godmother from Cinderella, flitting around and blinging all of the women who participated in The Sisters Project so that, by the time the interview was over, something in them had changed. Shannon, who e-mailed her questionnaire from Wisconsin, wrote, "I realize from this study that I really don't know my sister and that saddens me. It also sets me into action and makes me want to get to know her."

Life with Sister

In the course of talking with participants in The Sisters Project, I collected stories, vignettes, and reflections about many different aspects of being a sister. Here are some general vignettes women related about the experience of having a sister.

Amanda, the oldest of four sisters, aged thirty-seven to forty-three, described what it was like to grow up in a family with a lot of girls: "We were very well known as the Fletcher girls. If I said my last name, someone would say, 'Oh, I know your sister, Carrie.' There were amazing dynamics. Everything was fun. Imagination was unlimited. We didn't need television. Crayons and clay would take you all day. Our dolls were real. 'Hide-n-go-seek' 'til late at night. We loved having a camera and taking crazy pictures. The best for me were the hand-me-downs. The hardest thing was getting married and moving out. I cried on my wedding night—my husband didn't know what to do with me. There was always someone to talk to. Always action."

Susan, thirty-one, told about the pleasure of having someone in her life who really knew her: "There are so many things that happen when you are a child—your school, your friendships, the basis of what you really are, and she knows all that. We'll often talk about something and I'll say, that's like such-n-such a thing. Our logic getting into it will be the same because of our experiences growing up. Or we'll laugh about whatever. We used to go on family vacations and my father could not get up early in the morning, so we'd leave in the middle of the afternoon and it drove us crazy. We'll laugh about that now. She knows my shorthand. There's always someone who will understand that part of you without you having to explain it. . . . There's always someone who can be there—it's unconditional—it's not about impressing or worrying about stepping on someone's toes. She's there."

Twenty-seven-year-old Charlene's story was about the hidden competition between sisters made visible: "We shared a bed for five years and a room for nine, so we had to get along or be miserable. One rainy Saturday, we were bickering all day and my mom was sick of it, so she took us to the backyard and gave us each a 'weapon' (I had a wooden spoon and my sister had a spatula) and told us, 'Fine, if you want to hurt each other, go ahead and get it over with. I'll watch!' Of course, we threw down our weapons and started crying and saying how much we loved each other and didn't want to hurt the other. We were hugging when my mom looked at us and said, 'Remember this!' And we always did. I have to say that it must have taken a great deal of trust on her part to know that we would react the way we did."

Audrey remembered how, fifty-two years ago, she yearned to be like her big sister: "When I was ten and my sister was twelve, our grandmother gave us two dolls that she had made clothes for; one was brunette like we were, and the other was blonde. My sister said I could choose which doll I wanted and she would take the other one. I agonized for days over which doll was the better one, which doll she would choose. Finally, I figured that maybe she would think the better doll was the brunette one, so I chose the brunette doll. Then my sister said, 'Good. I wanted the blonde one.'"

Nadine, thirty-eight, reflected on the comfort of sharing the experience of being a female: "Female intimacy is entrenched if you have sisters. It's like something that you recognize immediately; you move toward it unconsciously. There's nothing woman-related that's foreign to you. Things to do with body image, eating, sexuality, relationships, and the intimate things that women experience; very early on, we were sharing."

Aileen, forty-nine, told a very different kind of story: "It wasn't a good dynamic with my sister. Dina was a thorn in everybody's side. She was very dominant, very pushy, very aggressive, very attractive. A mean-spirited, bullying kind of person. I don't think that my parents could do very much about that. It was a matter of getting from one episode to the next. I was much quieter, maybe more passive, so the bottom line for me was never to cause any trouble, no matter what."

And there were the many children I interviewed. I felt that it was extremely important to hear from kids and teens because they were living the day-to-day sister experience that the adult women were summoning up from memory. The teens and kids still have to deal with each other every day, which means that their passion and frustration is very close to the surface.

I interviewed Jessie and Chloe in their family's formal TV room on a rainy Friday afternoon while their mother was cooking in the kitchen, preparing for a huge family dinner. The house felt warm and busy inside with the dark cold outside. Eleven-year-old Chloe went first, jumping and bouncing on the soft leather sofa as if she were about to propel herself onto the floor while we talked. Then I talked with thirteen-year-old Jessie. Earlier I had explained to both girls that I would change their names to disguise their identities if I used what they said in the book. At the end of her interview, Jessie instructed me that, if I did quote her, the name she wanted me to use for her was "Lindsay." I said, "Okay, now let's get your sister back down here and ask her what name she would want." In typical big-sister fashion, Jessie said, "You don't have to ask her. Call her 'Brittany.'" Taken aback, I ventured that I'd love to hear what Chloe would choose, but Jessie was firm: "Call her 'Brittany'!" Pushing the point, I called Chloe down from her room and asked what name I should use for her. She turned immediately to her big sister and said, "You choose!" That's when the family therapist in me kicked in. Bucking the established order, I said, "C'mon, Chloe. What name would *you* choose for yourself?" Chloe hesitated and then said, of course, "Brittany!"

In addition to the 165 face-to-face interviews and the 235 e-mail questionnaires I received, I interviewed some women who didn't have sisters at all, in an effort to get a sense of what they thought life would be like if they did. For example, one New Year's Eve, I was at a dinner party, talking enthusiastically about my research for this book. When we got up from the table, Jennifer, a woman I had just met, took me aside and confided: "I am the oldest of five—my four younger siblings are boys. When I was a little girl, every time my mother went to the hospital to have another baby, I would beg her to bring me home a girl. I spent my whole childhood disappointed that I didn't have a sister. I love my brothers, but it's not the same. I always wanted a sister."

I also interviewed other family therapists to hear what they have learned about sisters from their women clients and to canvass their opinion on the question, "Do you think that blood is thicker than water?" Their thoughts on this question are addressed in Chapter 7, "Star-Crossed Sisters," on conflicted sister relationships.

My Journey: The Nikki-Vikki Story

As The Sisters Project continued, it became much more than a cultural study for me. My understanding of women and their sisters deepened and so did my knowledge of myself. The Sisters Project became, for me, a journey.

My interest in the "blood is thicker than water" question grew out of my own experience with my only sibling, my sister, Nikki, older than me by five and a half years. Nikki has what could generously be termed a strong personality, and my parents were at a loss as to how to handle her. There was a lot of high drama and tears, particularly on the part of my mother, in my childhood home, a place punctuated regularly by fireworks.

I remember how awful I would feel when Nikki and my parents would fight. My mother would yell at my father, "Julian, get the strap!" My father, who wouldn't hurt a fly, would chase Nikki half-heartedly around the apartment with his belt in his hand until she ran into my room and hid behind me for protection. Those memories are typified by one horrible incident that took place when our family was in the car going to see the stage production of *My Fair Lady*. My sister and my parents were having such a screaming fight that I remember feeling like my head was inflating and about to explode.

The roles that Nikki and I played in the family became polarized. I was seen as the "good" one, and she was seen as the "bad" one. I felt so sorry for my parents that I had to be perfect—I couldn't add to their grief—and therefore was often Nikki's target. Her resentment of my parents' obvious babying of me served to polarize us even further. I must have blocked out a lot of the chaos in my childhood because I don't remember many details about Nikki when I was young. That's pretty remarkable, considering that we shared a bed until I was nine!

The concept of "sisterly feeling" has always been alien to me because of the conflict that continued into adulthood and also the large age difference between Nikki and me. I've spent my life, however, trying to balance my need to protect myself from what I perceived as my sister's jealousy with my belief that family members need to be connected. Nikki is unmarried and doesn't have children, and my children and I are her only blood relatives (she is completely alienated from our cousins), so my sense of responsibility for her is heightened.

To her credit, Nikki believes in honesty and gave me carte blanche when she heard that I was writing this book. She said that I needed to tell it like I see it or else this book would be empty and hollow. I salute her for her courage in that.

In conducting The Sisters Project, I wasn't a disinterested researcher as I sat with woman after woman, learning about the quality of her sister bond. I had something personal to sort out, and that is why I describe The Sisters Project as my journey. I met women who, like me, struggle to maintain a connection with their sisters and I've learned a lot from them. I also met women whose eyes glowed as they described their loving sisterly connection; I often felt like a spectator talking with them. I am definitely at a different place now than I was at when it all began.

How the Book Is Set Up

Throughout the book, I'll refer frequently to a woman's family position as an older, middle, younger, or twin sister. To keep from repeating that mantra until you're bored to tears, I've developed a shorthand term—TOMY position. A woman's TOMY position will refer to her place in the family as a twin, older, middle, or younger sister. Additionally, I want to clarify that, although the stories you will read are true, the names and identifying information of most of the participants in The Sisters Project have been altered to protect their privacy.

Chapter 1, "That Sister Mystique," explores the emotional connection between sisters and how that relationship shapes each of our lives. Chapter 2, "Brains, Boobs, and Black Sheep," explains the results of The Sisters Project in depth. You will learn how our TOMY position shapes how we feel about our bodies, influences our choice of occupation, and has an impact on the dynamics of our friendships, among other things.

Part II, "Your Spot in the Sister Hierarchy and Its Effect on You Today," will devote a chapter to each TOMY position. Part III, "Three Unique Relationship Styles and What It All Means to You," examines the particular dynamics of conflicted, bonded, and caretaking relationships. It includes the final chapter, which clarifies the profound, and often hidden, extent to which being a sister shapes us.

In some chapters, you will find questions developed to help you reflect on your own sister relationship and guide you, should you feel the need, in making changes. I recommend that you grab a pen and write down your answers on a sheet of paper. Like anything, the more you put into it, the more you'll get out of it. As a start, take a look at the general Sisters Project questionnaire located in Appendix A or the questionnaire for twins in Appendix B. Not all of the questions will relate to your special sister relationship, but, on a separate sheet of paper, answer those that do. The process of reflecting on the questions will enrich your experience of reading this book and deepen your understanding of your own unique sister bond.

Awake, the girls were always squabbling, their natures at once as fluid as air and as fixed as concrete and, above all, eternally opposed to one another. But asleep in their singlets and knickers, beneath a tartan blanket, their small, pale arms overlapping, they seemed to share their dreams and to be content.

—Claire Messud, from *When the World Was Steady*

After all, don't we all fear our sisters to a certain extent— for whatever reason? Fear their harsh words, fear their kind words, fear their beauty, fear their ugliness, fear their age, fear their youth? Fear that we are too much or not enough like them?

—Jessanyn Miller, Sisters Project participant

I

Women, Teens, and Girls Tell Their Sister Stories

That Sister Mystique

The Emotional Charge of Being a Sister

A few years ago, I attended the funeral of the elderly mother of a friend. Taking my seat, I was puzzled to see that there were two caskets at the front of the chapel. As the service began, I learned that the funeral was for two sisters—my friend's mother, Violet, and her older sister, Rose. A couple of days earlier, Rose had suffered a stroke. When Violet received the telephone call telling her the bad news, she had a heart attack and was rushed to the very hospital in which her sister was being treated. The two sisters died in the same emergency room within a few hours of each other.

The eulogy recounted how Violet and Rose had been connected both literally and figuratively since they were little girls. Eighty-odd years before, their mother had roped them together at the waist so she wouldn't lose one of them in the thick fog of London. As adults, Rose moved to Boston and Violet followed. They lived in the same neighborhood. Their kids went to the same schools. They telephoned each other every day, and when they got off the phone, each one turned to whomever was around and proclaimed, "That's the last time I'm *ever* going to speak to that woman again!"

Such is the power of sisters.

The Invisible Force Made Visible

Like Violet and Rose, your relationship with your sister or sisters shaped your life. *My Sister, My Self* will help you understand why and how. Based on the stories of four hundred women, teens, and girls who were interviewed during The Sisters Project about their sister relationships, this book will shed light on a reality that you may instinctively know but rarely consciously reflect upon—that your childhood relationship with your sister or sisters greatly influences your identity as an adult. Merely having grown up as a younger, middle, older, or twin sister leads to the development of fundamental character traits that affect how you feel about yourself and how you relate to other people. Qualities such as independence or dependence, comfort with risk-taking, confidence in your abilities, a need for closeness or distance, a tendency to under- or overfunction, or even the desire to be taken care of, these all often develop as a result of your sister role, but rarely do women recognize that fact. Rather, we attribute those characteristics to our individual personality style, without being aware that these traits were preprogrammed into us the day we were born, just because we appeared on the scene either before or after our sister(s).

As you come to understand how your position in your childhood family and the quality of your connection with your sister(s) imprinted your identity, it will become clear to you why you keep bumping your nose up against recurring problems in relationships or in your work environment. Little by little, this invisible force in your life will become defined as you recognize how your sister relationship shaped you. You will see how it influenced your choice of partner, your relations with friends and coworkers, the job you chose, and your body image. It even has an effect on how a woman relates to her mother and deals with her children! Additionally, the quality of that childhood sister relationship is a powerful determining force in your self-esteem. A girl naturally measures herself against her sister(s), and girls who grow up with a loving and admiring sister feel very differently about themselves than those who have a jealous, conflicted, or caretaking connection with their sister(s). Sister relationships are somewhat like computers. When they work, nothing can bring you more pleasure and make you feel more competent. When they don't, nothing can make you more miserable.

For example, thirty-three-year-old Vanessa, one of the participants in The Sisters Project, has been able to see clearly how her little sister identity comes into play in her relationship with her boyfriend. She has given a lot of thought to how she both wants and doesn't want to be taken care of: "My boyfriend is the oldest of four siblings, and he has an older sibling personality through and through. The way we relate to each other on a daily basis is very much within the roles we're used to, and it drives me nuts sometimes! The funny thing is, he's five years younger than I am, but you'd never know it from our behavior. He's the 'adult' and I'm the 'child' in the relationship, but it works, because it's what we're both used to.

"He's definitely the nurturer and needs to be needed; he gets pleasure out of helping me. I often find myself saying, 'I can do it,' or 'Let me!' sounding like I'm five years old. It makes me mad when he tries to do things for me, but strangely, I like his attempt at nurturing. I fight it, but I like fighting it, if that makes any sense. It's as though I don't like being taken care of or having things done for me, but I like someone trying to, so that I can resist it. I think I enjoy proving myself, but in order to do that, I need someone to try to baby me. Getting something done alone, with no one else involved, is productive, but doing it when someone is trying to do it for you, when you can say, 'Let me do it myself!' followed by 'Ha! See? I did it!' is far more rewarding. This sounds so silly, but I think it's pretty accurate."

Vanessa has articulated how she is replaying with her boyfriend those old familiar dynamics from her childhood. Her older sister was constantly trying to help her, and she both invited and fought that help. She got a lot of pleasure from her sister's attentiveness when she was little and enjoys reliving it in her adult couple relationship. The little sister imprint on her identity means that she will probably instinctively gravitate toward people who permit her to remain in that role. Things may not be so smooth, however, when she comes in contact with others whose comfort level also requires that they be taken care of. She may try to get other people to treat her the same way she was treated by her sister, and some won't want to fill that role. If Vanessa can continue to recognize her unconscious motivation, then the level of conflict with others will be reduced.

Right on, Sister!

When we hear the term *sisterly feelings*, we assume that what is being referred to is the affection, loyalty, generosity, and protective love that make up the idealized sister bond of our fantasy. We think of little girls and their clapping games, whispered secrets, pillow fights, and giggling. We think of teenagers trading clothes and makeup, hanging out together, sharing an illicit cigarette, and discovering the body-truths of becoming a woman. We think of women, secure in the knowledge that there is someone in this world who is unconditionally *there* for them—someone who really knows where they come from. The one who will walk with them through life.

It's not all roses, however. To understand the full range of sister relationships, it's also important to explore the tense and tortured situations that reveal a different kind of truth. For the many women whose sister relationships are not the stuff of fuzzy-focused greeting cards, there is a sense of having missed out on something special. If no one can make you feel better about yourself than your loving sister, then no one can make you feel worse about yourself if you are cursed with sisterly feelings at the other end of the spectrum. Relations between some sisters are characterized by ugly rivalry, jealousy, frustration, and guilt. By the age of three or four, little girls who bitterly resent the attention paid to their rival are locked in a life-and-death struggle for their parents' approval. Teenagers mock and tease, sniffing out any latent vulnerability that could be used to squash a sister's self-confidence. Women continue to compete, comparing jobs, children, and waistlines long after Mommy and Daddy are dead and gone.

In between these two extremes lie the everyday sister feelings that no one writes songs or stories about. These workaday ones manage to bring the family together a few times a year to mark special events, when the closeness is somewhere between "tell all" and "tell nothing" and the sisters are firmly fixed in each other's orbit for life, but maybe not circling too closely. A certain measure of ambivalence is typical of many sister relationships.

Sister is a word that evokes a lot of emotion, so much so that it has become a metaphor for an intimate connection between women who are not even blood relatives. It has come to mean "women who have traveled the same path in life, who have suffered the same things, and who really understand each other's reality. As a result, they have a fundamental connectedness." *Sisterhood* has a hugely positive connotation in our society, and women exalt that bond of sorority. There is comfort in feeling that women have a special understanding of each other. Inherent in this concept of sisterhood is the belief that all women need to stick up for each other and unite in the face of millennia of unfair treatment. Just because we are women, we belong to a club, connected by a common fight against oppression. If we can be so intimate with strangers—*Right on, sister!*—we are expected to be even closer with a blood sister. We have internalized that expectation to the point that women are miserable if they can't fashion their own real relationship to resemble the fantasy one. But that doesn't stop them from trying.

Your Closest Living Relative

Let's take a look at what we women expect from our sisters:

- She's always there for me.
- She really understands me.
- She supports everything I do.
- She's like another mother to my children.
- She's sincerely interested.
- She's so much fun.
- She makes me feel good about myself.
- I trust her with what's important to me.

Do those expectations sound like a tall order? They are. But a surprising number of women could check five out of eight on that list for at least one of their sisters. Some women almost experience a blurring of identity, so that part of their self-definition includes their sister. Maria described it like this: "It's like I have a wonderful, warm best buddy who is sweet and tart and altogether my equal. When we were kids and she cried, I would start crying immediately. Still today, if she gets teary, I do, too. It's as if she is me. We share a piece of each other's heart, even if we can't talk about it."

That blurring of identity is not surprising. When you think about it, little girls spend a lot of time during childhood with their sisters. When they're small, they take their bubble bath together. They often share a bedroom and sometimes sleep in the same bed. They play the same kinds of games using the same toys. They travel to and from school together on the bus. They have similar kinds of chores around the house, some of which they do together ("You wash, I'll dry"). They often have only each other to play with on family holidays. They swap clothes—or try to. If their parents are divorced, they go back and forth together to each parent's house. They experience tragedy together when Fluffy, the turtle, dies and Zilch, the rabbit, runs away. Girls may be close to their brothers, but, as they pass through the same physical and psychological stages growing up, they look to their sisters to learn about themselves.

Genetically, a full sibling is your closest living relative. Emotionally, she's the one who knew you when you were a child and may be there with you to turn out the lights at the other end of life. More important, she and you were taught those taken-for-granted things about life by the same parents: things like how to brush your teeth, how to iron a shirt, whether to store potatoes in the refrigerator or under the sink, and whether to handle crises in life with anxiety or aplomb. She learned the same tricks and ways that you did without even realizing that you were learning them, and that fact contributes to the inherent sense of familiarity with your sisters that you either celebrate or despise.

Surprisingly, that sense of familiarity sometimes transcends a shared childhood. Twenty-nine-year-old Kim from Asheville, North Carolina, was adopted at birth. She only met her two half-sisters when she was twenty-six and they were twenty-three and twenty-two. Meeting them was a profound experience. "When I received the first letters from them, it blew me away. It was almost as if I was writing to myself. Everything was exactly like me. When we met, it was mind-blowing. I can't even tell you how we understand each other—we hardly have to speak—and when we do, we often say the same thing—it's almost as if we have the same thought process. We don't always agree, but it's almost as though our minds work in the same way. We like to think about deep things, emotions, why we feel the way we do. We can go so deep." Following that moving interview with Kim and her two half-sisters, I happened to glance over the forms they'd filled out agreeing to be part of The Sisters Project. Now it was my turn to be blown away—Kim's handwriting and that of her younger half-sister were virtually identical!

Closeness and Distance

During the interviews, women frequently raised the issue of boundaries and questioned to what extent sisters should respect each other's privacy. How much do they have the right to criticize or tell each other what to do? Many women referred to the challenge of balancing the drive for intimacy with the need for separateness; they felt that their lives were braided with alternating ropes of closeness and distance. Twenty-two-year-old Stephanie gave a good illustration: "In high school, my younger sister was sleeping with a guy that I liked and we ended up having a physical fight about it. That ruined our friendship until this year, when I had a baby and she came to help." Several women remarked that they felt comfortable weaving in and out of the relationship without fear of losing the connection.

The issue of boundaries was raised in one of four ways:

- To illustrate that the sisters are so terrifically close that they have no separation between them at all
- To point out that the sisters have such a good relationship because they are careful not to trespass into personal issues
- To express a feeling of desolation because one woman yearns to have a closer relationship but her sister keeps her at arm's length
- To describe how guilty one of the sisters feels because the other is always pushing for more than she is willing to give

Here's a perfect example of the first style. At the beginning of each interview, I would solemnly promise each participant that the contents of her interview would never be leaked to her sister, and most women would nod seriously in acceptance. One afternoon, I was interviewing Karen and Jane, two young adult sisters whose mother is one of five extremely close sisters. I was about five minutes into my separate interview with Karen when I became aware of a pair of feet in striped socks peeking out from the open doorway to the next room. Jane and her mother were sitting right outside the room, eavesdropping. I lowered my voice to try to protect Karen's confidentiality, but at a certain point, the two snoops burst out with whoops of laughter at something Karen was saying. Karen grinned and said, "I know they're listening. I don't have any secrets from them, so they might as well come in and get comfortable." We completed the "confidential" interview with Karen's mother and Jane seated in the room as the peanut gallery. The family culture of closeness and the lack of anything to hide between these two sisters (as well as between their mother and *her* four sisters) was a tremendous point of pride for them all.

Many women permit their sister an honesty that they reject from anyone else. She's somebody that you can bounce things off of—someone "who will call you on your bullshit." She is the one person who will tell you the truth when you ask, "Do these pants make me look fat?"—and from her, you can take it.

Interestingly, some of the healthiest relationships were structured to include the second style—a very clear "No Trespassing!" sign. Many women who described a close relationship reported that there were certain places they just wouldn't go—they wouldn't discuss their couple problems with a sister and they wouldn't talk about their sex life. They may feel that if they complain about their spouse, the sister will turn against him and stay angry long after the problem is patched up. Or, if the full extent of the marital discord were known, the sister might insist that something be done about it.

It may be harder to open up with a sister because, unlike with friends, the sister relationship is not optional. If you don't like your sister's response, it's harder to distance yourself from her. Additionally, you're at risk that your secret will be spilled to other family members; that frankness may come back to haunt you. Finally, having established the sister relationship long before adolescence, some women feel embarrassed to reveal their sexual side—they're just not comfortable being viewed in that light by a sister. It's sort of like hearing the details of your parents' sex life—do you really want to know? That area of discussion may be better left for friends.

"Why Don't You Just Grow Up!"

The quality of sister relationships tends to improve in adulthood and continues to strengthen as women age. Among other positive changes, the level of anger often dramatically decreases, particularly for older sisters. Judy, the oldest of four sisters wrote, "As kids, they were pests. As adults, they're my life!" One reason for that improvement is that the sisters usually no longer live together as adults; much of the petty jealousy and competition is eliminated. As women face troubles in life, they come to appreciate having someone whom they can rely on, with no strings attached. A sister in the background provides a kind of savings account tucked away for a rainy day, even if the women are not particularly close.

In researching these relationships, I found that there is a critical switchover point that occurs when sisters are in their early twenties; they often refashion their childhood dynamic. As teens move into adulthood and start establishing themselves as independent women, the age-related hierarchy starts to blur—a younger sister may have a baby before her older sisters do, a middle sister may train for a professional career and get a high-status job. As adults, it's not unusual for women to have friends who are a few years older or younger. The bridge that has to be crossed requires that the sisters permit themselves to step out of the childhood roles and renegotiate the contract as peers. If this doesn't happen, because either one or both are reluctant to take the leap, then there will more likely be dissatisfaction with the relationship as adults. Younger sisters often complain that they continue to be treated like a baby; older sisters complain that they don't want to be depended on to the same extent anymore.

On the other hand, a sister is a great person to regress with! My two daughters, Michele and Lauren, both in their midtwenties, have a tradition of going to see the stupidest, most ditsy movies together—ones that they would never bother to see with friends. Sixteen-year-old Ginny described the fun she has with twelve-year-old Zoë: "We goof around a lot, a lot, a lot. If I didn't have a sister, I'd be a lot more serious. I don't know if I'd be as comfortable having fun in the way I do with my sister with someone else. We always watch our favorite show together every morning—'Arthur'—a cartoon. My brother doesn't watch it, and I would never watch it with any of my friends."

From an adult point of view, the permission to get down and silly is priceless. One of my favorite vignettes was told to me by forty-three-year-old Genevieve: "I go with my sister, Sabine, to the Orchard Beach for a week every September, and we do nothing but scream and laugh and pee in our pants almost. We have a blast in the car all the way. The same route every time, the same place; there's nothing to do there. We can't wait—we're like kids. We sleep at my mom's house the night before we leave and get up at four in the morning. I'm sure my kids don't get as excited as this. We bring old tapes of singers we listened to at seventeen. We sing and dance in the car, and sometimes we have to pull over because we're laughing so much. We have a ball!"

Surviving the Family Storm

One of the questions that I asked all of the participants of The Sisters Project was, "Could you say how your life would be different if you didn't have a sister?" There was an easy answer to that one. Most summed it up in one word: *bor*-ing. A certain percentage, however, said that they couldn't have survived childhood without their sister—and some meant that literally. I received these heartfelt responses by e-mail from two sisters who hadn't consulted each other before answering the questionnaire. The younger sister wrote, "I think the harshness of my father would have completely broken me and I might have committed suicide as an overweight eighth grader if I didn't have a sister." Her older sister independently said, "I probably wouldn't be alive to answer this survey. In the middle of high school, I considered suicide but decided against it; I didn't want to desert my sister or hurt her."

Another older sister, who had survived incest at the hands of her father, said that she "shudders" to think what life would have been like without her sisters.

What's to Come

My Sister, My Self will take us all on a journey to understand ourselves as women who were hammered and shaped during a million different childhood moments, stamped by our roles as big sister, little sister, middle sister, or twin. I hope that no one is left out (not being left out is very important to sisters) as we listen to the voices of other women and girls telling us their sister stories and exploring the effect of that primordial relationship on their identity today.

Having the luxury of four hundred interviews to work with, I was able to do a lot of detailed analysis. The results have been really surprising—the influence of a woman's family position really runs deep. There are the archetypes: the oldest sister is maternal and protective from the early years of childhood and remains so for the rest of her life; the youngest sister is catered to, "the baby"; the middle sister is torn and fighting to be noticed; and the twins are in a world of their own. But in real life, each individual situation is unique, often much more intriguing than you'd expect.

Kelly, Crystal, Wendy, Kim, Mary Beth, and Peggy

Brains, Boobs, and Black Sheep

What The Sisters Project Revealed
About Sister Roles

"When we were in our teens, my two older sisters and I played on the same AA soccer team for three years. It started when I was approached by a scout who said, 'I really like the way you play,' and I said, 'If you like the way I play, you're going to like the way my sisters play even more!'

"We all played different positions. My oldest sister, Martina, was team captain—she did the coin toss. She was in a very responsible position because she was halfback, which means you're not defense, you're not a forward—you make all of the plays. My middle sister, Gaby, was defense. She did her job; she did what they requested, but don't ask her to do anything else 'cause she's not going to commit. And me, Billie, I had to be very versatile—I played every position. Sometimes I was goalie, sometimes I did defense, and sometimes I was halfback. I had to get along with everyone because I never knew when I would have to replace someone.

"And I guess that's how our life is. Martina has to tell everyone what to do and that sometimes causes friction. She has to be in the middle of the action, making all of the plays. Gaby, my middle sister, is very black and white. She likes to know what people want from her, but don't expect her to volunteer for too much. And me, I'm adaptable. I get along with everybody, which really gives me a certain amount of power."

—BILLIE, thirty-seven years old

Tracking Trends

What would you think if I were to tell you that your choice of employment might have been influenced by your TOMY position? You'd think that I'm nuts, right? How about if I were to suggest that you might feel differently about your *own* body had you been born before or after your sister? What if I demonstrated that the very words you use to describe who you are depend on where you fall in the sister hierarchy? You're probably thinking, "What does my sister have to do with all of that?" As it turns out . . . a lot! When I compared the thousands of answers from participants in The Sisters Project, what became clear is that a woman's childhood relationship with her sister makes an indelible impression on a range of unexpected areas of her identity.

In this chapter, we will explore The Sisters Project results, highlighting five of the twenty-one questions on the questionnaire:

- What is your occupation and that of your sister(s)?
- Did your relationship with your sister(s) have an effect on how you feel about your body and, if so, how?

- What roles did you and your sister(s) play in the family?
- If you could have said just one sentence to your sister(s) growing up that expressed your true feelings about her, what would it be?
- If you could say just one sentence to your sister(s) now, what would it be?

For each question, I compared answers based on whether the woman responding was an older, middle, younger, or twin sister. Because of the extensive sample of four hundred participants, I was able to track trends in terms of how a woman's family position affects her life choices, her self-image, and her experience of the world.

I found strong trends, but in no way do I want to imply that *all* younger sisters are like this or that *all* twins are like that. Position in the family has a significant influence, but many other variables affect relationships between sisters and alter the extent to which a girl's emotional development will be consistent with her place in the hierarchy. For example, the oldest sister in a family of six girls in which both parents are employed will probably develop a very different sense of responsibility than the oldest sister in a family of two where the mother is home most the time or than the oldest sister in a family of six kids in which four of them are brothers. Age spread is also important— when there are more than five years between sisters, the effect of the TOMY position is sometimes watered down. As we move on, we'll look at all of the possible permutations.

Occupations: TOMY Position and Job Choice

The other day, I met with a new accountant. In the course of describing my work, I told her about The Sisters Project and she mentioned that she was one of four sisters. I said to her, "I'll bet you're one of the two middle sisters." She looked at me in surprise and said, "How did you know?" I explained to her that it was an educated guess because she works in finance. Although statistically, she has a 50 percent chance of being a middle sister in her family of four girls, the fact that she works in finance told me that her chance of being a middle far exceeded 50 percent.

I came to that conclusion based on my analysis of the occupations chosen by women in differing family positions. Three hundred seventy-two women listed the kinds of jobs in which they and their sisters were employed. I assigned each occupation to one of five categories: education, professional, creative, healing professions, and business. I found that a relatively equal percentage of women in all TOMY positions chose to work in the fields of education, the professions, or creative pursuits, so it appears that position in the family does not influence the choice of those particular occupations. Things get interesting, however, when we look at the other two categories.

Healing Professions

Results from The Sisters Project show that a woman's position in the sister hierarchy does affect her decision to work in the healing professions (such as therapists, doctors, nurses, and dentists) and in business. Twenty percent of older and younger sisters in The Sisters Project went into the healing professions, but only 8 percent of middles and twins did. Out of ninety middle sisters, *not one* said she worked as a nurse, whereas a good percentage of younger sisters work in that field. More dramatically, only a miniscule percentage of middle sisters chose to become therapists of any sort—psychotherapists, physiotherapists, massage therapists, occupational therapists, and so on. On the other hand, younger sisters identified themselves as therapists *twelve times* more frequently—the highest concentration of one TOMY position in a particular occupation in the whole Sisters Project!

We can speculate about why younger sisters like to work as therapists. They spent their childhoods observing the family dynamics swirling around them and, with a younger sister's enthusiasm and grandiosity, they believe that they can help. Being a therapist gives one a certain cachet—people think that you know things. People turn to you when they need help; they listen to what you have to say. Perhaps younger sisters go into the healing professions and, more specifically, become therapists, because the job itself gives them the authority that they had to fight for as children. I frequently heard younger sisters complain that they felt disqualified growing up. Louisa, the youngest of three, said, "I always felt to a certain extent that I was vying for air time, and I never really feel, even to this day, that people in my family put credence in what I have to say and my opinions."

Jobs in Business

With regard to choosing to work in business, middle sisters were clearly overrepresented in management and, even more, in the non-management side of business. Twins also chose business as their field of endeavor, but rarely in management positions. Well over a third of the twins in my study work on the nonmanagement side of business, and the combined percentage of twins who work in both areas of business is 46 percent—almost half!

Middle sisters may not be interested in working in a field, like therapy, that involves a lot of unstructured emotional expression. My study results have shown that many middle sisters feel comfortable blending in and don't like to draw a lot of attention to themselves. They are accommodating and often independent, preferring to be free to do their own thing. Perhaps they don't enjoy being in the position of influencing others on an interpersonal level.

Business also may make sense to middle sisters because they are often the practical ones in the family. They're used to getting along with both older and younger people and work well in groups. Middle sisters have told me that they like being part of a team and enjoy making sure that everyone's voice is heard—a trait that would certainly be an asset in a management setting. Here is what Hayley said about her role: "I look for the solutions and possibilities to resolve conflicts. I act like a middle—I wait to see who tries to take the lead, and if no one does, I am willing to step up."

The same may be said of twins, who see the world through peer eyes. Twins are used to being on a par with the important other person in their lives and are not comfortable being in a position of authority. A twin may feel guilt if she outperforms her sister. That guilt may explain why twins are so underrepresented in the area of business management, a field that is defined by hierarchy.

What do we make of all of this? It's clear that, in some cases, a woman's TOMY position makes her more likely to choose certain endeavors over others. Something about having grown up as an older, middle, younger, or twin leads a woman to develop either a set of skills or a self-image that causes her to seek fulfillment in arenas different from those of a sister who is older or younger.

By the way, you won't be surprised to learn the occupations of the soccer-playing sisters who introduced this chapter. The oldest, Martina, is the vice president of a company; the middle, Gaby, is an engineer; and Billie, the youngest, is a social worker.

Body Image: Her Body, My Self

Maude relayed the following: "When I was about age ten, a friend and I were playing putting on nail polish. My sister came in the room and told me that Mother would be very upset to have me grow up too fast. Looking back, I think it was clearly a matter of a child playing dress-up as opposed to a precocious preteen yearning to be a teenager. Yet with that one sentence, my sister conveyed to me a whole set of expectations. I knew I was expected to be modest not flashy, discreet not provocative. All of my life I have been well covered so my body won't betray me."

Many women answered the question, "Did your relationship with your sister have an effect on how you feel about your body and, if so, how?" by saying that they were influenced by their sisters' opinions big-time and, sometimes, that that influence fundamentally affected how they feel about themselves. Girls frequently turn to their sisters, rather than to their mothers, for information, encouragement, and comparison. It is often a sister who tells them what to expect when they get their periods, teaches them the trick to inserting a tampon, and explains the nitty-gritty of what *really* happens with a boyfriend in the backseat of a Chevrolet. A couple of women told brave stories of how their sisters, although teens themselves, "saved their lives" by organizing clandestine late-term abortions.

While analyzing the 229 responses to the question on body image, I became aware that women in different TOMY positions are influenced by their sisters in different ways. Three-quarters of younger sisters, two-thirds of older sisters, and half of middle sisters said that their sisters affected their feelings about their bodies. Middle sisters were most often influenced negatively (remember, they have at least two sisters with whom to compare themselves), followed by older sisters, and, last, younger sisters. With regard to twins, body image is such a central issue that we will give it the attention that it requires in Chapter 6, "Wombmates," the chapter on twins.

Younger sisters are the most influenced by their sisters, but in the least negative way, and middle sisters are the least influenced, but in the most negative way! It's understandable that younger sisters would be most influenced, as they watch in fascination as their older sisters develop, get their periods, and become sexual before their eyes. The transmission of attitudes and information and the weight of approval or disapproval by older sisters toward younger ones are powerful. The girl trailing behind assumes that the trailblazer really knows the truth about issues related to the body. Youngest sisters are also the ones most likely to receive encouragement, support, and advice. Middle sisters are the least likely to receive that kind of buoying up.

Boobs and Beauty

Based on family role position, women focused on different body-related concerns. For example, older sisters often talked about their jealousy related to issues of beauty, although beauty hardly showed up *at all* as a central theme for younger and middle sisters. Older sisters typically contributed sentiments like, "I know my sister is beautiful—she's really gorgeous, like model material . . . but I'd never tell her that!" and "Growing up, I felt uglier than my middle sister, who was tall and blonde." The worry about being eclipsed by a younger sister is evident in this college student's concern: "I sometimes feel inadequate because she is prettier than I am. I have mixed feelings about hosting her at college because I know that, even though she is younger, she'll upstage me. Everyone will say, 'Your sister is so hot!' which is what people (especially guys) already say when they see her photo in my room."

The runaway bestseller issue for younger sisters was . . . boobs. Younger sisters devoted a lot of space to discussing who had bigger breasts and whether that was a good or a bad thing—most felt bigger was better. There must be a lot of teasing of younger sisters about their bra size going on in the kitchens across the civilized world! One woman said that she was a "late bloomer" and her sisters teased her mercilessly but that she grew to have a bigger bust size, so "who's laughing now?" Here's Simone's take on the theme: "I was always jealous of the fact that all of my sisters have nice big boobs and I have none. I never developed big boobies, and they all did—nice ones, with cleavage! Growing up—yeah—I always felt underdeveloped."

The other hot topic for younger sisters was sex. Several women referred to the discomfort they felt when they became aware of their sisters as sexual beings. Some disapproved of their sisters' choices sexually, and some had sisters who disapproved of them, occasionally causing them to become more reserved about their sexual expression. It was not unusual for sisters to be divided up into the sexy sister and the proper one, each disapproving of the other.

Sexual behavior that seems normal to older sisters can be quite shocking to younger ones. I remember visiting my sister in Boston when she was an eighteen-year-old college student and I was twelve. She was sick with a cold, and I was completely shocked when her boyfriend came to visit and walked *right into the bedroom* (gasp!) while she was in bed in her pajamas. Of course, I didn't complain too much when, because she was too sick to go out, he took *me* to dinner on the back of his motorcycle—a thrill I'll never forget!

Fat and Skinny

You can probably guess the most common theme across the board—weight. Close to half of the women surveyed in all categories talked about weight as an area of worry, competition, or despair. Some women bemoaned that they were always heavier than their sisters; others worried that they were in the process of becoming heavier than their sisters; and others felt guilty because they were thinner than sisters who were jealous of them! Brooke contributed this variation on that theme: "My sister used to be overweight and lost the weight about three years ago. I used to feel comfortable because, when we were both overweight, we would eat together. Now that it's just me who needs to lose weight, I feel more alone. It feels like she is a traitor in some ways." Caroline confessed her guilty pleasure at winning (at least temporarily) the thinness stakes: "My oldest sister was always thinner than me. When I saw her last Christmas, she had gained weight and I had lost it and looked skinnier than her and I loved it. I've been overweight all of my life until recently, and now she is gaining and I secretly dig that."

Styles of Influence

Either overtly or secretly, we learn things about our own bodies by reading the messages sent by our sisters. A sister may affect our own body image by transmitting her values in one of the following ways:

- She may be outright critical.
- She may be encouraging.
- Her insecurity about her own body may be contagious.
- Just by existing, she becomes a yardstick to compare oneself to.

was in fourth grade and my sister was in seventh, I heard her complaining of the largeness of her thighs, and I automatically became self-conscious of mine at the same time." Sally recalled her sister's lament: "Her boobs were too big. I can remember her standing in the mirror and saying, 'My boobs are too big, my boobs are too big,' and it made me worry that mine might get to be too big, too."

The Walking Yardstick. The most common thing I heard women say with regard to body image was that they just couldn't stop comparing themselves to their sister. Feelings about themselves were so intricately linked to their assessment of their sister that they felt that everything body-related had a reference to her. For example, if a woman loses weight, the first thing that may come to mind is whether she is now thinner than her sister. A sister's mere existence provides a woman with a constant source of comparison.

Tanya, the middle of five sisters, continually compares herself to her next older sister, who seems completely oblivious to the competition: "Could my poor body image come from the fact that I'm a size 10, maybe an 8 now, and Gabriella's always been a 2–4? She never had to worry about her weight—ever! She's always been small. She had her babies; she lost the weight. Never dieted, never worried, never looked at a scale. If anything, 'I should eat more—I'm too thin.' And I was always struggling. Always!"

Here's Linda's lament about how she could never measure up in her own mind to her two sisters: "Well, one looked like Cher and one looked like a model and I looked like Howdy Doody. I think I will always feel like the 'fat, but cute' one."

Roles Within the Family: Growing in Counterpoint

As a family therapist, I've always been interested in the roles people play in their families and how one person's role affects another's. A typical example would be when parents unconsciously divide themselves up into good cop and bad cop. If one parent is overly indulgent of the child, the other parent feels like he or she has to enforce the rules. The more the second one is busy being the enforcer, the more the first one feels sorry for the child, becoming even more indulgent. As years go by, their roles get increasingly polarized. However, if the soft one decided one day to get a bit stricter, the bad cop parent could feel more comfortable lightening up. And vice versa. There you have it—Family Therapy 101!

The same holds true between sisters. I'll give you a very benign example of how limiting sibling roles can be. When my kids were little, Lauren had the reputation of being the family artist and Michele, the family writer. When there was a competition for teens to write a movie review in the local newspaper, we'd suggest to Michele that she try her hand, but when it was time to make Grandma's birthday card, we usually turned to Lauren. Lauren liked movies a lot and probably had plenty she could have said in a review, and Michele liked to draw and could certainly have made a lovely card, but we kept slotting them into roles that prevented them from fully exploring other talents. In the prosaic mind of a parent, it's easier to keep track of everyone if they all have different roles!

Along those lines, when one sister develops a particular reputation in the family, the other sisters grow in counterpoint because the first role is already taken. And once one's reputation is formed, it's very difficult to shake. Pauline, the second youngest of five sisters, described it like this: "One of the hardest things growing up is that you get put in a box. Ronna is this way. Valerie is this way. Brenda is this way. Everyone has their box that they fit into, and it's almost impossible to get yourself out of that box. It's like, 'no,' I'm not the same person I was as a kid. When I was eleven, I said I wanted to be Miss Universe. Well, that stuck like glue, for god's sake. I was a child when I said it! I mean, like, c'mon. But, that's the way they are—they take snippets of memories and attach them to you, and it's like they're all over you and it takes a very long time to pull them off."

In an effort to explore this phenomenon, I asked Sisters Project participants the following question: What roles did you and your sister(s) play in the family growing up? This question seemed to really unleash the participants' creativity and passion, but one woman put it very succinctly: "I was the do-gooder. She was the pot-stirrer." I analyzed the responses to this question by taking all of the words that women assigned to themselves and their sisters (a total of 695 words!) and putting them into categories. For example, one of the most common designations for older sisters was "smart," so I put all of the times an older sister was called "smart," "good student," "overachiever," or "the brain" into one category. I did this with all 695 words and came up with a comprehensive picture of the roles that girls play in their childhood families and how remarkably different they are based on their TOMY position. (Once again, twin sisters are not included in this discussion, as their role in the family is most often described as a unit.)

Here's a sampling of how women described the roles played by each of the girls in their family:

• Ruby, twenty-nine, from Halifax: "The oldest was the brain. I was the clown (and artistic). Next was 'Miss Popularity' with many friends and a busy social life. The last was a sweet, likable 'Little Miss Perfect.'"

• From Grace, a thirty-six-year-old horticulturist and older sister from Denver: "I was the rebel, the screamer, the passionate one. She was more of a loner, quiet, conformist, and suffering on the inside."

• Debra, in her early thirties, interviewed in San Diego: "The oldest is a typical 'big sister' and has opinions about *everything*. The middle is considered 'the bitch' but is also the one to count on when family business needs to be taken care of. She's the first to help in the kitchen. I am considered 'the anchor'—mellow and stable. Everyone knows that I'm a comfortable place to be."

Roles of Older Sisters

I was flabbergasted when I saw how often expressions like "surrogate mother," "mother's helper," "mother associate," and even "mother's surrogate mate" were used to describe older sisters. Along with similar terms like "responsible," "bossy," "nurturing," and "protective," this category made up one-third of all of the terms attributed to older sisters. Add that to the second most frequent set of categories—"smart," "goody-goody," "role model," "trailblazer," and "mediator"—and you have a description of two-thirds of all older sisters! The picture that develops is one of a smart, caretaking, serious girl loaded down with a huge amount of responsibility in her family.

The vast majority of terms attributed to older sisters were positive, and only a small percentage of these girls were described as playing negative roles, such as "drama queen," "rebel," and "the storm." In the 316 roles attributed to older sisters, not once was one described as "fun" or "funny." As to "carefree" and "easygoing," those terms came up only twice among olders, much less frequently than for the other two positions. And "brat" does not come up at all!

Roles of Middle Sisters

When we look at the results for middle sisters, the results are really surprising. Time and again, middle sisters were described as being "the clown," "funny," "jester," and "comedian." I surmise that middle sisters adopt that role as a way of staking their turf in the family. If the oldest is most often "surrogate mother" and the youngest is most often "the baby," the girl in the middle makes her mark by being funny.

A colorful choice of words was used to describe middle sisters when they're acting up and not being so funny—"wild one," "evil child," "rebel," "riot squad," "brat," "pest," "squeaky wheel," and "demon seed." Twice as many negative terms were used to describe middle sister than were used for older sisters.

Middle sisters were also described by a large assortment of odd categories, many in a psychological vein—"compassionate," "low self-esteem," "crybaby," "neurotic," "vain," "loner," "iconoclastic," "scapegoat"—words that seem to have a different flavor than the descriptive terms used for olders and youngers. I think that it has to do with the independence encompassed by the middle role. This sister feels freer not to conform to expectations, and as part of charting her own course, she sometimes crashes upon the rocks.

The term that I expected to come up most often for middle sisters, "invisible," was not strongly represented. But middle sisters did win the prize as most commonly called the "black sheep."

Roles of Younger Sisters

The most frequent role for younger sisters was, as expected, that of "the baby," "favorite," and "pet" of the family. As it is with olders, their second category was "smart," "the student," and "genius," followed by the somewhat snide "Little Miss Perfect." One category that was prevalent among younger sisters but did not show up at all for middle and older sisters is "sweetheart." The tenderness is palpable in the terms chosen by older sisters to describe their kid sister—"kind heart," "sweet," "cute," "precious," "affectionate," and "loving."

Just One Sentence: The Essence of Feeling

In an effort to get The Sisters Project participants to distill their sisterly feelings down to the essence, I asked them the following question: If you could have said just one sentence to your sister growing up that expressed your true feelings about her, what would it be? Later, in the interview or questionnaire, I asked for just one sentence that expressed their current feelings. I thought it would be interesting to see the progression from childhood to adulthood, how things changed over time. I separated the answers, once again, based on TOMY positions, and then broke them down further to isolate the negative and positive themes that appeared. Certain types of sentiments showed up repeatedly and are good indicators of how a lot of girls and women feel about their sisters, although I want to again underline that these statements do not reflect the feelings of everyone. I'm highlighting just the dominant ones.

Older Sisters' Statements

The big sister is apparently tremendously proud. Out of twenty-eight positive statements made by older sisters as adults, ten of them actually used the word "proud." A typical statement made by an older sister is "I'm proud of the woman you have become, Munchkin." If we look at the fifty-nine positive statements made by middle, younger, and twin sisters, however, only three of them used "proud." Older sisters have cornered the market on pride, and there is often a parental flavor to it.

Older sisters also have a side business in love. Out of the twenty-seven positive statements that older sisters would have made as kids, the phrase "I love you" was used nineteen times—that's 70 percent of the time! In comparison, out of the fifty-nine positive statements by all of the middle, younger, and twin sisters combined, that phrase was used only fourteen times—23 percent of the time. The wholehearted warmth and tenderness conveyed by older sisters was phenomenal. It's summed up in this statement by one of the participants: "I absolutely and totally love you, Chicky Babe."

Last bit about the older sister: it seems odd, but many of the negative statements have a positive twist to them—or are these positive statements with a negative twist? Women said things like:

- "I love you, but you drive me crazy."
- "I love you, but you get on my nerves."
- "You're a very outgoing kid, but stop following me around!"
- "I love you very much, but I'm not your mother."

- "You're a pain in the ass, but I still love you."
- "You're kinda annoying, but I really think you're cool."
- "I'm glad you're here, but I certainly enjoy it when you're gone."

From these statements, it seems that the older sister has trouble getting completely out of the nurturing role and has to soften the kick with a pat on the head. That caretaking, nurturing stamp is so deeply ingrained that older sisters can't completely shake it, even when they're annoyed.

Middle Sisters' Statements

On the other hand, middle sisters often expressed what can be one of the most painful emotions to tolerate—regret. Many middle sisters felt badly that they had been mean to their little sisters growing up and, as adults, wish that they had done it differently. Some responses that reflect that bitter reality are:

- "I'm sorry I can't take better care of you."
- "I'm sorry I made you uncomfortable."
- "I am sorry I never understood you."
- "I'm sorry for all of the fighting we did while growing up."

It seems that sometimes there is an inherent jealousy in the middle sister role that is so overpowering that these girls can't stop themselves from tormenting their little sisters. Perhaps this feeling is particularly strong because, when the younger sister is born, middle sisters not only lose their status in the family as the baby, but they also lose their older sister's undivided attention.

Middle sisters are both older and younger sisters themselves and share some of the sentiments of both groups. Some of the sentences from middle sisters toward the younger ones do express tenderness ("You make me happy just by walking into a room!") and some, annoyance ("Stop being such a brat!"). Toward the older sister, the longing to be as cool as she appeared to be was captured in the recurring refrain, "How can I be more like you?"

Younger Sisters' Statements

A lot of younger girls felt that they would have really been in a mess if they didn't have big sisters, so they want to say "thank you"!

- "Thank you for being there."
- "Thanks for giving me your old driver's license to get into bars when I was underage."
- "Thank you for being my guide."
- "Thank you for always being so sweet to me."
- "Thank you for molding me."
- "Thank you for all of your help and protection."
- "Thank you for liberating me from Brooklyn."
- "Thanks for eating all of the yucky things on my plate I hated!"

Younger sisters' statements often reflected the other side of the coin to those submitted by their older and middle sisters. Younger sisters were full of thank-yous, but also a certain amount of hurt about having been treated badly, particularly by middle sisters.

Another strong theme ran through the sentences younger sisters would like to say. They reveal their frustration that the relationship hasn't jumped the gap to become more peerlike in adulthood. The theme is represented by statements such as:

- "I'm an adult now—please treat me like one."
- "You don't have to be the 'big sister' anymore."
- "I can manage without your advice about everything."
- "It would be wonderful if I could get one sentence in sometimes."
- "Please see me as a real person, not just your little sister."

Twin Sisters' Statements

Feelings conveyed by twins were something else altogether. Both as kids and as adults, their sentiments were overwhelmingly positive and frequently had an otherworldly quality to them. Statements like the following were not unusual:

- "Incredible love—incredible connectedness."
- "I wouldn't know what to do without you."
- "I'd rather die than have us grow apart."
- "You are my light at the end of the tunnel."
- "I can't imagine life without you."
- "Some people search the world for their soul mates and we're so lucky—we came into the world together!"
- "With you, I don't need anyone else!"

Both Sides of the Coin

I was particularly interested to compare the "just one sentence" responses when I had heard from both sisters, expecting to see a consistency between the older and younger sisters' experiences. I was surprised that there were very few in which the older and younger sisters' sentences were specifically related (except for all of the general "I love yous" on both sides). Here are a few examples of some that were:

- The older sister wrote, "Stop following me!" Independently, her younger sister wrote, "Calm down! Nothing is that serious and getting angry doesn't help."

- In another case, the older sister wrote, "You don't have to ignore your family to get attention from guys." And her younger sister said, "I sometimes wish you'd do more understanding than judging."

- And finally, an older sister wrote, "I see you even though you don't think I do." Her younger sister sent in, "I wish you could accept that God made me for a reason."

The Influence of Your TOMY Position

In this chapter, we've looked at the answers to four of the twenty-one questions asked in The Sisters Project. We've seen some of the ways a woman's TOMY position influences her choices and feelings about herself. As we continue, you'll develop a much richer understanding of your unique spot in the sister hierarchy.

II

Your Spot in the Sister Hierarchy and Its Effect on You Today

Rose-Andrée and Jennifer

Blazing the Trail

The Oldest Sister

"When I was about thirteen, I asked my mother if I could get my ears pierced. My mother said I was much too young but she would agree to it when I turned sixteen. All those years I looked forward to my sixteenth birthday, and when we were finally on our way to the jewelry store, I can't tell you how excited I was. But . . . my sister came along—she was eleven—and when she saw all of the pretty earrings, she started to nag my mother and nag my mother to let her get her ears pierced, too. I couldn't believe it when my mother finally gave in. I got so mad, I was furious, and then my mother got mad at me for being selfish and making such a big fuss, and she said, 'What's the big deal? You got your ears pierced, didn't you?'"

—CORETTA, eighteen years old

At the Head of the Pack

One of my most memorable interviews was with the six Mayo sisters, who invited me for lunch at the home of the eldest, Peggy. Paddy's girls, as they were called, ranged in age from forty-one to fifty-three. All but one still lived on the Mohawk reserve where they had grown up, and that sister boasted that she could "floor it" back to the reserve in ten minutes, provided the police weren't out on the highway. They had endured a really rough childhood and had depended on the older sisters to make it through. They continue to count on each other as adults, even though life is now sweeter. As we sat around the dining room table, Peggy reminisced about their past: "When I was a child, we had very little money. I remember collecting bottles to sell, and when I'd made a few dollars, I would take all of my sisters to the five-and-dime in town. I would give them each a quarter and they'd spend hours deciding what to buy. Then we'd go to Norm's Bar-B-Que Shack to have a hot dog, a bag of french fries, and a Coke—one—and we'd split them between us." At this point, I glanced around the table, registering the fact that everyone was crying. Then Wendy chimed in, "We'd always buy a 45 record, and, to beat it all, we didn't even have a record player . . . but we were planning on getting one!" With that, everyone burst out laughing, and Mary Beth added, "Not only that, we didn't even have electricity!" By then, we were all in hysterics!

What motivated Peggy to do so much for her sisters? She was a child herself—only twelve years old—when the last one was born. It was very important to her that her sisters have something special in their lives; if their parents weren't able to provide it, she took it upon herself to do so. She loved those girls and felt sorry for them, and, by making their lives a little bit better, she felt more positive about her own life. Little girls often have big shoulders and take on burdens without being aware that the weight may be too much for them to bear. They sometimes end up paying the price years later as adults. The sisters around the table that day were quick to laugh and quick to cry, remembering those hard times and the sacrifices of their older sisters, which made life more bearable.

Peggy took on the surrogate mother role voluntarily, but that mantle is placed on many girls' shoulders whether they like it or not. It is widely expected that the first girl on the scene *should* be loving and nurturing—anything less than selflessness is subject to disapproval. In decades past, when the work of a family was too much for one woman, the contribution of elder daughters made a critical difference as to whether or not a household functioned well. We are only a few generations away from the days of the coal stove and wringer-washer, and ten thousand years of human patterning doesn't change overnight. The expectation that big sister will play "little mother" remains in many families even today.

The older sister role, although extremely complex, is also the most defined of all of the TOMY positions, both within the family and within society. The burden of being expected to pick up the tasks of surrogate mother may feed a lifetime of resentment, but that is not the only scenario for the older sister. Her level of job satisfaction depends largely on the extent to which being the eldest confers more status than suffering. An eldest sister who has a tremendous amount of responsibility may truly enjoy her role if some measure of power, glory, or pride comes along with the sacrifice.

Besides being a surrogate mother, the older sister is often described as the trailblazer, and, again, there are two sides to this role. The trailblazer may deeply resent that she had to work so hard to cajole her parents into permitting her some privileges, but once they've been softened up, her little sisters breeze along to reap the rewards. On the other hand, she may love the freedom and flexibility of not having to live up to anyone else's example. This chapter looks at the challenges of life as the oldest. We'll examine the many facets of the caretaking and trailblazing roles and learn how they affect sister relationships as adults. We'll also take a good look at how having been the oldest sister profoundly affects a woman's self-image in all aspects of her adult life.

The Sister Relationship as Children

Whenever I ask a roomful of women to define the dominant role of the oldest sister, there is never a second's hesitation in the answer. The extent to which the oldest sister is identified with caretaking is startling.

The Burden of the "Surrogate Mom"

Bianca, a younger sister from Houston, sent me these thoughts about the role of her eldest sister, Jenna: "My sister was the dutiful oldest child who met all of our parents' expectations. She had to take on many adult responsibilities in childhood and was required to make sacrifices on behalf of us younger children. From the age of six on, it became her job to help Mother carry diaper bags and kiddy supplies when we went out, and her assigned seat in the car was the middle of the backseat, so the little ones could look out the window. I think her childhood was very circumscribed."

As mentioned in Chapter 2, fully two-thirds of older sisters in The Sisters Project were described as playing the role of "surrogate mom," "mother's surrogate mate," "mother associate," "parent representative," "in loco parentis," or "trailblazer" or were said to be responsible, bossy, nurturing, and protective. The majority of women in this group were not happy with having had to play the "little mother" role, because they felt that it had constricted their childhood. Many talked about their efforts, as adults, to undo the personality traits that they had acquired; those hyperresponsible, controlling habits got in the way of their other relationships.

In most families, it is just assumed that the firstborn girl will be the mother's helper. Underlying that assumption is a set of unspoken beliefs:

- Females are natural caregivers.
- Sacrifice is noble.

- Jealousy is ignoble (corollary: if you can't avoid it, disguise it!).
- The eldest sets the example (corollary: she could screw up the whole family by taking the wrong path).
- Older sisters are more competent.
- Mothers and fathers approve of girls who nurture (nice girls do . . . change diapers).
- Selfishness is the worst evil and is to be avoided at all costs (see the corollary on jealousy).

Some of the women who had played that surrogate mom role found it painful to talk about. Their childhoods were riddled with guilt, anger, frustration, fear, and helplessness. I talked with women who had felt guilty because, in a frustrated effort to get their sisters to behave, they were mean to them. I met women who were resentful because they were given responsibility but not authority; they couldn't be sure their parents would back them up when they tried to discipline a younger child. I talked with women who, as children, were angry because they would be blamed for the naughty antics of their little sisters. I met with women who spent their childhoods terrified that some disaster would happen to a younger sister in their care.

For example, Leila, now twenty-six, was five when June was born. Leila and June had different fathers, and neither man was long on the scene. The girls shared a bedroom and a bed with their mother, who was loving but struggled with depression. She could often be found asleep on the sofa for twelve to thirteen hours a day. Very early on, June looked to Leila for mothering. Leila described her relationship with June:

"I was very focused on trying to make her happy. When she was about four or five, I would make a piñata out of a paper bag and put little things I found around the house in it—a barrette, a little pencil, a jelly bean, things like that. Then I would stand on the sofa and she would try to hit it with a little plastic fork. At a certain point, I'd drop it and all of the things would fall out, and Junie would love it and laugh.

"When she started school, I did her hair every morning, gave her breakfast, made her lunch; I walked her to her class; I taught her school on weekends. I was extremely overprotective of her. I had a very stern personality that stemmed from the fact that I took responsibility for everything that went wrong. I grew up with a tremendous amount of pain inside of me, trying to protect myself and everyone around me.

"I never relaxed with June. She would never hear me swear; she would never see me smoke. I was trying to lead by example. It took me a long time to let her make her own choices, her own mistakes; that was a constant head-to-head for us. It was not uncommon for us to have huge, huge, huge arguments. It's only in the past three years that I've tried to pull back and learn to let things go. Talking about this makes me sad—I feel I'm holding back tears. I live with it every day—it makes me very emotional. It has threaded itself throughout my life."

Leila was in the caretaking role because of her mother's emotional problems and because she had no father around to help out; there really wasn't anyone else around to parent her little sister. Her story illustrates themes common to many older sisters. Leila talks about having been tough on June in an effort to get her to listen, causing June to resent Leila. She talked about the need to control situations to feel safe herself. She alluded to the guilt she feels because of how she handled things. On the other hand, Leila had a lot of freedom because she was not accountable to anyone. She could make her own decisions and run things pretty much as she wished.

The Guilt Reflex. The silent partner of responsibility is guilt. It's not possible to feel that everything depends on you and not feel, as Leila described, guilty when things go wrong. Some older sisters said that they even felt that it was their fault when their kid sister got into trouble in high school, such as becoming anorexic, addicted to drugs, or pregnant, because they had failed to keep the younger girl on the right track. Older sisters feel that they have to set an example, either because they are told to or because, like Leila, they assign that task to themselves.

It's not easy for parents to get their kids to behave, but it's often twice as hard for an older sister to get her younger siblings to do so. She is a child herself and has limited authority to keep the kids in line. Many women talked about how they had to be tough, even mean, to get their sisters to listen to them. Some older sisters were treated harshly by their parents and took out their anger on their younger sisters, sometimes to the point of being abusive. They talked about being mad at their sisters for misbehaving, which forced them to yell. One woman, the oldest of three sisters, said: "When I was a teenager, all of the responsibility was dumped on me. I was very bossy. I scared my sisters a lot. I used to tell them the boogeyman was coming. They didn't give me a hard time, because they were too afraid of me. I feel pretty bad about it. But I loved them; I just adored them. I still do." Now, as an adult, she is grieved because her relationship with her sisters is so poor that one of them no longer even speaks to her.

The eldest sometimes feels that she has to hide her light under a bushel so that a younger sister won't feel bad about herself. Margot e-mailed this subtle analysis of how she tried to avoid feeling guilty: "There is a bit of irony in this. I remember wanting all of these conflicting things—wanting to do better than her but also feeling badly if I did achieve something that was seen as an accomplishment that she couldn't achieve. I felt that I had to either be less successful than she was; help her reach the same level of success; or hide my successes, if she didn't achieve the same."

Rebecca, twenty-four and contemplating medical school, reflected on the delicate balancing act that takes place in her mind in an effort to protect her twenty-one-year-old sister who chose not to go to college: "I don't want to do too much, because it might make her feel bad. I would hope that if I do great things, she wouldn't mind, but it's always in my mind. I wouldn't want to start being critical of her choices or do something that would indicate that I thought less of her. I wouldn't hide things from her, but I wouldn't boast either."

In Loco Parentis. When Tamika's baby sister was born, her father told her that she was also responsible for the baby. She was twelve at the time and felt overwhelmed by the prospect, which she took very seriously. Like Tamika, many older sisters internalize their role in such a way that they feel that they can never lay down the responsibility, even when they're away from home at school or camp. For example, I interviewed a woman who, as a solemn fourth grader, would check on her sister's progress every day with the younger girl's kindergarten teacher.

In some other cases, teachers or camp counselors assigned the eldest responsibility for her sister. Some reluctant girls tried to wriggle out of that role. Donnalyn sent me this story: "In elementary school, my little sister was once so furious at the lunch lady who asked her to finish her lunch that she threw a horrible tantrum. I was called out of class, and when she was brought to see me, I pretended I didn't know her. Yes, in a school of only a hundred kids, that didn't work too well."

My friend Agnes recounted a lovely vignette about an incident that took place when she and her older sister, Ruth, were away at summer camp. Eleven-year-old Agnes had climbed to the top of the diving tower at the lake intending to jump, but when she looked down, she froze in terror. The camp had a draconian policy that forbade any child from retreating back down the stairs—once you were up there, you had to jump or dive. Dithering tearfully, Agnes was stuck up there a good part of the afternoon, until someone ran and summoned Ruth, who coolly sized up the situation. Ruth decided to jump off the diving board to show Agnes how it was done. She climbed to the top and jumped. No go—Agnes was still too scared. So Ruth just kept climbing up the stairs and jumping off the board, over and over, until, after about fifteen jumps, Agnes finally got up the courage and let fly. Of course, when her head bobbed to the surface, she shouted excitedly to Ruth: "Hey, that was fun!"

Disqualified as a Surrogate Mom. Several women spoke with bitterness about how they had *wanted* to be seen as a surrogate mother, but their little sisters wouldn't play along. The older one yearned to be important in her sister's life—she longed to be needed—but the younger one was just not interested. Barbara told of the pleasure she had derived from caring for little Lucy when they were young children. Both were gymnasts, and Barbara enjoyed spending long hours patiently helping Lucy with her routines. When Lucy reached adolescence, however, something changed. To Barbara's disbelief, Lucy dropped gymnastics and seemed to drop her as well. Lucy developed a very active social life and lost interest in her quiet, homebody older sister, who experienced Lucy's new preoccupations as a rejection. The pattern has continued into adulthood, where it seems as though Lucy, now a successful economist with three children, has little time for or interest in what Barbara has to offer.

I was surprised to see the pattern of a younger sister rejecting the ministering attentions of her older sister already well established in the relationship of little girls. Nine-year-old Charlie had this to say about her seven-year-old sister, Alexandra: "It's really hard to take care of her because she doesn't listen to me. I once told her, 'Don't use this thing,' but she used it anyway. That gets on my nerves because I really like babysitting, but she won't listen to me. Sometimes I try to help her because my dad says, 'You're older so you should take care of her,' so I try, but she just doesn't listen to me." Later, when I asked little Alexandra what she learned from Charlie, she said, "Just one thing— she showed me how to hold her frog."

The Protective Instinct. Some older sisters just revel in their surrogate mom role. For these girls, the burden of being in charge pales in comparison to the pleasure of being in control. These older sisters usually have willing subordinates, keen to go along with the rules of their games. Their younger sisters seem to really need them and appreciate all that is done for them. The older sister feels protective in a loving way; she feels that the younger one brings joy to her life. Accorded the status of being almost on a par with her parents, she has the power to make decisions and is given backup when she does. She may feel good about herself because her little sister looks up to her. And having a little sister offers her a legitimate excuse to get back down on the floor and play with dolls.

You can hear the delight in the tone of this e-mail sent in from Toronto by Mary-Lou: "I was so excited when I found out my mother was pregnant that I ran around telling everyone, 'I'm going to have a baby!' I wanted a sister so badly and prayed for it, so when Mom had a baby girl, I felt my prayers were answered. I always felt very proprietary; she was *my* little sister. Simone DeBeauvoir said exactly the same thing about her sister's birth, 'I had a little sister; that doll-like creature didn't have me.'"

Like Mary-Lou, girls who are five or six years older than their sisters often have vivid memories of them as babies. An extremely protective impulse in the older girl is stimulated as she gazes upon the helpless infant. The need to nurture is powerfully hardwired in some females; having a newborn around is a dream come true. Allegra, thirty-three, sent in this lyrical vignette: "I remember when she was born. I looked into her crib while she was sleeping and had this overwhelming feeling (and I was not even six years old) that she and I had a very deep soul connection, like I knew her forever. Like she was mine, not in a parental kind of way, but like I loved her unconditionally and wanted to teach her things and be there for her. Like we were going to have a special bond throughout our lives."

Twenty-year-old Theresa was also five when her sister was born. She recalled her nervous protectiveness toward the baby, a sentiment that reveals her own fear of hurting the delicate infant: "I remember all of my friends begging to come over to see the baby, but I didn't want them to hold her. I was afraid that they were going to hurt her, but Mom said, 'Don't worry.' So they'd come over and they'd hold her, and I'd be so nervous. I'd be standing over them saying, 'Don't drop her!' I was very overprotective. Even when family came over, I'd say,

'Be careful with my sister! Don't hold her too tight! Stop touching her head!'" You can feel the intensity of that emotion, even though Theresa was just a little girl herself. Mary-Lou's devotion and Theresa's overprotectiveness toward "her" baby reveals the profound nature of the bond that develops in some older sisters, one that will shape these relationships throughout their lives.

Even when the age difference is not as marked, older sisters can feel vividly protective. Melinda described how she was always slim as a teen while her sister, Carrie, one year younger, struggled with her weight. Melinda was hypersensitive to the remarks people would make about her sister's weight problem in high school. It upset her as much or possibly more than it did Carrie, but she made up her mind that she would "never, never, never" mention her sister's weight, and she never did. Carrie, in her interview, said, "She's never, ever commented on my weight. She's the only person who's never bugged me about it, and I respect her a lot for that."

Several women said that having their younger sister look up to them helped their own self-esteem. Cicely told how she came from a poor family and had a hard time in school. She had few friends, struggled with schoolwork, and often felt awkward and shy. In the outside world, she had little status, but within the family, she was important. When she would walk in the door from high school, her two little sisters would come running, delighted to see her. They thought she was so mature and sophisticated, and they turned to her for help with their problems. The fact that they were so impressed with her gave her something priceless—something she could hang on to during the long, lonely days at school.

Bossy Sergeant Major

The older sister role gives some girls free rein to take charge. The oldest of four, Willa, who breezily called herself a "bossy sergeant major," giggled when she said, "I organized everything to a tee!" Her sisters cheerfully accepted her direction, so she could plan things in a way that made perfect sense to her. When they went on long car trips, she would decide who sat where, who lay on the floor with a pillow, and when they would rotate positions—it was all timed and all of the girls were happy to go along with Willa's plans.

Being in a position to arrange everything as they'd like it sometimes leads older sisters to lord it over the others, and there were some who admitted that they would playfully manipulate their kid sisters to get what they wanted. Melinda, the protective slimmer sister mentioned earlier, laughingly recounted how she tricked Carrie into giving up the brand-new Polly Pocket purse she had just gotten for Christmas. She told Carrie that it was too bad that it was so small, then graciously offered to trade Grandma's roomy old purse so Carrie would have plenty of space for all of her things. Wide-eyed with appreciation, Carrie made the trade, and Melinda slinked off with her stylish new treasure.

Playing Like a Little Kid

Part of the fun of being an older sister is getting to regress. Many women told me that they had little rituals and games that they would play with a younger sister that they would have been too embarrassed to suggest to their friends. In the guise of entertaining the littler ones, girls could continue cutting out paper dolls and playing house. Susanna started working delivering newspapers when she was nine and spent most of the money that she earned on Fisher-Price people for her little sister. She acknowledged that she was a bit too old to be playing with little plastic dolls, but saying that it was for her sister gave her the perfect excuse to continue to do so. The two girls would fashion a high-rise out of a board-and-brick bookshelf, pulling out every fifth or sixth book to make separate apartments and elevators. Then they would make up stories about the "people" who lived in the building, creating a whole world for themselves. It gave Susanna, a serious and studious girl, a chance to prolong her childhood. This was particularly important because she was the main support for her divorced mother.

Describing herself as a "mother associate," she felt that she and her mother raised her sister together. She was very matter-of-fact about it, saying that she doesn't remember having many feelings about having to be so responsible for her sister when they were kids: "She was more just something to take care of, like, you vacuum the floor, you water the plants, you take care of your sister."

The Practice Kid

Resentment runs high in older sisters who struggle to get concessions from their parents only to watch their younger cohorts be granted the same and more—*and* at a younger age. Like Coretta, the outraged teen whose anecdote about piercing ears introduced this chapter, everyone had a story to tell about the privileges they had battled for. It's human nature for new parents to be more conservative with their firstborn daughter. They're understandably nervous, not having raised a girl before, and tend to err on the side of overprotectiveness. They're often idealistic, expecting their daughter to follow the rules without question. They may feel the need to prove to the world that they know what they are doing. The first daughter in the family has more of her parents' energy and attention than subsequent ones; it's harder to wriggle out of things. They tend to measure her level of freedom against their own when they were her age and, typically finding her life easier, tighten up the reins as a result. With later children, there's more action in the household. Parents are worn out and reconciled to the fact that the world won't stop if their daughter stays out past eleven.

Interviewing kids and teens for The Sisters Project was particularly fun when the interviews were conducted in their rooms. Kids' rooms are always expressively decorated, revealing much about the girl living there. Eighteen-year-old Mickey's bedroom, for example, was festooned with dance posters. A glass cabinet contained her collection of turtle sculptures, and hanging from its knob was a battered pair of pink satin toe shoes. Her eyes shone with passion as she told me how important dance was to her and about her plan to continue ballet classes, even though she was already in college. That smile faded, how-ever, when the talk turned to the double standard in her family regard-ing the rules her parents had set for her and the much more lenient ones currently in place for her thirteen-year-old sister, Tina: "We're allowed to do the same things, but she's four years ahead of me. My parents were always tougher on me than they are on her. Like, I remember my first date. I was set up by my best friend, Pat, when I was fifteen. When I told my parents that I was going out with Pat and this guy, Gino, they literally stopped. They were like, 'What??!!' They couldn't believe it. And now my sister has already started going out with guys and my parents say, 'Oh, it's okay—no problem.' Where did the grilling go? I had to answer a thousand questions, but with her, it was like, 'okay.'"

Participants in The Sisters Project used a variety of terms to describe this feature of the older sister's role, such as "the practice kid," "the guinea pig," and "the one who breaks the glass ceiling." That their parents tend to be more lenient with younger sisters is the number one reason for resentment and jealousy in older girls. Depending upon the extent to which older sisters view their parents as having been unrea-sonably strict, that resentment can range from mild to bitter and, in some cases, completely poison the relationship between the girls. For some older sisters, detecting unequal treatment (real or perceived) on the part of their parents becomes their raison d'être—they spend their lives sniffing out whether a younger sister got more privileges at an ear-lier stage.

Princess Dethroned: The Nikki-Vikki Story

My mother used to tell the story of the day I was brought home from the maternity hospital. At that time, women remained in the hos-pital several days after delivering babies, so my sister, Nikki, who was five and a half years old at the time, was waiting impatiently outside the apartment building for our mother's return. When the taxi pulled up, Nikki ran exuberantly to greet her mom, who was carefully maneuvering out with me in her arms. Our mother shrank back and sharply told Nikki, "Be careful—don't bump into the baby!" In a flash, Nikki was unceremoniously dethroned and a new princess was anointed. In later years, my surprisingly psychologically minded mother rued that moment, attributing to it the origin of the jealousy that I perceive to have threaded through Nikki's relationship with me.

It is moments like this that cause so many older sisters to be supercharged with jealousy. How parents handle jealousy, either by normalizing it or by demonizing the child who suffers from it, makes a big difference in terms of how much of a hold that awful feeling will have on the older sister. Girls whose parents can empathize with their feelings may still feel some resentment toward the baby, but the intensity is tempered by knowing that, at least, "Mommy and Daddy understand and don't think I'm an awful bad girl."

For children whose parents view the jealousy as naughtiness, the girl not only suffers from her feelings toward her sister but is also alienated from her parents, who punish her for having those feelings in the first place. She becomes angry—angry with her sister for being born, angry with her parents for blaming her, and angry with herself because she knows that nice girls don't feel as vengeful as she does. These feelings develop into a negative spiral. The more the older sister is angry, the more her parents punish her. The more her parents punish her, the more she blames her younger sister and seeks revenge. As she takes out her frustration, her parents back up the younger girl, shaking a disapproving finger at the bitter older sister, and the whole cycle is reinforced. Often, as in my case, the younger girl doesn't want to disappoint her parents and so aspires to perfection, cementing her role as the "good" daughter in counterpoint to the "bad" one.

The Trailblazer

If the concept of "practice kid" relates to parents learning to lighten up with their younger daughters, then the role of trailblazer refers to the influence of the older sister on the younger, over and above their parents' involvement. The trailblazer gets there first (in life), surveys the situation, and decides how to handle it. She can then graciously pass on the wisdom gained from her hard-won experience to help out her little sister, or the little sister can just observe and copy!

When I asked Kate to choose just one sentence that she could have said to her sister when they were kids, she said, "Stop following me!" She was particularly irked when the little brat not only copied her but also surpassed her! "I always felt like she started out walking in my shadow but ended up outshining me in everything she imitated me in. I got 1495 on my SAT in high school; she got 1515. If I did well in my horseback riding competition, she did even better. I graduated with honors in political science from Michigan. My sister graduated a year later, from the same college, in the same degree, magna cum laude! As a kid, it felt like I was trying to hack my way through a dense forest with a tiny, little machete, not knowing where I was headed, not knowing how to get by. I fumbled a lot in the dark, trying to find my way, and then my sister, only a year younger, plowed effortlessly behind, sitting comfortably on a lawnmower, following my already trodden path."

Kate does sound a little jokingly bitter. But many older sisters embrace their role as trailblazer, mentor, or role model and take it very seriously. Ballet-dancing Mickey said, "She looks up to me—it was never really said—but it's fun that I can show her that there's a right way and a wrong way for everything. I don't want to let her down and do something that would make her disappointed in me. I don't think I'm a bad kid; I don't do drugs or smoke or anything, so it's not like she's going to get bad habits from me, but I do want to make her proud of me. I care about her."

For other girls, the job of scout weighs on them. Patricia, the oldest of three, complained that she always had to be the resource for her sisters, but she had no one to guide her. On her first nervous day at the local college, she had to summon up her courage to enter the daunting maze of buildings and find her way around. When her sisters followed her there in subsequent years, she led them by the hand and gave them a personal orientation. She regrets that she never had anyone to ask and resents how her sisters always took her support for granted.

The trailblazer leads the way in areas other than values. Eleven-year-old Jeannie explained how her thirteen-year-old sister, Carla, keeps her up-to-date on the important things in life: "None of my friends have an older sister—I act different from them and I think that's because I have an older sister. Sometimes, I go to school and my hair has, like, mousse in it or something, and my friends say, 'Whoa, what's with your hair? It looks really weird.' And I say, 'I don't know, this is how I like it, this is how my sister showed me.' And a lot of the times, they say, 'Your sweater is so short!' and I say, 'Yeah, but that's how I like it.' I wear it short because my sister said, 'You should wear it like that,' and they're not used to it—it didn't get to them yet. Carla shops at this clothing store, and so I ask, 'Can I buy something from there?' and my friends go, like, 'That's weird!' and then a few days later, you see them wearing the same thing. So I tend to start a lot of trends because I have an older sister."

The Shock Absorber. The trailblazer often camouflages her worry or fear to make her sister's life more secure. When my two daughters were kids, they would frequently fly as unaccompanied minors from Montreal to New York. Michele, who hates turbulence as much as the next girl, would hide her fear so that Lauren wouldn't get even more nervous.

When there is turbulence in the family, the oldest sister often absorbs the shock. Sherry told how she had to become the "rock of the family" when her parents divorced. She had to be the listening post, try to maintain some normalcy for everyone, and, as she tells it, "suck it up." Rebecca, the twenty-four-year-old who was contemplating medical school but worried about outshining her younger sister, related her dilemma caused by her father's recent serious illness. Her sister lives in the same town as their parents and helps out a lot, but Rebecca questions whether she should return home because, as the older daughter, it's really her responsibility.

The Serious One

The sense of responsibility that older sisters carry lead many, dare I say most, of them to describe themselves as being more serious than their younger sisters. Remember how older sisters were never described as being "fun" or "funny"? Reading the following statements made by older sisters is like watching two girls on a squeaky seesaw:

- "I'm an introvert; she's an extrovert."
- "I was a goody-goody; she was a rebel."
- "I was the quiet, studious one; she was outspoken and demanding."
- "I was shy and reserved; she was spontaneous and fun."
- "I was serious, hurried, an overachiever; she brings joy wherever she goes!"

One worried older sister said that she doesn't allow herself to be frivolous because she has to live up to the oldest good-girl image. She described her younger sister, however, as being "like oxygen when she walks into a room!" The younger girl had a lightness and carefree attitude that her older sister could never even dream of emulating.

Ivy's e-mail, however, sounded glum: "As the oldest child I was always more responsible, which I think has led me to be a more serious adult. I have less of a fun side than either of my sisters. I'm the one who is usually pointing out what could go wrong."

Setting the Bar

I've talked about freedom in the older sister role, and in some families, there's no doubt that it is she who sets the bar, particularly if she is a high achiever. Unlike Patricia, who hated being the first girl in her family to find her way around the local college campus, some women enjoy the sense of adventure of being the pathfinder. These women probably had a pretty good sense of themselves to begin with—they have the confidence necessary to feel comfortable in new situations—and they like not having to follow in anyone's footsteps.

Twenty-year-old Cassandra from Iowa wrote that her "just one sentence" expressing her feelings toward her sister growing up would be: "I love you, man" (adding, "You have to have the 'man' there for effect"). Her "just one sentence" as adults would be: "I love you, mannnnn!" The word she would use to describe their relationship was "hilarious." Her affection for her sister bubbled out all over her e-mail, as well as the confidence that being the oldest has afforded her. She had this to say: "I'm way more independent than my sister, and I have always learned things the hard way, or 'my own way.' Even when on a sinking ship, I've always been sure that I would know the best way out. I like my role and I really like myself; I've always been confident. I'm an idiot like that, but I love it—confident when things are bad, confident when things are good! Whatever, I'm just me. I think that I'm something of a leader, although I would never be a dick about it. I'm not bossy, just suggestive."

The Sister Relationship as Adults

The intensity of the childhood relationship often mellows as little girls grow up and move out of their parents' home. Sometimes it becomes sweeter, but sometimes it becomes more distant.

Switchover Point

In the first chapter, "That Sister Mystique," I talked about a switchover that ideally takes place when all of the sisters reach adulthood and the relationship between them reorganizes to become more equal. In reality, however, many older sisters do remain in the nurturing role, and some resent that their younger sisters continue to look to them for the same support and guidance that was the hallmark of their childhood relationship. Even though thirty-three-year-old Kara was a business partner with her younger sister, Deedee, she still couldn't escape that nurturing role. Kara remembered a time when Deedee came to her with a request: "She asked me if I could cover for her at a meeting that she'd scheduled, and I said that I couldn't. She got so annoyed. I felt like I was with a child who asks, 'Can I have a cookie?' and you say, 'Yes,' and ten minutes later, she asks, 'Can I have a cookie?' and you say, 'Yes,' and ten minutes later, she asks again, 'Can I have a cookie?' and you say, 'I'm sorry, I just don't have any more,' and she says, 'Whaddya mean, you stupid bitch!' That sort of thing would happen pretty often when we were working together."

Older sisters may also feel that their younger sisters are selfish as well as demanding. They feel let down when younger sisters put themselves first. Some elders worry that this self-centeredness extends to their sisters' treatment of their husbands and children and wish their sister was a better wife or mother. Sixty-seven-year-old Isabella, whose sister still lives in Italy, said sadly: "She doesn't have a good relationship with her daughter, although I have a good relationship with my niece. She has two gorgeous grandchildren, but the way she talks to them—she's so severe. They know she loves them, but it bothers me."

Many women try to get out of the caretaker role with their younger sisters as adults, but it's so ingrained in them that it's practically impossible to shake off. This following quote sounds like it comes from a woman much older than Keisha: "I catch myself looking after my sister a lot: helping her move from apartment to apartment (which she doesn't do for me), cooking her meals when she comes to visit (when I visit her, we go out to a restaurant), and telling her she should stay in school (which really isn't my place to say, she should make her own decisions, but I can't help it). I think being the older sister has made me act older than my age—I'm twenty-four years old, a homeowner, in graduate school, and getting married in three months. I just feel so . . . settled."

Wanting the Best for Her

One of the most pervasive sentiments expressed by older sisters was a passionate wish that their little sisters' lives would turn out well. Many women said that they could not enjoy their own success if their sisters were not equally as successful. This wish grows out of the loving connection that older sisters feel but also out of the sense of responsibility that makes it hard to imagine being able to feel comfortable if a sister is troubled. Perhaps there is a subconscious desire to be able to lay down the burden of needing to make life good for a younger sister. Melinda described how she cried with joy at Carrie's wedding: "I didn't cry like that for my own wedding, but at her wedding, I was so happy for her and so emotional about my sister. I want the best for her so much!"

Lisa poured out her big-sister worry in her e-mail: "Nobody else, other than my sister, could I love and despise equally in one person, and I mean that in the sweetest way. I get annoyed with how flippant and indecisive she is about life. I worry about her future, yet she doesn't seem to care. I wonder why she doesn't date, and when I mention it, she gets defensive. I hope she eats well, eats right, takes care of herself, dresses warmly. She stresses me out so much sometimes, worrying about her!!!"

Carmella's younger sister had to laugh about her big sister's determination to find her a husband: "It's a joke how she was trying to fix me up. She would stop people in the bank; she went to a book review and the author was single—she gave him my card—or the congressman for our district—his wife died—she's calling him up. So I know that she means well, but puh-lease! Give it up!"

The Oldest Sister Stamp

Being an oldest sister naturally imprints such an indelible stamp on a woman's identity that many spend their lives replicating that role of responsible caregiver, the person in control, whether on the job, with friends, or in love relationships. That impulse suits some women just fine—it enhances their lives and doesn't seem to get in their way. Many, however, are burdened by it and feel that it limits them in a variety of ways. Those overfunctioning elders have often remarked to me that they are working hard on themselves trying to change that compulsion to control.

Natural Nurturers

Women who are comfortable with their caretaking traits talked about how they learned to be independent thinkers and problem solvers, skills that they enjoy applying. They are self-confident, natural nurturers and have learned to parlay their abilities into successful relationships. Perhaps they are not so bossy that they alienate people, or maybe the people around them are happy to look to them for leadership. A university professor proudly said that she feels protective of younger women in general and experiences a sense of satisfaction when she helps them develop their potential. Another participant said that she likes crisis management and that is why she became a clinical psychologist.

Because they are naturally independent, some older sisters are unaware of the extent to which others in their circle depend on them for caretaking. When my elder daughter, Michele, was twenty-seven, she went through an illness serious enough to necessitate that she move from her apartment in Toronto back to Montreal to live with us. One of the hardest parts of that difficult time for her was coping with the way her friends in Toronto dealt with her leaving. They seemed far more preoccupied with their own sadness about her departure than they were with the trauma she was experiencing. They even expected her to comfort them! Michele was flabbergasted—if she were in their position, she would have done anything in her power to encourage a sick friend. After shaking her head about this for several months, something remarkable suddenly dawned on her. She counted on her fingers—one, two, three. Her closest friends were all younger siblings and had typically looked to her to make things right. Now she was leaving them and they felt abandoned.

Fear of Making Mistakes

Some older sisters, rather than being confident, find themselves very hesitant and fearful of making mistakes. They may have spent their childhoods second-guessing themselves—"Am I doing this right?"—and, as adults, can't shake that impulse. This is particularly true of women whose parents were critical and demanded perfection. These women felt that they could never measure up.

As a child, Juanita had struggled to help her younger sister, who was developmentally delayed, and always felt bad that her help was not enough to significantly improve her sister's school experience. That fear of failure continues to pervade her adult life: "I have always felt enormously guilty about not being able to fulfill all of my responsibilities. As a result, I am too serious and often depressed, even when things are going well. This is my oldest sister syndrome, I guess. I lack self-confidence, even when others praise me, and I resent being asked for advice or for other kinds of help because I doubt my ability to give what is being asked for."

Women who can use their older sister traits to their advantage without too much internal conflict, however, were probably girls whose place in their childhood family was secure and valued. The reactive emotions of guilt and fear of failure were not cultivated by their parents or family circumstances growing up, so they did not incorporate those reflexes into their psyches.

Overfunctioners

Women often have a love/hate relationship with that part of themselves that overfunctions. Everyone agrees that it's good to be responsible, careful, and protective, but only to a point. When those qualities are fueled by guilt, anxiety, and fear, the charm fades fast. For many older sisters, to feel comfortable in their skin, they need to know that everything is under control. But before they can relax, it all has to be under *their* control, so they can be sure it's safe. They have been conditioned since childhood to expect disaster if they let down their guard, and the belief that apocalypse is imminent is pretty hard to change. As one woman said, "I have a high need to ensure security for those I love."

These things, learned in early childhood, have become so much a part of the fabric of a woman's thinking that she often can't take the necessary step back to challenge the absurdity of them. Forty-seven-year-old Annette describes the strange forces that drive her: "I feel responsible for everyone and everything. I have a tremendous amount of guilt about things over which I don't have control, never did have control, and have no reason to expect to have control. I tend to act as an older sister to everyone. I like being in charge of things and taking care of everyone. I try to curb those tendencies but sometimes fail miserably."

Self-Denial

Perfectionist thinking pushes older sisters to be hard on themselves. When you have had too much responsibility before you were old enough to handle it, you come to believe that if you don't succeed at something, it could lead to disaster. It's hard to give yourself permission to be less than exemplary. Older sisters are often so busy taking care of everyone else that they forget to pamper themselves. They have become experts at denying their own needs and at delaying gratification. As Helen wrote, "Being the older sister created a sense that I was the one in charge and that I had no one to turn to beyond myself; that I should hide any insecurity, fear, or sadness because people are counting on me."

Another take on the same theme came from twenty-four-year-old Keisha: "I catch myself telling my friends to watch how much they drink at bars—I don't drink because I'm *always* the designated driver. I watch out for the guys my friends hook up with. I always make sure they call me when they get home safely. I don't smoke. I don't do drugs. I adamantly lecture about condom use to all of my friends. I guess I feel protective of them!"

The Perfectionist: Ruby's Story

I went to Ruby's financial consulting firm on a beautiful, sunny March morning, the kind of day in Montreal that makes you really believe that winter will eventually end. Her office is located in the basement suite of her home, and her amber-eyed Angora cat kept tapping to come inside and then to be let outside and then managing to sneak back inside again. Ruby must really like cats—her computer makes a meowing sound when she receives a new e-mail.

Thirty-seven-year-old Ruby is the oldest of three sisters; the others are nine and eleven years younger. As a kid, Ruby was always expected to look after her sisters whenever she wasn't in school. Their mother was a nurse and did shift work, and their father was certainly not interested in child care. Even when her mother was around, Ruby was not impressed with her mother's parenting skills and felt that she had to spend a lot of time protecting the younger girls from their mother's hot temper: "I participated enormously in the raising of these children. The youngest one was almost like my child because I would feed her and bathe her, and, I remember, her first steps were with me. When she was five, she had a little car accident and hurt her shoulder, so she slept with me for a month. She was very close to me then and I'm still very close to her—a special bond.

"Until I went to therapy when I was thirty, I always felt extremely responsible for my sisters. We grew up in Kentucky, and when I left home at twenty-one, they were still quite young. I was worried about them and felt I'd abandoned them. There was a lot of guilt—it was not normal. In therapy, I worked through the fact that they're not my kids and I'm not responsible, and that intense guilt stopped.

"But because of what I went through growing up, I'm a caretaker. I'm a caretaker in my job, and I even see it with my assistant, who is the same age as my youngest sister. I have good people skills, and everyone here depends on me. I'm a very take-charge kind of person and have a hard time knowing my limits. If I'm not careful, I'll let my job take over completely. I even have a problem of feeling guilty when I'm having fun. When I go on holiday, I usually find myself regretting having gone and need to talk myself around into relaxing enough to enjoy myself.

"I'm independent—sometimes too independent. I haven't had a love relationship in a very long time. I think that I kind of scare men in the sense that I know what I want and I'll just do what I have to do to get it. I don't wait around for somebody else to do it for me, and that makes men feel uncomfortable. I would have a hard time letting someone else take care of me even if I wanted to. It probably wouldn't feel natural. I have to do things in a proper way—I'm a perfectionist.

"And it's funny, I don't have any children, but I always felt I've had my kids already. If I had had the opportunity, I probably would have had kids, but I don't think I'd be such a great mother. I probably would have been way overprotective and maybe stifling."

That Self-Reliant Muscle

The character traits of older sisters like Ruby don't always lend themselves to smooth personal relationships. The need to be in control in order to feel comfortable means that partners, friends, and colleagues may have to make compromises that they are not always willing to make. These others have to permit the adult older sister to have things her way or risk conflict. Adult big sisters are aware, at times, that they give advice too readily, without being asked, and that it sometimes puts people off.

As Ruby described, adult older sisters often have trouble depending on others. They spent their whole childhood flexing that self-reliant muscle, so by the time they are grown up, it's overdeveloped. Not only do they feel uncomfortable when they are not in control, they also cannot really believe that anyone else would *want* to take care of them. It feels like too much of a luxury to permit themselves to relax back into another's care—a guilty pleasure, but also a bit scary, like they're asking too much. That older sister discomfort with being cared for can cause problems for friends or lovers who try to get close and perhaps meet their own desire to be needed.

Pressure from friends and family sometimes forces some older sisters into acknowledging that they need to unlearn some of the interactive patterns they developed as kids. This unlearning process can take place either through self-reflection or by participating in therapy. Diana wrote about her process of change: "I've had to learn how to let go and not overmanage situations, and it has been a journey! I've had to learn how to just be. My whole view is about what have I done and I literally can't believe I am offering anything to a group if I just sit there quietly. I am glad to be unlearning some of this."

The Older Sister Unmasked

We've explored the gamut of the older sister personality, both as a child and as an adult, and can see that it covers quite a range. As the one in the family often called upon to care for the others, the older sister may feel either privileged or pressured. How she experiences those early responsibilities goes a long way in explaining the character traits that are evident in her in adulthood. An older sister may develop a tremendous feeling of self-confidence and may find that her leadership qualities contribute greatly to her ability to achieve things. On the other hand, she may have suffered through a childhood awash in anger and guilt, leading to an adulthood in which she is crippled by jealousy and resentment—or somewhere in between. But we can track a clear line from her role in her family to the ways in which she deals with the world as an adult.

The next chapter will look at the life experience of her mirror image, the youngest sister, and see how the girl on the receiving end of the caretaking grows up with a very different set of personality traits. Then we will have set the stage to understand the middle sister, who is affected by the dynamics of both the older and the younger. Finally, in this part of the book on the sister hierarchy, we will look at the very special relationship of twins.

In Her Footsteps

The Youngest Sister

"I remember that my older sister, Emma, used to walk me to school when I was in kindergarten and she was in sixth grade. One particular day, it was so windy that I was literally lifted off my feet. Emma told me to walk behind her and hold on to her waist. I remember feeling so safe, anchored to her, with her breaking the wind for me. It's a perfect metaphor for our relationship."

—MAUDE, fifty-eight years old

From Powerless to Princess

Fifty-eight-year-old Maude's simple story illustrates the comforting sense of security that she enjoyed around Emma. She was little and cared for and loved. If only younger sisters' emotions were always that uncomplicated. In reality, they run the gamut from total powerlessness ("Being the baby meant to me—it's like a dog. Kick the dog away; it's not important.") to a sense of entitlement typically accorded to princesses in fairy tales, and feelings from younger toward older sisters can range from total trust to terrified.

A family is a living organism, constantly in a state of change. The mind-set of the parents at the time their youngest daughter is born is not the same as it was when the oldest girl made her appearance. The family has evolved. The parents may not only be in different financial circumstances (often improved), experience better or worse health, or have a stronger or more fragile marital relationship, but they will have learned a few things about parenting from the experience of raising their older daughter.

Most parents' parenting styles change over time. They tend to become more relaxed as they realize that children will not easily be coerced into doing what's expected of them. Parents for whom rigid rules seemed to make perfect sense when their older daughter was fifteen are now chuckling, "What *were* we thinking?" when the next girl in line reaches the same age; their old rules now seem out of date.

The Sister Relationship as Children

The role of the youngest girl carries with it a strong emotional charge for her older siblings. They tend to feel either extremely warmly or intensively negatively toward her; her position is rarely neutral.

The Cuteness Factor

Claudia, the middle of three thirty-something sisters, had given a lot of thought to the question of why Dale, the youngest, was so indulged. Claudia speculated that her parents just got tired of fighting by the time Dale was approaching her teens. She hypothesized that there is a "twinkle in the eye" that parents reserve for the youngest. She called it "the charm" of being the littlest girl—the cuteness factor—and said that in her family, the youngest extended the spirit of childhood in her parents' lives. Dale's mere existence kept their parents young longer.

Some older sisters dote on the little princess as much or even more than their parents do. An older girl's eyes may also twinkle when her little sister walks in the room. There may be a lovely complicity between the older sister, who cherishes her live doll and enjoys being needed, and the younger girl, who is more than happy with the doting attention she receives.

For some older sisters, however, that glint in the eye is a glare rather than a twinkle as they watch the goalposts being moved to accommodate their spoiled little sister's demands. As parents are busy fawning over the newcomer, the older girl's agenda may include a plan to cut this young pretender down to size, using the power inherent in her superior age—she is more experienced, more competent, and more savvy.

Whether feted or deflated, the hallmark of the younger sister is powerlessness. It's easy to see how she might feel powerless when her big sister is lording it over her, but a dose of helplessness comes with being indulged as well. Psychologists know that self-esteem develops when a person is challenged, rises to the test, and succeeds. If everything is presented on a silver platter, she's robbed of the opportunity to enjoy that pride of accomplishment. I remember, as a child, saving my babysitting money to buy a record player. I was only a few dollars short when my mother surprised me by buying me the exact one I had had my eye on. I was furious, but she was baffled. How could I not be happy to effortlessly receive the very thing I had wanted for so long? Because (the lament of "little Vikki") "I wanted to do it myself!"

Under Her Thumb

It's difficult for a child to develop self-confidence when she is constantly being told by an older, more powerful sister, that she is spoiled, stupid, ugly, or just plain wrong all of the time. Younger sisters in The Sisters Project readily recounted some of the sarcastic put-downs they had to put up with, muttered comments along the lines of "You think you're so smart!" and "You're such a baby!" and far worse.

Women talked about not being taken seriously by their older sisters, about feeling that they didn't get much respect in the family growing up. In some cases, older sisters were mean and cruel, intentionally keeping their thumbs on the younger one so she wouldn't get "too big for her britches." Daisy, eighty-four, is the woman who made the "kick the dog" comment earlier. She was the youngest of four sisters whose mother died when she was a small child, leaving her sisters free rein to take out their frustrations on her. She said, "I always felt that I was a failure. I was never told I did anything well. In fact, my older sister used to say, 'Why do you talk so much when you have nothing to say?'" Those hurts are still there eighty years later.

The bitterness is palpable in Jan's e-mail in which she described growing up in a home environment similar to Daisy's: "For a long time, I had little self-confidence. My sisters had labeled me a misfit and I bought it. Their way of 'helping' me was to tease, coerce, and shame me into being more like them. The result was that I largely avoided relationships. I really wasn't interested in being around other people, because I thought I lacked the skills to relate to them." Another woman e-mailed, "[My sister] used to humiliate me in front of my friends by yelling at me like I was ignorant and childish, even though I was a 'leader' with my friends."

The Bottom of the Totem Pole

One of the focal points for younger sisters' laments about lack of respect centered on the cavalier manner in which their older sisters messed with their stuff. These frustrated younger girls might find their best new clothes rolled up in a ball on the floor of their big sisters' closets. Here's a sample of what different women wrote:

- "She went through a phase of stealing my clothes. I found an outfit of mine mildewed in the garage. I was furious and cursed her out."

- "She read my diary when I was in grade school. That was not a good point in my life."
- "She didn't respect my privacy; she'd go into my room and just take whatever she wanted!"

The older sisters described here didn't take the concerns of their younger sisters seriously. They knew that the younger girl wouldn't like what they were doing, but that was not enough of a deterrent to get them to stop. They probably subconsciously felt that they had the right to take what they wanted from their younger sisters' rooms, justifying it in their own minds with a rationalization like, "Well, she always gets everything *she* wants from Mom, so why shouldn't I?"

Along the same lines, some younger sisters felt taken advantage of because their older sister sought their company only if nothing better was available. Della sent in the following: "A lot of times, my sister and I would make plans to go out, but if something better came up, she would just dump me. I was the fallback plan. I don't think I was like an eager puppy, but it was more like, 'Okay, we already made plans—let's do it.' Not to say it didn't hurt when she would dismiss me and disregard me. I went through several years of that. At that point in our lives, I didn't like her much."

Billie, the soccer-playing youngest sister from the opening story in Chapter 2, adopted a philosophical tone when telling about her role in the family: "I wasn't a threat to anybody. I had no power, no status. If my sisters wanted to beat up on someone, I was always available because I wasn't strong. They picked on me—well, not really—but they knew they had power over me. Anything—'You have to make the salad.' Not that they were cruel or mean, but in the sense that nobody felt threatened by me."

Billie's family didn't worry much about her feelings in all of this. They were just too busy living their own lives, and it seemed like the natural order of things. If you'd tapped Billie's mom on the shoulder back then and suggested that her youngest daughter needed some support, she probably would have looked at you in surprise and explained that things were the same in her family growing up, too.

The Slave: Gayle's Story. I arrived to interview Gayle at her impressive East Hampton house and found everything in turmoil. There were workmen everywhere and the entrance was guarded by a housekeeper who, for some unknown reason, seemed to have more status than Gayle. A Great Dane greeted me at the door, keen to show me her saliva-covered toy, which I duly admired. It was the day devoted to cleaning all of the rugs, so to my surprise, Gayle ushered me into her and her boyfriend's light and airy bedroom, which overlooked the beach. The room had that intimate disorder of an unmade bed and crumpled pajamas lying around. At the foot of the human bed was an enormous plaid dog bed. After I got over the strangeness of being entertained in the bedroom of a woman I had just met, I felt very relaxed. I was installed in a big, white, overstuffed chair—at least we weren't sitting on the bed. As Gayle went to get an extension cord for my tape recorder, I reflected on how only a younger sister would assign her own meeting such low priority that she would hold it in her bedroom so as not to inconvenience the workers.

As the gray ocean light filtered through the window, Gayle detailed for me the dynamics of her childhood home. She is the youngest of three; Joanne, the middle sister, is four years older, and Livia, the oldest, is five years older. She described Livia as having been a very serious student and not one for dating—the kind of teen who worried about World War III. Joanne was the party animal. And Gayle's role? "It's still a joke in our family that my parents babied me so terribly that I actually only got out of my crib when I went into kindergarten. I wasn't allowed to bathe myself until high school. Literally!" She had the lowest status in the family and reminisced about what that meant: "I ended up being 'the slave.' Nobody ever went to get a drink for themselves. Friday night meals, it was 'Gayle, go get me a ginger ale.' They forgot their glasses when they were watching TV downstairs, 'Gayle, go get my glasses.' I remember every week saying to myself, 'That's it; this is the last week. I'm going to say something!'—which I never would do. I was at the bottom of the totem pole. There was only a downward movement in the hierarchy; so, let's say, if my sisters were angry, they could express it toward me, but I could never express it toward them. They could say 'shuddup' to me; I couldn't say 'shuddup' to them—that kind of stuff. There was a lot of frustration.

"I think, as a result, I'm an underachiever from way back. I have laziness in me; I lack confidence. My sisters think they can accomplish things, but I'm afraid of a lot of things. To me, the world is a fearful place. I've got phobias; I've got idiosyncrasies."

Gayle attributes her role as the powerless youngest sister in her family as a major cause of the problems she has faced trying to get ahead in life. Her confidence was constantly undermined. Day after day during her childhood, the message was reinforced that the youngest was the least important.

Vying for Air Time

It's just natural that for most small children *big* means "better" and *little* means "less." We tend to use the word *little* as a put-down— "You're such a little *blah-blah-blah*"—and the word *baby* . . . don't ask! Babies have no power whatsoever. That's why there is such a strong drive among children to get big! Some women follow their sisters through life, always being referred to as so-and-so's little sister, feeling as though the standard has been set by the older one and now they have to live up to it. Even at eighty-six, Sharon bitterly recalled how she limited her options to avoid coming up short in comparison to her scientist sister: "My sister was brilliant and beautiful, and her deportment was perfect. How could I compete with that? Never wanting— or daring—to vie with her, I steered clear of science and math, although I later learned that I had real talents in those fields."

All of this engenders insecurities in these younger sisters. They are vulnerable to being diminished at will by older sisters who need to boost their own self-esteem by lowering their sisters'. The younger girl may become hesitant to voice her opinion. She has to fight for air time at the dinner table; when she does speak up, she may be ridiculed. For some girls, it is easier to adopt their sister's opinion than it is to come up with a justification for their own that will be taken seriously, so they just follow the party line. Mary Jane wanted so much to be accepted that she was ready to compromise her position at a moment's notice if it meant that she could be seen to have fallen into step with her sister: "I remember looking through the Sears catalog with my older sister when we were kids, and she pointed to something and asked me if I liked it. I said, 'Yes,' but then she said, 'Oh, I don't,' and I felt I had to change my mind to agree with her so she wouldn't think I was stupid."

Thirty-year-old Vanessa wrote about the pressure of having to live up to an older sister's accomplishments: "Always feeling you have to prove yourself can be quite tiring and take up a lot of energy. If you just focus on accomplishing something, you do it and it's done. But when you feel you need to do it to prove something, because there's an older sibling watching you, it takes twice as much energy and effort. It's not enough to do well; I have to do well because I have to prove that I'm capable, and that's a pressure."

Vanessa's sister, Bridget, only two years older, was one of those older sisters firmly planted in the surrogate mom role. Their family had lived overseas in various cities due to their father's job, so Vanessa naturally turned to Bridget for everything when they were kids. Vanessa talked about the push and pull of trying to become independent, fighting her natural tendency to just let her big sister take over: "I think Bridget, being the older sister, just wanted to help and be needed. But sometimes, I read it as her thinking that I was not capable of accomplishing things on my own. If someone is always trying to do things for you, you think that they don't have faith that you can do it yourself. The message is, 'Don't worry if you can't, because I'm here for you and I can.' That's not such a good thing. I think it actually lowers your self-confidence.

"In a sense, I had the feeling that she was waiting, expecting, almost hoping that I'd fail, so that she could step in and save the day.

It's as though you have a cheerleader behind you, but she's not saying, 'You can do it!' Instead, she's saying, 'It's okay if you can't, because I can do it for you.' It almost encourages you to fail. Sometimes it's just easier to give in and say, 'Okay, you do it,' which doesn't really build self-esteem."

Vanessa went on to say that her childhood struggle to believe that she could accomplish things on her own has affected her confidence as an adult. She still has an old reflex that tells her that if she doesn't get the job done, someone else will come along to mop it up for her.

Entitled to the Best

Some younger sisters, like Gayle, the family "slave," have been trained to believe that they are entitled to very little. They occupy the bottom of the totem pole, and no one is overly concerned with their needs. But others, like Vanessa, develop a sense of entitlement because they expect that their older sisters will always be there to smooth the way. They grew up with parents who predictably took their side in any sisterly argument and believed that the biggest piece of cake *should* go to them. Their parents typically chastised the older sisters, saying things like, "You're older—why can't you just let her watch her show?" and "How could you take the last cookie when you knew your sister would want it? You're so selfish." The younger sister understandably comes to believe that it's her older sibling's job to make sacrifices on her behalf; if she is aware of the injustice being perpetrated, she keeps it to herself and enjoys her guilty pleasure.

Thus, the structure in some families becomes very clearly defined. Even in cases where the age difference between the girls is minimal, the older one may have been told that she must always defer to the needs of the younger. Parents often want to avoid the youngest throwing a tantrum and do so by getting the older girl to acquiesce. Some parents feel sorry for the younger for some reason and want to even things out by using the heartier-seeming older girl as a counterweight.

A nine-year-old girl who has to give up the red jelly beans to her seven-year-old sister will have to continue giving things up two years later, when her little sister herself is nine. The back wheels never catch up to the front wheels on the cart; the front wheels will always have to take the bumps first. This trains younger sisters in some families to believe that the correct order of things is that they are entitled to the best.

Shielded and Protected

We saw in the last chapter how an older sister had to summon up her courage to find her way around college on the first day and how she took her younger sister by the hand and escorted her around when she entered the same school a few years later. Some younger sisters enjoy a wonderful sense of security, knowing that there is always someone whose mission in life is to back her up. Some have said that having that backup made it easier to take risks when they were young.

An older sister's protection may, at times, be necessary in some situations. I heard more than once from women whose sisters helped them when, as teens, they became pregnant. This vignette from forty-three-year-old Melanie from Virginia illustrates how an older sister summoned up her resources and courage to, literally *and* figuratively, save her sister's life: "The first time I had sex, I got pregnant. I was sixteen. I didn't know what to do and even contemplated suicide; I had a gun. Finally, after months of doing nothing about it, I told my sister. She made arrangements for me to have a late-term abortion out of state. She let me use her ID, somehow raised the money, organized the transportation, and got me a place to stay with some friends of hers in Kentucky, where I had to go. She never judged me or acted disappointed in me; she never made me feel bad. When I think of it now, although only eighteen, she was wise beyond her years. She stepped up to the plate, knowing I was totally overwhelmed, and came through for me."

Surrogate Baby

If two-thirds of older sisters are described as surrogate moms, then we need to look at the experience of the legion of girls who were "parented" by these sisters—the "babies" of the surrogate moms. Often their "just one sentence" as kids was "Leave me alone!"—a hollow refrain that is the anthem of younger sisters everywhere when face-to-face with a bossy big sister.

One of the prerogatives of surrogate moms is to make the rules for those in their charge; along with responsibility often comes power. Some younger sisters talked about feeling terrorized by an older sister and fearing her discipline even more than that of their parents. Chi-anna, from London, e-mailed this: "My angry memories center around the fact that she was allowed to discipline me if I didn't obey her. She would often hit me or call me names. I hated being belittled by her. I wasn't always able to predict her moods. Sometimes she would let me get away with things, and other times she would be all over me; I hated her unpredictability. Although deep down I loved her and respected her, she sure knew how to make me fearful."

Beverley spoke about how her older sister, Adra, bossed her around and how much she feared the older girl's anger. They shared a room until her sister moved out; even at night when she was in her bed, Beverley still had to be careful. Adra was crazy about Elvis, and Beverley had to be sure to avoid intruding on her nightly ritual: "We shared a room, but there were clear boundaries. I wasn't to look at her; I wasn't to touch her. If she ever caught me looking at her when she was kissing her great big picture of Elvis on the wall above her bed each night, she'd scream, 'Turn around!' She bossed me around terribly."

Cherished Kid Sisters

Surrogate moms, like real moms, come in all varieties and are certainly not all as scary as Chianna's and Beverley's. I received e-mails from two women who credit their older sisters with nurturing their love of literature and writing. Caitlin, fifty-eight, told how her sister introduced her to the classics, from A to Z: "One of her assignments was to supervise my chores, so it was from her that I learned how to clean house, cook, and iron. But it was also my sister who got me enrolled in a school for gifted girls. She guided my reading from age twelve through the end of high school so I would not be disadvantaged, as she had been. She brought me four novels a week from the public library, selecting classics alphabetically by author, starting with Jane Austen through to Emile Zola!" Sixty-nine-year-old Meg, who became a journalist, credited her sister with starting her off in that direction: "One memory of my older sister was when I was about nine or ten and decided I wanted to be a writer; she was very encouraging. She bought me my first copy of *The Writer's Handbook* (which I still have!), and that made me feel special."

Vanessa told what life was like for her as a surrogate baby: "Bridget definitely mothered me a lot, which sometimes drove me crazy. She would try to get me to do things her way, learn from her mistakes, but I wanted to learn for myself and do things my own way, so I often ignored her advice, which made her really frustrated. There was a lot of her saying, 'Listen to me!' and me saying, 'Leave me alone! I can do it myself.' My grades weren't as good as Bridget's, and although I did far less work, I didn't do too badly and I think that drove her nuts. I would be on the phone with friends all night, not studying, and she'd be on my case, remembering how difficult the test was when she'd done it two years before. She'd try to get me to study, warning me how hard it would be. I wouldn't study and then I'd panic. She would do the whole 'I told you so' thing and would probably be more nervous about my taking the test than I was. Then I'd do fine, which would piss her off even more."

In another dimension of their relationship, you could hear the loving "mom" quality as Vanessa told how her sister would tuck her in at night: "When Bridget would come to tuck me in at night, she'd play a game that we called 'Make Me Cold.' She would lift up my comforter and shake it around above me, while I lay in my bed. The draft from the cover would make me all shivery and then she would drop the comforter back down on top of me and tuck it in all around me, so that I was all cozy. I loved that!"

Role Reversal

Younger sisters love it when the power balance is reversed, even temporarily. Francine sent in this demonstration of her younger sister's use of blackmail: "My funniest memory of my sister is of when I was in the sixth grade and she was in kindergarten. She found an old frilly apron at my grandma's house and announced that she was going to wear it to school so that everyone would know that she was going to grow up to be just like her mom. Well, I had a complete and total hysterical breakdown, running around the house screaming, 'You're not allowed to do that!' My five-year-old sister totally silenced me. She said, 'If you don't let me wear the apron, I'm going to tell the whole school that you wear Smurf day-of-the-week underpants.' It was a tactical coup, and I had to let her wear the apron."

In a different kind of role reversal, the younger girl takes pride in being in the protective role. Several women described how they would do the talking for the both of them in public because their older sisters were shy. One woman even ran interference with their parents: "When we used to go shopping for school clothes, I would say, 'Catherine, do you want to try on that shirt?' and she'd say, 'Yes,' so I'd say, 'Mom and Dad, that's the shirt she likes.'"

When my own daughters were little, I once took them to the Museum of Natural History with a friend and her seven-year-old son, Max. All afternoon, Max delighted in tormenting five-year-old Michele by hiding behind exhibits, yelling "Boo!" and jumping out to scare her. As we wandered around the displays depicting prehistoric life, three-year-old Lauren, buckled into her stroller, would exasperatedly squeak to this much older boy, "You leave my sista alone! You leave my sista alone!"

The Wind Beneath My Wings

Three younger sisters who participated in The Sisters Project said that their sisters were the "wind beneath my wings." In the song by that name, Bette Midler sings about her hero, the one who helps her fly high and accomplish great things. This lovely sentiment is felt by some younger sisters who talked in reverent terms about all that their devoted sisters had done for them. I was particularly moved by the passion expressed in the interviews of children and teens toward their in-house heroines. Ten-year-old Ramona sounded incredulous as she described the special qualities of her thirteen-year-old sister, Amy: "First of all, I think she's gorgeous, and second of all, I think she's got a great lot of friends and a great lot of respect. At camp, I was 'mini-Amy' for a while and I felt envious that a lot of people knew her so well that they would call someone they didn't know so well after her. I feel jealous and sometimes I feel sad, but not angry, because there's nothing she could do. She has an amazing personality, which I envy, and I talked with her about it, and she said, 'I'll help you with your personality.' We talked about it a bit, and she told me what I should do in made-up situations."

What comes across loud and clear from Ramona is both her adoration and her envy, as if she fears she could never be as "great" as Amy. She wants and needs so much to be important in Amy's universe that her love is tinged with a fear of loss.

Ramona went on to recount the lessons that Amy has taught her about life: "My sister is always telling me 'be yourself.' If 'yourself' is someone who likes to read all day and that's what people call being a nerd, you're not a nerd—that's you. It really made sense to me then. Even if you're the most popular person in the school, it doesn't matter, because they don't love you; they love what you're acting like and that's not the real you. And that's the most important lesson she taught me."

Being Left Behind

The painful disappointment that comes when an older sister's attention is withdrawn was spoken of frequently in younger sisters' interviews and e-mails. A common pattern was one in which the girls were quite close as young children, but when the older one moved into the next stage, the preteen or teen years, and her love life or friends become primary, the younger one was bewildered and hurt, feeling left behind. That feeling became heightened at the point at which the older sister left home or married. Some younger sisters felt betrayed. The cozy familiarity of after-dinner strolls to get ice cream or watching a video together on the old couch in the basement was forever changed.

Meredith, twenty-six, recalled her distress as boys started to move in on her exclusive relationship with her sister: "I was looking for that close, close relationship with her, and, when she was quite young, she became interested in boys while I was still interested in toys. I got very upset because I felt these guys were taking my sister away from me and it really, really bothered me. I remember when I was ten and she was twelve, my parents were out somewhere and we were washing dishes. One of the boys she liked stopped by and was talking to her in the driveway, and I went outside and grabbed her and shouted, 'Get in the house and do the dishes!' I was just so upset that this guy was sort of taking my sister away from me."

Sunny, in her early twenties, described that same frustration but with an awareness of how normal it was to be in mismatched stages: "It was very hard for me when she moved on to the next stage where her friends became more important, because I wasn't there yet. The family was still the top priority for me. She first started dating her boyfriend when she was eighteen and I was fifteen. I saw her lean on him and go to him for advice, wanting to spend all of her time with him and that was tough for me. I would have wanted to be part of that self-definition process with her, but I guess that's unrealistic. She was still seeing me as just a kid."

These young women were quite close to their sisters as kids, and, although they may have felt left behind in their midteens, they resumed a different kind of close relationship as adults. For other women, however, that nurturing attention was gone forever. Even if the age difference was as little as just one year, the younger girls in these families longed for their older sisters to play that caring role. This is the mirror image of those older sisters, described in the previous chapter, who long for their indifferent little sisters to accept their ministrations. Zsuzsi, sixty-seven, always idolized her sister, seven years older, but felt largely invisible in her sister's universe: "I vividly remember her wedding. I was thirteen—old enough to be a bridesmaid but she didn't ask me. It was a large wedding with lots of bridesmaids (our other sister was maid of honor), but she didn't invite me to be in the wedding party. I was crushed."

Following the Path

Younger sisters have a lot to be jealous of; along with being a second, third, or fourth daughter, they often have to put up with second-hand clothes, bikes, skis, and all of the rest. They watch from the sidelines as their older sisters get to do things and go exciting new places, while they have to sit patiently and wait their turn. Things have lost their mystery by the time they get to the younger sisters—the shock of the new has worn off. Summer camp, the senior prom, driving lessons—they're all old hat when the younger ones finally get there, so they may feel that it's silly to get all excited.

Most younger sisters in The Sisters Project, however, would not have chosen to change their TOMY position as children. They liked having that older girl clear the way with her little machete so that they could follow the already trodden path. They liked feeling protected; the burden was on someone else's shoulders. This reflection on the younger sister role came from sixteen-year-old Sandy, who sounds wise beyond her years: "I know that I would always wish I had an older sister if I didn't have one. I need the advice and I need her to give me a heads-up on what's going to happen. I like to think that I'm independent and do stuff my own way, but then again, I like using my sister's old textbooks that she's already underlined, and I like babysitting for the people she used to babysit for, so that they immediately like me. I would hate to have the sole job of leading the way for those behind me. Instead, I would rather follow some of her paths and some of my own."

The Sister Relationship as Adults

Younger sisters have the most to lose when the sister hierarchy doesn't flatten out in adulthood. Although being adorable works great for children, adults are typically measured by a different standard, one that values assertiveness, decisiveness, and authority.

Still in the Backseat

In spite of not wanting to change TOMY positions as kids, younger sisters are, without a doubt, the most dissatisfied with their relationships with their sisters as adults. Powerlessness is etched in high relief on the faces of women closing in on forty but who can still be made to feel fourteen by their sisters. Whether the relationship has been loving or not, the complaint is always the same, "I wish she wouldn't still treat me like a child." Anne, a forty-three-year-old university professor, couldn't believe the scene when she was driving back with her two sisters from a visit to the family cottage: "I'm still a little kid in their minds, and maybe that's because we all slip back into old roles when we get together. For example, last summer, we rented a car to go to my parents' cottage. My oldest sister was driving and I was in the backseat (I always get the backseat). They were picking on me all weekend and I started crying—like a twelve-year-old. I told them, 'You guys were picking on me. You always pick on me!' I listened to myself and thought, 'Oh my god! I'm a grown woman with a Ph.D. What am I saying?' They both were looking at each other with smirks on their faces, as if to say, 'Can you believe this!?!' Is it that I'm behaving that way or that they interpret it that way? Was I acting like a child, or was it just because they have me in this little pigeonhole and I will always be this way and there is no hope for change for little Annie?"

Pigeonholed

The "kid sister" pigeonhole is a hard one to flutter out of, perhaps because *both* the older and the younger sister collude in keeping the younger sister in it. Not only is the older sister maintaining the status quo by being bossy, but the younger one also continues to slot herself in the helpless role long after she has actually gained equal power. A younger child at home may, in fact, be at the mercy of her older sister, but as an adult, she has equal access to what the world has to offer.

If we think of the older sister hacking the path with her little machete and the youngest one taking the easy route by following behind, we can see how hard it would be for the younger sister to deviate from that route, even when she has a full array of tools at hand. Her natural instinct is to plod behind. If she wanted to hew her own course, she would have to, first of all, change her thinking about herself so that she could believe that she has the skills to be an intrepid explorer. Second, she would have to do the path-clearing work with her own machete, and chopping down trees is hard.

Parents tend to pigeonhole, too. Particularly as they grow older, they may look to the oldest daughter for advice and support far more frequently than they do to a younger one. Charlene, an older sister, told about a time when she was out of town and her elderly father had a bad fall; he needed to be moved immediately from his apartment to a

facility for assisted living. Her younger sister, Toni, spent days researching appropriate seniors' residences, but when she offered her recom-
mendations to their father, he mildly said, "We'll just wait till Charlene
comes home to make that decision." Toni, who was well over fifty at
the time, was just livid.

Changing Neural Pathways. When my daughter Lauren was
about seven and Michele was about nine, I once tried an experiment
in role changing, with very interesting results. One afternoon, Lauren
was in the basement feverishly trying to stuff a week's worth of piano
practice into the hour before her lesson. That was, of course, the exact
moment at which Michele decided that *she* had to use the piano. With
her big sister authority, she started banging on the lower keys, eventually ordering Lauren to "get off!" Lauren (true to *her* script) started
whimpering and whining at Michele in her typical ineffectual little sister manner. Eventually, Lauren came up to the kitchen to complain to
the boss (me), "Michele won't let me praaactice!" Instead of marching
downstairs and ordering Michele off the piano, I told Lauren, "I want
you to pretend that you're the big sister and Michele is just a little kid
who wants your attention. She doesn't understand how important it is
that you practice for your lesson. Now, try to explain it to her in simple words so she can understand." Lauren disappeared downstairs and
in a couple of minutes, Michele appeared. She jerked her thumb
toward the basement door and asked, incredulously, "What's with her?"
Apparently, Lauren had temporarily shed her little sister role and spoke
to Michele using a more authoritative tone. Michele was so taken aback
that she just got up from the piano bench and left. For that one brief
moment, Lauren read from a new script, and the play took an unexpected turn.

Role changing takes conscious thought and persistence. Many
women in The Sisters Project lamented that, like for Anne crying in
the backseat of the car, things don't change. Older sisters may remain
critical, motherly, or superior throughout a lifetime. Anne told how

her oldest sister, Vivian, is always surprised when Anne accomplishes anything, even something as simple as cooking a meal, because she always thought of "little Annie" as the one who doesn't know anything. Even when Anne provides her with evidence to the contrary, Vivian's default position kicks in and returns Anne to her long-established, if obsolete, position as a child. When Anne does things competently, rather than revising that view, her sister sees it as an anomaly—an exception to the true picture of incompetent Anne (who, you remember, has a Ph.D.). For Anne to change her sister's opinion of her, she would need to consistently demonstrate a new behavior, while also verbally pointing out (in a nondefensive way) whenever her sister is pigeonholing her again. It takes a lot of repetition to change neural pathways.

"Don't Mother Me!"

Kathleen's frustration was evident as she described how her sister, who lives on the other side of the continent, continues to assume an unwelcome motherly role: "There are times when I talk to her and it's this age thing—I feel like she's being my mother. 'You never look after yourself. You need clothes. I know you—you don't buy yourself clothes.' She's telling me this from two thousand miles away! Why is that? That frustrates me and makes me a bit angry. I'd like her to respect me more. She's not my mother. I want her to be my sister and my friend. I wish I could tell her, 'I'm almost sixty. Don't mother me!' but it's hard to come up against her because she gets angry right away. She intimidates me and I don't like to hurt people's feelings."

Twenty-one-year-old June, whose sister made the piñata for her when they were kids, still struggles to feel like an equal when they're together: "Leila's always been the leader and I always feel like the little child—even until this day. When she's around, it's like I'm in the background. I almost feel like I have no personality, even though I know I do have a personality, but when I'm around her . . . grrrr." June hates that she depends on Leila to take the lead, but the structure of their relationship is such that June doesn't trust herself; she trusts Leila. The well-established reflex that big sister knows best can often persist well into adulthood. When June has a decision to make, she second-guesses herself until she runs it past Leila. June needs the "Leila Certified Stamp of Approval" to feel comfortable; without it, she can feel insecure and even miserable.

Appreciating That She's There

Vanessa is amused when she sees herself falling back into that old role with Bridget: "Yesterday, my father telephoned from Mexico, where he's spending a few months. And at the end of the phone call, he said, 'Okay, keep in touch and let me know how you're doing,' and, without thinking, I responded, 'Oh, you don't have to worry. Bridget looks after me like I'm two!' It was just a spontaneous answer. I laughed after I hung up when I realized what I'd said. I've just spent two years teaching in Japan where I was quite able to feed myself, take care of myself, and so on, but since getting back to Los Angeles one week ago, Bridget and I have spoken at least three times a day. She checks in to make sure everything is okay. I didn't even really realize it; I guess we're just used to it. Anne-Marie [Bridget's partner] pointed it out, so it made us aware, but to us, it's just second nature."

Some women talked about how their sisters have inspired them by courageously facing the tough things in life. Sally, whose vignette in the first chapter told about her giggling sister, Jeanette, ditching their skating routine, is now in her sixties. It pains her to watch her once-powerful older sister cope with illness. She said, "If there were wind beneath my wings, it would be her because she's so very brave with this arthritis. She's waiting for surgery, yet she says to me, 'A year from now, you watch me, I'm going on a Panama cruise!' And she will, if she can. She's always uplifting; she never, ever complains. If she's hurting, we never know. 'Hey, Jeanette, how're you doing?' 'Oh, not too bad.'"

Partners and Kids

Getting involved in a relationship, getting married, or having children is sometimes the jolt that changes the dynamics between sisters. Being in the same role, such as mothers running a household, is a great leveler for many women. They are at the same stage for the first time in their lives, regardless of their ages. Even if just one of them has a child, the balance changes. One younger sister e-mailed this thought: "My sister becoming a mom has somewhat changed our relationship. Now that I'm an adult and she has a child, we need to learn how to be sisters without the mom-baby dynamic we've had for so long." On the other hand, some women sheepishly admitted that they felt some jealousy toward their older sister's baby because the child had taken over their own role.

Jealousy may also play a role when an older sister marries or moves in with a partner and gets all wrapped up in the couple life. As the older one's life gets busier, there just may not be enough time for the sisters to hang out like they used to. Meredith, who was still interested in toys when her sister got interested in boys, loves being an auntie to her sister's three kids, but she still longs it to be just the two of them: "I can't get enough alone time with her. Often, when we go out, she gets a phone call and has to go home because of something with the kids. I just wish that we could have more time, just her and me, when there's nothing that she has to rush back to."

I'm the Big Sister Now: The Nikki-Vikki Story

Although I am fiercely independent now, I had a real little sister personality when I was a child. Nikki, being five and a half years older and far more dominant, imposed her will with impunity, and I was always afraid of being put down by her. There wasn't even a hint of a protective surrogate mom in her demeanor with me. As adults, even though we lived in the same neighborhood, we pretty much went our separate ways, meeting mostly at family events. On those occasions when we would have a meal together, always with our parents, I would revert from my typical confident self back to being nervous about whether she would get angry about something. As a rule, she did, and in that way she maintained a certain amount of power over me.

About twelve years ago, my widowed mother and sister were both living in New York, but I had already moved to Montreal. My mother was having fainting spells and could no longer live alone. We all hastily decided that the best thing would be to move her up to Montreal where I could look out for her. I took a week off from work and packed up the apartment in which she had lived for thirty-six years. Thirty-six years of stuff to be sorted through, furniture from a three-bedroom apartment, papers, photos, dishes, mementos, and only five days before we had to drive back to Montreal! I was working frantically, from six in the morning until late at night, trying to get it all done. My sister would saunter in around eleven and, looking for things she wanted to take, dump the boxes I had packed that morning and rummage through them. Meanwhile, I was worried about her getting annoyed.

We were both playing out another tired old script—me in the role of the long-suffering, helpful daughter and her in the part of the "anti-goody-goody," the self-interested one. Finally, after she had spilled out the contents of yet another carefully packed box, I lost it and exploded. I said, "Okay, that's it! I've been patient long enough! I'm takin' over! I'm the big sister now!" Feeling tremendously liberated from her for the first time in my life, I stopped caring what she thought. It was like something went "click" in my head. I stopped feeling sorry for Nikki because our mother was moving away. I stopped making allowances. I stopped analyzing the situation. I stopped rationalizing her behavior. I stopped giving her all of that power, and I stopped trying to please. It was really a significant moment in my life, and I can clearly remember how good it felt.

Trading Places

One of The Sisters Project participants was only able to cut free of her older sister's influence after that troubled sister committed suicide. Clara was twenty-nine at the time but felt a whole lot younger: "You know how you could emotionally be a certain age even though physically you're another? When she died, it's as if I had been sixteen and then overnight, I became thirty. I took over her role. I said to myself, 'Okay, she's dead and gone, and now I'm the eldest and I have to take on the family problems.' My sister's suicide forced me to do and be what she wasn't—responsible, parental, independent, fearless. It catapulted me into adulthood. After my sister's death, I did a sudden U-turn. I was approaching thirty and I was depressed. I wasn't doing what I wanted in life. Her death was the catalyst for me to make a profound change. I needed to make some boundaries for myself, because when my sister died, I felt I really didn't know who I was. I was determined then to find out."

When Clara's sister died, it was as if a vacuum had been created in the family. The role of the eldest needed to be filled, and Clara felt like she had to grow up quickly to fill it. She looked at the traits her sister had been lacking and consciously chose to develop them within herself. She could no longer enjoy the luxury of feeling sixteen at twenty-nine.

The Youngest Sister Stamp

The Sisters Project originated from a comment made by my daughter, Lauren, in which she said that no matter whom she's with, she always feels like she's a little sister. Hearing her, I realized that I feel the same. Through the process of interviewing and receiving e-mail from over 130 other youngest sisters, I found out that Lauren and I are not alone. Woman after woman told me that she had a "younger sister mentality," which caused her to replicate with others the same role she played in her family growing up. Many said that replaying their younger sister role with friends, lovers, employers, and colleagues often caused them problems. It didn't matter whether the childhood role was one of having felt insignificant or entitled—it tended not to translate well in the real world.

The Peter Pan Syndrome

A "younger sister mentality" was neatly defined by forty-nine-year-old Rachel, the youngest of four: "It is my natural inclination to function as the youngest, the 'baby.' I tend to defer to others and assume (without thinking about it or examining the facts) that others know more than I do. I tend to have a 'someone will take care of me' worldview." Along the same lines as Rachel, other women admitted that because they are younger sisters, they don't make waves and they act immaturely at times.

Vanessa was intrigued by how she has been influenced by this "Peter Pan syndrome": "I don't know if most people's inner child stays with them so blatantly in adult life, but mine is definitely present, loud and clear. And more so, the older I get. I think there was a period in my late teens and midtwenties when I wanted to be adult and to be taken seriously, so I acted mature. Then, all of a sudden, I realized I was an adult and getting older and then I longed to be a kid again. So lately, I've reverted back a bit to that kid inside. Strange phenomenon!"

When women talk about their younger sister mentality, they are referring to an internal perception as well as to how they act with others. Some tend to feel younger and less competent than the people around them. In actuality, such assumptions may not be borne out, but because the women experience it that way, they then act as if it were true. One woman said that in her workplace, where she is ten years older than the next younger person, she still feels like she's younger than most of the other employees. She doesn't like to take on a lot of responsibility. Twenty-four-year-old Nicola wrote, "At work, I often find myself slipping into the role of 'little sister' and acting more immature than I should. I play the part of the little annoying one. I crave attention, ask a lot of questions. I 'misbehave.'"

By acting younger and more dependent, women like Nicola lead others to believe that they are less competent. That causes the people around them to treat them that way, and thus their view of themselves is reinforced. It's a negative feedback loop: The younger sister acts hesitant, making other people think that she's not capable, so they're reluctant to trust her. She senses that other people are holding back, assumes that she can't meet their expectations and, therefore, becomes even more hesitant. She's actually inviting people around her to view her the same way she views herself due to the manner in which she deals with them.

Anne, the university professor, described her hesitancy: "It doesn't matter who's in the room, I always feel like I'm the youngest. I have a tendency to let others talk first before I'll express my opinion. I suppose I'm cautious in expressing mine because I care very much what they think."

Dependency

Having grown up with someone else leading the way instills in some adult younger sisters a feeling of dependency, the "someone will take care of me" worldview described by Rachel. Women who give in to this impulse tend to feel bad about it—it's not their finest trait. One described herself as a "fragile little person" who needs to call someone as soon as anything happens. Alex, who is ten years younger than her sister, wished that she had the motivation to be more independent in general: "I have trouble making decisions. I should actually be figuring things out for myself, whether it's what movie to go to or something important about school, but I get lazy and just ask others for advice and let them take care of me. I really need to gain more independence. I think I'm getting better at it, but I fall very easily into letting people decide for me."

Clara, who had to grow up quickly when her sister died, doesn't like facing new things or even going to new places alone: "Even today, I look for a companion if I'm going somewhere. I know that this comes from my relationship with my sister, who was always there for me to take me places. I have to find the courage. I always manage, but I find it very hard. I'd rather have a friend come with me."

The Me-Me-Me Quality

In his film *Deconstructing Harry*, Woody Allen's character, Harry, commented to a friend, "I think you're the opposite of a paranoid. I think you go around with the insane delusion that people like you." A similar delusion seems to afflict some younger sisters. They go around with the unrealistic expectation that everyone in the world will adore them, just like their parents did, and assume, therefore, that others will step aside and give them top billing. When it doesn't happen, they get insulted. Older sisters have a word for that—*spoiled*.

Marcelle, thirty-nine, from Vancouver, admitted, "I always got my way, and I think I still expect to get my way now. When I don't, I'm not happy. I think that since my parents thought that I was perfect, I have the sense that I am and that I should always be treated that way. I like being taken care of and I like getting my way!" A further confession from Vanessa: "I think being the baby, I definitely have that me-me-me quality to my personality. I don't expose it too much (outside of the family), but it's definitely part of my inner thought process. For example, if anything goes wrong, I don't hesitate to think 'No fair!' or 'Why me?' and get annoyed."

Of course, the me-me-me quality can provide a feeling of confidence for some women. As Marcelle said, because the family thinks that she's great, she thinks that she's great, too. Twenty-five-year-old Deidre's submission describes how being pampered led to high self-esteem: "I think being the younger sister gave me a higher self-confidence. I was given lots of opportunities, lots of cool activities, and didn't really have to push for things. I knew I was loved and I feel good about that." One women wrote that if two parents are better than one, imagine how confident she feels having grown up with three "parents" to nurture her!

Running with the Big Kids

Paradoxically, some younger sisters were spurred on to achieve *because* they were the low girl on the totem pole and things weren't handed to them. Several women sent in e-mail that went something like this one: "In everything I do, I always view myself as the youngest and most inexperienced (usually I am anyway), so I try harder to do my best so I can 'run with the big kids,' so to speak. That has made me more confident."

Part of running with the big kids is observing how other people handle things and learning from their mistakes. There seems to be a general consensus that younger sisters perfect their skills just by watching. Some of the skills that women attribute to their younger position are being tolerant of others and knowing when to hold their tongue— "some things just need to be left unsaid"—being open to options, being able to take turns, standing up for things they believe in, and knowing "how to ignore folks at times." The woman who made this last comment added, "With two parents and two older siblings, I could get bombarded with information and directions, so I had to learn how to sort through and ignore some stuff." Women also said that being younger made them risk-takers: I watched the older kids make choices, both good and bad, and I realized that most stuff wouldn't kill you. Therefore, I like to try new things."

Having been beaten up by her older sister a fair number of times growing up, twenty-seven-year-old Tawanna said that she learned not to take people's crap: "Being a younger sister taught me balance so that if people say things I don't agree with, I'll just let it fly, but if it's important enough, I'll speak up until I get heard. It taught me to choose my battles."

Nadia, thirty-six and the youngest of three, reflected on what she learned by watching her sisters: "I think being the youngest has allowed me to take a 'wait and see' approach to life. I'm a very good listener, and I've honed the craft of watching and learning from others and their mistakes. Once I figure things out, I'm more confident about what I want in life, unlike my oldest sister, who forges ahead and then has regrets."

Lovers and Friends

In an attempt to replicate that comfortable role from childhood, many younger sisters either gravitate toward people who are natural caretakers or try to nudge their reluctant partners and friends into that role. One woman even said that she checks out the birth order position of any prospective new boyfriend and at one point in her life would probably have run from guys who were the youngest in their family. Otherwise, she would have constantly been dueling with him, each in an attempt to get the other to be the caretaker.

June has trouble even finding friends with whom she can connect. She is always looking for a trace of Leila: "I want a leader, a taker of initiative. I guess Leila's been the model in my mind—kind of up on a pedestal—and she's always been so selfless with me that I find it hard to be in relationships with other people who are so self-centered. I'm used to being taken care of."

Vanessa was bemused by how she and her boyfriend have such different views of dependency: "It always amazes me that what I try hard to avoid in people, that is, neediness, my boyfriend almost looks for and gets excited by. He's constantly telling me to call him if I need him, no matter what time it is, even in the middle of the night (we live in different time zones, so his nights are my afternoons and evenings).

He's almost disappointed when he wakes up in the morning and I haven't called. I, on the other hand, can think of nothing worse than being woken up in the middle of the night by a phone call! It's just a different mentality. He's sadly thinking, 'She doesn't need me!' and I'm proudly thinking, 'I didn't need him!' "

Although in her thirties, Vanessa is still fighting an old reflex—the one that tells her, "It's okay, go ahead, depend on other people; they really want you to." The theme song that has accompanied her life may be the one that the Lost Boys sing in the musical *Peter Pan*, "I Won't Grow Up!" although she seems to be looking for another melody at this point—perhaps "I Did It My Way!"

Taking Initiative

Younger sisters who have integrated childhood messages about the special position of the youngest girl or the "baby" may have been coopted into believing that they don't have the muscle to do important things in the world. They may then spend their adult life either seeking to recreate a dependent relationship with the important people around them or, on the opposite side, trying to prove to the world that they can make their mark using their own initiative. For example, my reaction to growing up with a bossy older sister is that I became almost pathologically independent. I'll change the tire, cook the meal, paint the kitchen, and diaper the baby—all at the same time! Then I can say, "I did it all by myself!"

Jessica, Emily, and Danielle

Bridging Both Worlds

The Middle Sister

"As the middle sister, you have to be very resourceful in terms of finding your place in the family. You try to draw attention to the fact that, 'Hey, I'm here; don't forget me! I'm not the baby. I'm not the oldest. But I'm here! If you don't want me here, then, fine, I'll go out and make my own way,' which is basically what I did."

—KIM, forty-three years old

Monkey in the Middle

Kim, the exact middle of five sisters and the mother of three daughters, smiled wistfully as she talked about her position in her family as a "betweenie." She had to be resourceful in finding her place because the middle sister role is the least defined of any of the TOMY positions. Everyone knows what's expected of the oldest and youngest sister, but that middle role isn't as easily summed up. It is that lack of definition that is the hallmark of the middle sister. It strangely colors her self-image as a child and continues to affect her as an adult. The middle is both an older and a younger sister. Depending on the spacing between the girls in her family, she may be called upon to play the older sister role; in that capacity, she has to watch her step because she's a role model. As a younger sister, she may feel the need to prove that she can live up to the accomplishments of her older sister.

This lack of definition makes the middle role tricky. The middle girl is vulnerable to suffering the stress of being pulled in two directions. Seven-year-old Kaileigh's description of being the monkey in the middle captured the push and pull: "Having two sisters is cool, but it's also annoying because when you want to have privacy, one of them is bothering you and you say 'stop' and that one goes back to her room and then the other one starts to bother you. It's hard to have some privacy 'cause everyone is awake and you want some relaxing time and they're saying, 'C'mon, c'mon, play with me!' "

One of the features of being a middle sister is the reality that this girl comes by her position by dint of having been replaced. For some number of years, she was the youngest in the family, the baby. She may have been enjoying that special status and felt shortchanged when she had to relinquish it to the next in line. Although the oldest also had to suffer the indignity of being replaced, she retained a high status spot in the family hierarchy even after her little sister was born. The middle sister, however, saw her status reduced when she had to give up the "baby" position, and she received no compensation for it.

The middle is also affected by whether she is the only middle in a family of three girls, or, like my mother, the third among six girls, or, like thirty-six-year-old Scarlet, the fifth among eight sisters in a family of twelve children. Here is a taste of Scarlet's childhood reality: "The older sisters often acted in the role of 'mother,' taking responsibility for us 'little kids.' We shared a room (five beds, bunks, and trundles) and that often meant fighting over clothes, space, and ideas of neatness, as well as enjoying a shared closeness about stories, music, reading, imagination, and experience. Being number eight of twelve, I often felt 'invisible' and was a keen observer of my older sisters' lives and challenges. I also felt competitive with my next-in-line sister and, in turn, sometimes felt 'left out' of the rest of the family group."

Middle sisters are the only ones whose TOMY position is socially recognized as possibly being problematic. As a result they have their very own diagnosis—the Middle Child Syndrome. Summed up in a word, it describes how a child may feel if she believes herself to be "unspecial" in the family, or, like Scarlet said, invisible. Some parents are sensitive to the effect of this "syndrome" on their middle daughter, and that sensitivity may contribute to it being implanted in their child's mind; it becomes a self-fulfilling prophecy. Sarah's father made her aware of the drawbacks of being the middle: "My dad used to tell me, 'Oh, you're the middle child—you're going to be the sandwich in the family.' He's a middle child, too. He showed me this article when I was ten or eleven saying that the middle child tends to be sandwiched and they have to fight back more." Some girls just naturally adopt the view of themselves as unspecial even if their family does nothing to support it. It seems to go with the territory a fair amount of the time.

We have already encountered some of the terms middle sisters use to describe themselves. In this chapter, we'll get a better understanding of why middle sisters are described as being:

- Sociable
- Independent
- Balanced
- Mediating
- Creative
- Resourceful

or sometimes they are even described as being:

- Loners
- Black and white
- Invisible
- Black sheep
- Iconoclastic

or

- Nutsy!

The Sister Relationship as Children

The oldest girl in the family derives her power from being the repository of her parents' hopes and dreams for their daughters—she gets the most focus and attention just because she's the first. The youngest capitalizes on the cuteness factor; remember the twinkle in the eye reserved for the baby? And the middle? She somehow develops an awareness that there is no defined category to fit herself into. She's not this and she's not that, but what she *is* exactly is open to interpretation.

Lost in the Shuffle

Not all middle sisters grow up feeling unspecial in their families, but the ones who do deal with it in one of three ways. First, they may retreat into the woodwork, trying to take up as little room as possible. Second, they may "scream for attention." Third, they may take themselves out of the running and get their needs met outside the family.

Girls in the first category grow up feeling that they don't deserve very much. They have internalized the message that the needs of the younger and older are more important than their own. Rhonda described herself as a typical middle child: "I was always the one that people didn't remember as well. When Marlene did something—well, it was the first. And when Leah did something—well, she was so cute." Along the same lines, Paige, the second youngest of four girls, wrote that she always thought she could be easily discounted even though her family did nothing to contribute to that assessment: "I retreated a lot and always felt as if time, attention, and money should not be spent on me."

Screaming for Attention

Some middle girls cope with their undefined role by making sure that they are noticed. The opposite side of the coin from making herself nondescript is for a girl to become a shit-disturber. Middle daughters seem to be the ones that have the most conflict with moms, who sometimes feel they can't control this "squeaky wheel" or "wild one." Elana wrote, "I was the rebellious middle child, called the 'reactive child' by my old therapist. No one else in my family showed negative emotion, so I guess I took it on as my job to let everyone know when the emperor had no clothes. My oldest sister was the peacekeeper in a household that never spoke of anything if it was not happy, good, upbeat, and positive. I can remember her telling me I was a troublemaker and asking me why I always had to ruin things."

The number of older and younger sisters who described the middle as sneaky surprised me. Middle sisters may feel that family rules don't apply to them in the same way they do to their sisters, but they don't want to invite trouble, so they maneuver around them. One younger sister said that her middle sister, Shauna, developed a "false self." Their parents saw Shauna as a good girl. She did a bunch of stuff that would have angered them if they had known, but she rarely got caught. When she did, however, she blamed her antics on her other sisters. In a similar vein, Gayle, a younger sister, said that her parents thought her middle sister was "it" because she laughed at all of Dad's jokes. Little did the parents know that, away from the home, this middle sister was drinking and riding around on the back of her boyfriend's motorcycle. Gayle said, "I didn't like my middle sister during high school because I thought she was a phony."

The Black Sheep

Quite a number of middle sisters talked about how their friends took on central importance when they were growing up. Each described herself as "the black sheep" who strayed beyond the perimeter of the family fence to seek her identity elsewhere. Kim, whose quote opened this chapter, was one of those girls who strayed: "I was the middle of five and we were all two years apart. In our teens, the older two hung out together and the younger two stuck together, and it's still that way to this day. I kind of went my own way, made my own friends. Socializing-wise, I usually just stayed with my friends."

Middle sisters were often said to be social butterflies. Ellie, who is three years older than her middle sister, Lena, resented the different face Lena presented to the outside world: "She was funny outside the house, but she was miserable inside the house. She had this angry face when she was home, but she was 'Miss Personality'—that's what my mother would say, 'Miss Personality'—outside the home."

Independent from an Early Age: Claudia's Story. I met thirty-four-year-old Claudia at her younger sister Dale's quiet, elegant New York apartment. The foyer was decorated with Japanese prints and other interesting pieces of Oriental art. One wall of the living room was painted dark red, and another, burnt orange. Claudia graciously offered me green tea, just as Dale, three years younger, had done when I interviewed her the previous week. This meeting with Claudia marked the last of my meetings with the three Fitzgerald sisters; I had spoken with the eldest, thirty-seven-year-old Jenny, two weeks prior. I was looking forward to the interview, not only because I loved being able to speak with all of the sisters in a family, but also because I had found both Dale and Jenny reflective and articulate. I was keen to hear Claudia's angle on their family story.

I started the interview asking Claudia about the different roles each girl played in the family growing up. "Beginning in puberty, I would say that I was the 'demon seed' and Jenny was the more serious first-born, bridge-maker, peacemaker, parent-pleaser. Dale was 'the baby.' I think I saw myself as independent from a very early age. The classic story in my family is about my first day of nursery school. My mother walked me there with all of the other mothers on our street. All of the kids were clinging to their mothers' aprons crying, 'I don't wanna go to school!' while I was cheerfully saying, 'Bye! See ya! Later!' From four or five years on, I was like, 'Okay, I'm outta here.' My life outside the home was very different than inside the home. I felt quite at odds most of the time with what I was being offered at home. I felt very misunderstood. I didn't feel normal. There was a lot of anger, there was a lot of screaming, and there was a lot of fighting with my mother.

"When I was an adolescent, I thought Dale was pretty spoiled. She was parented differently. The older I got, the more I realized that she enjoyed a lot of freedom that Jenny and I hadn't; she got a sweeter, longer leash. That was probably the beginning of a litany of complaints, which went on for years, like, 'How come she gets to get her own room?'

"Our mother had this messy drawer that was stuffed with all of the family photographs. One weekend, when I was about eighteen and Dale was fifteen, while our mother was away in the country, Dale painstakingly went through every single picture, extracted a photographic history of her own life and put it in an album. Months later, I remember thinking, 'I want to do the same thing so I can look at my own life in pictures.' I went through the drawer and found that there were almost no pictures of me. There were a kabillion pictures of Jenny. There were a kabillion pictures of Dale. There were no pictures of me. There was like one here and there, and they were usually with Jenny. Or they were with Jenny and me straddling Dale. I remember being sooooo hurt and annoyed and incensed.

"Middle children are the black sheep of the family. They tend to be the creative ones who stray the farthest from the family fold. They're the most independent. They're the most tortured. It's a very amorphous role, and I think that if it is at all defined, it's defined by how much people reinforce that you are the middle child. Each of us is an Aquarius, we are the children of the same parents, we all grew up at the same address, but my life is characterized by wanting to define myself apart from the family. The minute I finished college, I went to work in Paris. Back then, I don't think I thought, 'Oh, there's always Jenny' that made it possible for me to leave. But now, she's the one who lives near my parents and has the grandchildren that keep our parents involved on a day-to-day basis in her life. I know that's a burden for her, and it fills me with an enormous amount of guilt that I'm not there to shoulder my portion of it."

Dispossessed

Claudia and her sisters are now very close, but her resentment of the special treatment that Dale received when they were kids comes across clearly. Among all of the TOMY positions, the most consistent reports of jealousy came from middle sisters toward younger ones. Some inherent fault imbedded in that relationship makes it hard for middle sisters to stop themselves from being mean to younger girls. It's similar to the animosity of the fabled wicked stepmother. It's not that stepmothers are evil; it's just that some inherent pressure in the structure of that stepmother-stepdaughter relationship naturally gives rise to resentment. Perhaps the jealousy is strong for middle sisters because with the birth of the younger one, they lose not only their status as "the baby" but also the undivided attention of their older sister.

My friend Dominique, who is a middle sister, told me that she was enjoying being the baby when her little sister was born. She already had a playmate in her older sister and didn't need another one. She said that if you're getting along well enough with your older sister, the third one not only takes your place but is also superfluous. It's like a man who has one wife. If he were happy enough, why would he need another? Duos in nature tend to be more stable than trios.

Like other older sisters, middles resent being burdened with the care of a younger sister, but in the case of middles, the feeling is even more bitter because the girl they're supposed to help is often also their rival. Abigail is eight years younger than her next older sister (there are five in total), but only two years older than the baby, who she was supposed to "keep in line": "I resented her. Obviously, she displaced me as youngest. In addition, it seemed to me that while much was expected of me, little was expected of her. If she fell short of our parents' expectations in school performance, for example, I was to fix it somehow, not she." When asked what "just one sentence" Abigail would have said to her little sister growing up, she wrote, "Unflattering though it is, it would have been, 'Drop dead!'"

It sometimes takes a long time for that resentment to fade. This youngest sister told it from the other point of view: "My sister, Wanda, who had been the baby of the family for ten years until I came along, hated and resented me throughout my childhood. She considered me the pesky baby sister. She finally forgave me for usurping her position as princess when I was about twenty-five and she was about thirty-five."

Madeleine, another younger sister, sixty-seven, can now see how she "stole" Daddy away from her middle sister, who is seven years older: "We were rivals for my father's attention. I think, because of her brilliance, she got the lion's share of his attention until I came along. Then he paid a lot of attention to me as the baby and his 'last' child. He loved babies, so I had a distinct advantage. I, too, was very bright, so maybe I stole some of her thunder."

Hand-Me-Down Blues

Middle sisters have very different feelings toward their older sisters than they do toward the younger ones. A typical "just one sentence as kids" toward a younger sister is "Stop being such a brat!" A typical "just one sentence as kids" toward an older is "How can I be more like you?" Carol's older sister took a page from *Tom Sawyer* when she'd had enough of Carol following her around: "I always wanted to do whatever she did. I would beg to be included when her friends came over to play. One time, she agreed and then said, 'Okay, we're playing house and you're the maid. It's Thursday and it's your day off.' So that way, she got rid of me."

Jealousy sometimes plays a big role in the relationship with the older sister too, and it often seems to focus on the issue of clothes. Fifty-nine-year-old Pamela recalled the unjust situation in her family: "I was jealous when my older sister got new clothes and I had to wear her hand-me-downs. My younger sister carried on so much about hand-me-downs that she also usually got new clothes. I didn't get new clothes very often. Most definitely being the middle child affected my self-confidence, from the clothes I wore to the relative lack of resources (timewise and moneywise) that I got from my parents." Kim had some strong feelings about the issue of clothes and what it represented to her: "I remember my mom came home from Minneapolis with two coats for my older sisters—in the '70s they had the 'wet look'—and I was so jealous. I always felt like the two older ones got more than we did. They got their own rooms before I did—although the two younger ones never got their own rooms. There were times when I thought, 'That sucks!' They always got everything before I did. I just got the hand-me-downs."

A Wonderful Place to Be

Although many middle sisters talked about the "lost in the shuffle" aspect of their role, a certain percentage also highlighted the positives. They benefited because the spotlight wasn't on them and used words like "independence," "freedom," and "resourcefulness" to describe what they gained. They weren't carrying the family torch, so they could take detours without disappointing others. One woman said, "There was no parental expectation that one of my sisters could not meet, so I was always free to be myself. I think that freedom shaped my adult view of myself as an independent person."

Some women said that being somewhat neglected forced them to become resourceful. There was an unmistakable note of sarcasm in Stella's enthusiasm about the virtues of the middle role: "I think it's a wonderful place to be! It was wonderful because nobody had time for me. It was absolutely perfect. I could be left alone to do what I wanted. My older sister would always be struggling to get permission to do things—going out with boys and things. I didn't have to do that; she'd already done it. And my younger sister was the one my parents wanted to hang on to a little bit longer—but not me! Nobody paid any attention to me. I wasn't considered pretty; I was smart. And I could be trusted to do my own thing. I had freedom and I decided fairly early that I was going to leave Quebec City, where I was born—it wasn't my bag. I didn't feel any ties to the family. I didn't feel I had to stay, because my sisters were there to mind the store."

Middle sisters often said that they enjoyed the options available to them. They felt that they could get along with both the older and younger girls—when one sister was busy or in a bad mood, the other one was available to play with. It was the best of both worlds! Middle sisters know less than older ones, so they could learn from them, and more than younger ones, for whom they could act as mentor. They developed the skill of evaluating things from varied perspectives because, structurally, they "looked both ways" to learn about life. They could act as a mediator or peacemaker because they could relate to both sides. This ability to see the world from different points of view also contributes to the creativity that many middle sisters tell about.

The Clown

As we saw in Chapter 2, the term used most often to describe the middle sister was "clown"! Women described their middle sisters as "the fun one," "a joker," "[having] a great sense of humor," and "comedian." One middle sister said of herself, "I was always trying to be a clown to get attention." That would explain the middle sister's need to be funny—along with being a "squeaky wheel," being a comedian is another great way of getting noticed.

The persona of a clown, however, is bittersweet. The clown in the circus gets applause by falling down and playing the fool. The concerns of the clown are not taken too seriously—it is often the jester in Western culture who is the one to speak the truth. Because of this disempowered position, people are not too threatened when the clown reveals, as we heard Elana say, that the emperor has no clothes. In my work as a family therapist, I've often observed that it is the troubled teenager who is the only one with the courage to reveal the truth about the family's secrets. In many ways, that is also the role of the middle sister, who stands a bit outside, observing what is going on and commenting in either a disruptive or humorous manner.

Surrogate Son

One of the surprising findings about middle sisters has to do with their frequent closeness with their fathers. They tend to have more conflict with their mothers but are frequently the girl in the family closest to Dad—several middle sisters in The Sisters Project were described as "Daddy's Girl." When a family has three girls, the oldest is often in the role of the "little mother," the youngest is in the role of the delicate little baby, and sometimes that middle girl is subtly encouraged to play more of a "boy" part in the family. She's the one that Dad chooses to kick the ball around with. In looking at the results of the questionnaire, the word *tomboy* was used to describe middle sisters but not older or younger ones. Middle sisters were found to be the most interested in sports, followed by youngers, and, last, olders. I questioned Kim, for example, about what it's like to have three daughters: "I like it because I know girls. We would have liked a boy for my husband, however, because he's so sports oriented. He really would have enjoyed a boy, but my middle one is a sports fanatic—she plays hockey with the boys, she plays soccer. He's turning her into a fine boy!"

Lee told about how she ended up being a girl with a boy's name: "Family myth was that my parents really wanted a boy and I came along instead, so they decided to call me a boy's name anyway." Samantha was given all of the responsible jobs to do in her family. It took her a while to figure out why: "Something as simple as going to the bank for my father, that responsibility never went to my older sister—it came straight to me. It would upset me. I would say, 'Why can't she do it?' and he would say, 'No, no, I trust you. You're old enough to do it.' Later in life, I realized why. They had given me the unspoken status of being the 'boy' of the family. Both my sisters were very much into grooming and looking good, and I was never into that. I think it was my role of being the 'boy' in the family that contributed to that."

Alliances

Having three girls or more in the family leads to alliances that are sometimes stable and sometimes shifting and that are often dependent on the spacing between the children. In quite a number of families of three girls, the two closest in age form an alliance against the third. It's often the middle who aligns herself with the oldest against her rival, the youngest, either to intentionally hurt her feelings or just because the youngest was not much fun to play with. (In the chapter on twins, we'll again see this dynamic of the youngest one being excluded.) Erin grinned, remembering how she and her older sister outsmarted the little one: "I used to play Barbie with my older sister all of the time, but we didn't want to play with my younger sister, so we used to try to hide. I'd go to my older sister's room and say, 'Do you want to play B-A-R-B-I-E?' and my younger sister couldn't spell at the time. Then we'd sneak into my room and play Barbie for hours."

On the other hand, here are two examples of middle sisters who feel pretty guilty about their childhood alliance with the oldest against the youngest. Lee described her treatment of her little sister, six years younger: "My older sister and I were very close and only one year apart.

Our younger sister would come to us and say, 'How come you don't let me in on your games?' She always felt she was left out, and that's been a bit of a bone of contention all of our lives. I've felt a mea culpa for many years because there were times that we did intentionally exclude her, not really wanting to be mean, but just that, 'No, we don't want our little sister.' Our parents would try to tell us, 'Look, she's little and she's alone and you guys have each other.'"

Jade, thirty-one years old, painted a picture of how two older girls can gang up to torment the youngest: "I never remember my younger sister doing anything to me, but my older sister and I made her unhappy. We used to have this toy called The Baseball Kid; it was a plastic thing that pitched to you. Well, we caught my younger sister dancing with it and we ripped her to shreds! She was lonely at that time—we didn't really want her around—so she was dancing with The Baseball Kid. We told everyone and made fun of her forever. That makes me feel bad."

Harmonious relations seemed to be the most difficult in trios. Some middle sisters talked about happy memories with an older or younger sister individually, but tension and jealousy was most pronounced when the three of them were together. These feelings were particularly difficult if the older and younger didn't get along. Then the middle felt like a Ping-Pong ball, bouncing back and forth, trying to keep each of them happy.

When there are more than three girls, the group tends to break into cohorts. One woman explained that she has one sister who is two years younger and three older sisters who range from eight to eleven years older. It felt as though the three older ones were from a different family—she didn't have much to do with them—so she was thrown together with her younger sister with whom she was constantly fighting.

A peculiar thing tends to happen in families with five daughters. If the spacing is relatively even, the two oldest stick together and the two youngest stick together; the exact middle girl is pretty much out there on her own.

An Estrogen-Filled Home

Over the course of one winter month, I went from office to home to café, separately interviewing each of the Evans sisters, five vibrant women whose age range was only seven years, from thirty-three to forty years old. They come from a traditional family in which Dad made the money and Mom took care of the household. I heard their childhood story from five different angles and developed a picture of a strict, safe, but hectic home with a bunch of spirited girls vying for space, clothes, freedom, and the bathroom. Evidently jokes and hairbrushes went flying in equal measure. I asked Jessica, the second youngest, if she felt some pride in coming from a family with so many girls: "Pride? Sure. Especially when the whole family was all together, walking around the neighborhood. It would be like, 'Here comes the Evans clan!' or 'Harry, you got yourself an army!' There's strength in numbers, and you sort of roll your eyes and say, 'Yeah, it's cool. We're all sisters.' People would say, 'You lucky guy!' or 'You poor devil!' It's funny because it was always directed toward my dad."

Participants in The Sisters Project who came from families with four girls or more had similar stories to tell. There was often a mix of frustration and fun. Dolly talked about all of the sisters "singing together in four-part harmony, which contributed to the camaraderie." Other sentiments were not so rosy. One woman said, "It's hard being the ugliest girl in a family full of sisters." Another grumbled, "It's not easy growing up in a home with so much estrogen running through it." Overall, however, most middle sisters remembered always having someone to hang with, the fun of holidays and camping, the feeling that there was always "action." Lizzie told about her family, in which all six girls shared a single large attic room: "It was bed, bed, bed, bed, bed, bed, bookcase, bookcase, bookcase, bookcase, bookcase, bookcase, closet, closet, closet, closet, closet, closet. I really wish I could paint a picture of what bedtime was like; all of us lined up in our beds, like we were in some kind of orphan dormitory. We'd all be trying to get to sleep, but with all of the talking going back and forth—the sharing of this and the sharing of that. Someone saying, 'Why don't you go to sleep!' and the other one saying, 'I don't want to go to sleep!' It was just ridiculous."

Twenty-five-year-old Alexis, the second oldest of four, shared this sunny vignette: "We lived in an apartment that had a pool, and every summer, we just lived at that pool. One of my happy memories is of the time when my oldest sister and I taught our younger sisters how to swim. We would teach them how to do flips and dives. I loved having them look up to me at such a young age."

Scarlet, the fifth of eight sisters, also has great memories of imaginative play and adventure: "We walked to grade school together, using a backwoods trail that we called 'the cinder path.' We would all walk together, rescuing hurt or dead animals, climbing trees, finding nature objects, involved in the discovery of life. Other happy times, we would play in the woods behind our house, where we freely spent hours, made up games, had trails and tree houses, imagined that we were orphans running from airplanes, and so on."

On the other hand, when you have four or five sisters and the power of that group is negative, then "ganging up" can take on a special resonance. Jessica usually had a thick skin, but sometimes enough was enough: "Sunday dinners, I was often the person to get picked on; I was the one who got ribbed. At times, it was like they'd all jump on top of me, subtly, laughing, 'It's a joke—can't you take a joke?' Jab, jab, jab. Ninety-five percent of the time, I was okay with it, but sometimes, I'd walk away and I'd be freaking out. You know, just really angry. 'They don't understand who I am! They don't know me!'"

Although sisters may fight within the family, they often close ranks when they get outside. Kim told about the fierce loyalty among her five sisters: "When we moved here, the kids picked on us, and we would really band together. We'd get on the bus and they'd call us names and we'd call them names right back. If one of us came home and said, 'Aw, this kid threw a snowball at me!' we'd all drop what we were doing and go out there and get 'im! No one messed with the Tremblay girls!"

That same sentiment was sent in by e-mail from Angela, one of six sisters in Washington, D.C.: "Whenever I hear the song by Sister Sledge, 'We Are Family,' I think it is about my sisters and me. I always say, I come from a long line of independent women. I also say, no good comes from a family full of women—it makes you think you can take over the world and do it better than anyone else. I can talk about my sisters and they can talk about me, but Lord help the fool who talks about one of us to another!"

The Sister Relationship as Adults

Several middle sisters, particularly from families of three girls, said that it often isn't easy to spend time together with their sisters as adults. Childhood tensions continue into adulthood, splitting the group along the lines of old alliances. Carol, whose older sister let her play house only if she would be the maid, said: "It's harder to have fun when it's all three of us. We went to New York City together one year and it wasn't fun. There was always some funny dynamic. It's better two at a time." Spending time together may be smoother when there are four or more sisters, as it's more likely that there will be at least one person with whom you're on good terms that day.

Backbone of the Family

An odd thing about the middle sister's role in the family as an adult is that although she may maintain a position that is a bit apart, she is likely to be the one who steps in in times of crisis. Kim fit that description: "Often my family accuses me of being too into myself—dealing with my own problems alone and not confiding in them. I find it hard to reach out. I think it's one of my faults. Funny thing is that if anything goes wrong in the family, healthwise or crisiswise, I'm the first one they call. My oldest sister was diagnosed with cancer and she called me from the hospital. So I said, 'Mary, calm down.' I got her in to see a specialist, and it all worked out fine. She looks to me for logical, calm-down kind of stuff. And if there's a problem with the other girls, someone will usually call me. I guess I take charge and deal with it and help them deal with it. They scatter and don't know what to do."

Tamara described the same phenomenon in her middle sister: "The middle one is considered 'the bitch,' but she's also the one to count on when family business needs to be taken care of. She is also the first to help in the kitchen." Samantha, the "surrogate son" who went to the bank for her father, has continued in that role in adulthood: "I realize that, over a period of time, I've kind of become the boss of the family. My parents have facilitated me adopting that role without me really wanting it."

Black and White

In the section on occupations, we saw that middle sisters are overrepresented in careers related to business. Perhaps that is because some middle sisters tend to be very practical. Soccer-playing Billie, a younger sister, described her middle sister, Gaby, like this: "She's very black-and-white and solution oriented. Everything's got to be very practical. With Gaby, it's all on the surface. The emotional is zero. She's a bit like a guy. She never liked girl things. She got her first degree in computer science and now she's an engineer."

Eighty-three-year-old Winnie said about her middle sister, ten years older, "She was not very pretty and was more of a tomboy. She could fix anything and was counted on to do so. She taught herself to drive—she was the practical one."

Flora, seventy-seven, remains troubled that her middle sister, three years younger, doesn't really open up to her: "My middle sister is closed-mouth and does not freely tell any intimate parts of her life to either me or our other sister. She does not share any information about her children, who are grown and married. I know that she is distant with them as well, as I have a good relationship with each of her four children."

They'd Move Mountains for Me

It's impossible to overestimate the sense of security some middle sisters feel, knowing that there are two or more people in this world who truly have their best interests at heart. As one woman said, "I've always known that my sisters would move mountains for me." Particularly in larger families and as women grow older and face difficulties, having several sisters becomes more and more precious. All of the bickering, anger, and jealousy is put on the back burner when someone in the family is in crisis. Jessica explained, "I can tell you that the security and the backup that I feel that I have in life are huge. I know that I'm lucky that I'm able to rely on them, that I can pick up the phone and say, 'I need you for this.' And even though it's not usually spoken of in our family, it's there. You go through life knowing that you've got a team of people behind you who only want what's best for you, and when we're older, they'll still be there. There's a real feeling of security." Emily, Jessica's next older sister, told about a new family tradition: "Just after Christmas, the five of us got together for the first time and had dinner—no kids, no husbands, no parents—it was really nice. We all brought something. I was really looking forward to it, and I had a really good time. Since then, we've all been getting together every couple of months. We have a 'girl's night out,' go to a restaurant, and it's a lot of fun."

Taylor, whose four sisters range in age from nineteen to twenty-nine, reveled in her sisterly feeling: "I just adore them and think the world of all of them. I admire them all in different ways and for different reasons. Most of all, I love us as a group. When we are all together, I sometimes like to take a step back and just watch us. I can't imagine how great it must be for our parents to watch us interact and see how much we love each other. I hope my sisters all feel the same way!"

In twenty-four-year-old Daphne's family, there is a large age gap between the three sisters. Daphne is six years younger than Janice and seven years older than Allison. Nevertheless, Daphne delighted in her connection to each of them: "They're my best friends even though we're all very different people. Allison and I are very much in agreement with regard to religion, politics, and entertainment, while Janice tends to be more conservative, politically and religiously. Allison is my friend; someone I would be friends with even if she weren't my sister, because we have a lot in common and because she's fun and funny and witty. Janice is my friend because she is my sister and I mean that in the best possible way. She is very much the friend that sisters are supposed to be. She offers the best advice, supports my decisions unconditionally, shares my inside jokes, and understands me the way others never will."

The Middle Sister Stamp

Middle sisters had to solve some of the necessary riddles of life back when they were children—how to navigate unchartered territory, how to juggle relationships with people of different ages, and how to think for themselves. These skills come in handy when the "monkey in the middle" grows up.

Plays Well with Others

Unfortunately, as adults, some middle sisters continue to feel unimportant and overlooked in their life at work and with friends and lovers. They have to fall back on the same coping mechanisms they used as kids. They choose between trying not to stick out and acting up to get noticed. Beth said that she has "acted out for attention as an adult. I sometimes say things I shouldn't, just for effect." Like the black sheep, adult middle sisters may choose to chart their own course. Hannah wrote, "I tend to 'go against the grain.' I never quite fit in, but as an adult, I'm confident about being different and happy to stick out."

Quite a number of middle sisters said that they tend to go along with what others want; they accommodate and, similar to younger sisters, have trouble making decisions themselves. Ida wrote, "As a middle child, I tend to be a pleaser. I worry about what people may think about something I've done and don't like it when people are angry with me. It's like I'm always waiting for the judgment." Paige's e-mail echoed Ida's sentiment: "I act like the middle child. I share, accommodate, and 'play well with others.' I usually opt to do what other people want to do. I am incredibly indecisive, so I prefer others to make the decisions."

Balancing Leading and Following

Being in the center of things and able to see the point of view of both (or all) of her sisters makes some middle sisters flexible when it comes to dealing with a variety of personality types. There are both negative and positive aspects to this. For some women, it means that they are too easily influenced (one woman called herself a chameleon); for others, it means that they have a rich and varied social circle. On the negative side, Juanita, second youngest of five, said, "I think, as a result of my middle childness, my self-confidence is a little low because I measure myself against everyone else's success. I morph into different roles with different people, relating to them according to their age and my role in relation to them, rather than taking on [my own personality traits]." Lynn said, "Being in the middle, I've been shaped by the traits of my older sisters (independent) and my younger sisters (less assertive). I act like a younger sis with women who are older than me (e.g., looking to them for advice) and like an older sis with those who are younger than me (e.g., giving advice back)."

On the positive side, the middle sister adapts well. One participant said, "It helped me outside the family to be able to balance leading and following, and knowing which to do when." Another said that she remains the peacemaker in most situations: "Being in the middle allowed me to have a balanced view of myself. I grew up thinking I knew less than Sister #1, yet more than Sister #2."

The Go-Between

While middle sisters rarely choose to become therapists, they nevertheless often describe themselves as mediators. They look for solutions and possibilities and try to resolve conflict. They are masters at multitasking. They're good listeners, and people seek them out to hear their opinions. Nili told how she uses her creativity to make everyone feel acknowledged in her group at school: "Being a middle child has allowed me to be a better mediator in and outside of my family. When I'm working in a group at school, I often find myself being the person who molds together everyone's ideas so they can all be used. Being the middle child has also helped me read people's emotions better. I have a better understanding how people are feeling because I play two conflicting roles in my family."

Getting "the Smarts": Scarlet's Story

Scarlet, the fifth in a Catholic family of eight girls (twelve children in all) had a lot to say about how her role in her unusually large family had an effect on how she feels about herself as an adult. Scarlet is the one who, at the beginning of this chapter, said she felt "invisible" and "left out" of her family at times. She also told how the gang of sisters would walk to school down the cinder path and play in the woods. Her reflections on her role touched on many of the primary issues central to middle sisters: "I think my place in the family made me very tolerant of lots of things going on and lots of differences and perhaps even developed in me a desire for justice. I became a listener and an observer. I was the kid invisibly, vicariously watching, taking it all in and learning. I had to get attention by coming up with something that was different than the sisters before me. So I got 'the smarts' and used them.

"Being in the middle's made me ambitious, perhaps more balanced with male and female energies than the others. It also has made me a 'doer' who takes initiative. I see what needs to be done, and I independently complete the task. I am well rounded, knowing how to cook and do domestic things, but also enjoy reading, music, culture, foreign countries, and traveling. I'd rather lead than follow. I'd rather have a party than go to a party, and I like to speak up for justice.

"In many ways, being a middle sister affected my self-confidence negatively because I am always comparing. I seem to see myself as 'less than' and 'not enough' in terms of social skills, personality, likability, and body image. I still hate my body and find myself too fat. I still think my sisters are prettier, more fashionable, more full of friends and fun. I'm most comfortable with myself when I'm in charge, when I'm speaking publicly as an authority or smart person. In social settings, however, I remain the invisible middle child."

Springboard to Growth

Scarlet talked about how being invisible pushed her to become more resourceful—she had to do something different than the sisters before her. She got "the smarts" and she's proud of that. It is an interesting paradox—some middle sisters who felt neglected to one degree or another used that as a springboard toward becoming capable and independent-minded. As Randy said, "Although it was tough at times being a middle sister, I think it made me into a self-reliant, well-adjusted adult." The confidence of the middle role can also encourage a certain amount of adventurousness and risk taking. Lee contributed, "I think I'm very independent-minded, and I guess I have a very hard time doing something just because everyone else is doing it. For example, if everyone says they have to wear pink, well, I don't like pink, so I'm not going to wear it. I take more risks, sometimes stupidly. I'm very curious and really like to explore and ask and look around."

Perhaps because of this paradox, most middle sisters said that they wouldn't change their TOMY position if they could do it differently. They often said that they hated it as kids but grew to like it as adults and, if given a choice, wouldn't switch. It's almost like a badge of pride. I can picture a T-shirt with the slogan: "I survived childhood as a middle sister and, baby, look at me now!"

Olivia and Michelle

Wombmates

Twin Sisters

"I get our memories mixed up. I can't remember who did what. I'll remember something and it feels like it happened to me, but I'm not convinced that it has, and my sister says the same thing. For example, one day, when we were in kindergarten, we were walking home from school and had to pass this older kid who was a bit of a bully. He was standing on the sidewalk with a branch in his hand. I remember him hitting me with the branch on the back of my legs and I remember it hurting, but I know it was her that was getting hit—not me. I remember feeling scared, all of that stuff as if it was me, but it wasn't. That happens a lot."

—DANIELA, thirty-five years old

Similarities and Differences

Thirty-five-year-old Daniela's preceding vignette illustrates how the psychological boundary that separates her from her twin sister sometimes gets blurred. She is so close to her twin that there is virtually no stimulus barrier separating them; it feels like what happened to her sister was happening to her, too.

Other twins in The Sisters Project said, however, that the emphasis in their relationship with their twin sister was more on "sister" than it was on "twin"—they didn't have that mythical twin bond. This raises an issue that was central to my interviews and questionnaires from twin sisters—the extent to which women who are twins either embraced a shared identity or struggled for individuality. Theoretically, each twin could plot her position at various points in her life on a linear graph that looks like this:

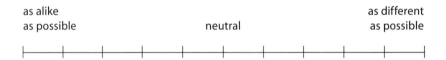

as alike   as different
as possible   neutral   as possible

I frequently found that twin sisters loved to play up the sameness when they were small, but went through a differentiating period in adolescence, often never to revive that wish for fusion. Seventy-year-old Olivia told me about the concept of "the reluctant twin," the one who yearns for a separate identity while her sister is very comfortable being identified as a twin. Olivia said, "I've heard theories that there is a reluctant twin and a not-so-reluctant twin. I must be the reluctant twin! I've tried so hard in my life to make my own mark; it's so strong within me that it feels like I'm driven! I almost have no control over it."

We will be examining twin relationships from two vantage points. Thus far, I have been talking about the interior need for sameness or difference. With twins, however, society imposes a huge set of expectations that also plays an important role. People are intrigued by twins, particularly identical ones, and love to remark on the novelty of two separate human beings who look alike. Total strangers on the street are so fascinated by the twin phenomenon that they tell their family about it at dinner, "I saw these twin old ladies on Main Street today, and they looked exactly alike and even had their newspapers folded under the same arm! It was weird!" Haven't we all (we nontwins, I mean) wondered at some point what it would be like to be a twin?

Having to put up with fascinated people who ask them, "What's it like to be a twin?" raises a sore point for twins. They are asked that question all of the time and often find it irritating. Corinne's annoyance came across loud and clear: " 'What's it like to be a twin?' is a popular question. What's it like not to be a twin? What's it like to be a man? What's it like to be Chinese? What's it like to be a horse?" You can picture twenty-five-year-old Pia and Bianca standing there with blank expressions, smiles pasted on their faces, as they endure some people's enthusiasm: "Bianca and I hear the most irritating things. We try very hard to just smile and nod while people go on and on: 'Oh, I've always wished I had a twin!' We're like, 'I'm so happy for you!' Or they say, 'I used to pretend I had a twin when I was young.' 'Good for you!' I don't know how to respond to that. Or when people are like, 'What's it like to have a twin?' I don't know! I have a twin! I don't know what it's like not to have a twin!" Now, I guess, a lot of us singletons will feel really stupid for having asked questions like that in the past!

The Sister Relationship as Children

As kids, twins are usually viewed as a unit. They're typically referred to as "the twins" both within the family and at school or other activities. Rules are different for them—a level of closeness and dependency that may be viewed as unhealthy between sisters of different ages is not only tolerated but also expected of twins. It's taken for granted that they need to be together.

Special Status

Society awards twins that look alike a special status, particularly when they are children. Olivia said that her mother got tired of being stopped on the street while people "oohed and aahed" over the adorable identical girls. Many twins admit that they get a lot more attention than their friends and are aware that they can control the extent of that by playing up the twin thing, what one woman called "milking the twinness." Thirty-three-year-old Monica sheepishly admitted how aware she is of the special power she and her sister have: "We intensely accentuated our differences when we were younger, choosing different styles of clothing, bristling if we were lumped together as liking the same thing or being the same way. Starting in college and since then, we've been wont to play up the twin thing in social gatherings and among friends. I guess it's a sort of a pride or ego thing (embarrassing to admit) to show nontwins what they're missing. We can slip very easily into assuming identical expressions or uttering the same response simultaneously, instinctively knowing that such a display of twinness will be received by others with interest and perhaps some jealousy (the 'I wish I were a twin' phenomenon)."

Whatever happens to one of the girls is often automatically measured against the experience of the other. Women who are twins told me stories about times when only one of them achieved or received something, and their parents felt the need to give something to the other to even things out. Carla explained, "Our parents wanted us to do the same things. When I didn't make cheerleading one year, they told my sister that she couldn't be a cheerleader. I objected and said it was only fair that she get what she earned and deserved. They conceded."

Parents have differing philosophies about how to handle the twinness factor. There's no question that mothers get a lot of attention from having twins and some may choose to play up their daughters' similarities to share in the limelight. Parents may give the girls rhyming names (people are always asking me whether Nikki is my twin). The final two participants that I interviewed for The Sisters Project were ninety-five-year-old identical twins who were given the same two first names, but reversed—Heather Anna and Anna Heather.

Some parents scrupulously reinforce the separate identities of the girls. They dress them differently, make sure they are in different classes at school (or different schools) and encourage separate after-school activities. They are sensitive to the need for the girls to develop as individuals. That doesn't stop grandparents, however, from turning up with matching dolls and dresses at Christmas, but parents can work around that. Polly appreciated that her parents let her just be herself: "Thank God my parents nurtured my free-spirited personality and didn't expect my behavior to match that of my sister. In school, however, all of the teachers would ask me why I couldn't be just like her."

That raises another drawback that goes with the territory—twins are constantly being compared to each other, and they find that hurtful, no matter whether they come out better or worse in the weighing. Daniela analyzed why people feel the need to do so: "People compared us all of the time. Who's prettier? Who's smarter? Who's nicer? When we're doing sports—which one's faster? Constantly! I think people do that because when they're struck with a similarity, they look for a difference. People naturally assume that no two people who are so alike could be equal. We're not equal, but we're very much alike. We didn't compete with each other, but others would do it for us and that was something that I used to find very painful. It was okay if she was better, but I found it very hard if they thought I was better. It made me feel guilty and protective of her, and she's told me that she had the same sort of reaction." Daniela has pointed out that people are uncomfortable with the thought that two people could be so much the same. They feel some urgency to identify disparities. I'm reminded of those puzzles in some newspapers in which two pictures appear to be identical and you're supposed to spot the differences. Don't we feel clever when we pick out that the sun has five rays in one picture but only four in the other?

Little Sis/Big Sis

Twins in The Sisters Project very often reported that they have a perception of one being older and one younger, depending upon who was born first. They're conscious of that timing from a very young age. You wouldn't think that three minutes would make enough of a difference to establish a hierarchy, but in the world of twins where every difference is finely parsed, even a minute or two is significant. It's hard to know how the dominance of some "elder" twins gets established, but I hypothesize that the girls (or their parents) seize upon the concept of older-younger and then their relationship develops accordingly. Once one girl starts to jokingly assert, "I'm the big sister!" she begins to integrate that role into her self-image and starts to act like an older sister might, even if, in truth, she's not really older. Of course, not every set of twins finds the "older" one more dominant, but a significant percentage of participants in The Sisters Project did. Twenty-one-year-old Charmaine illustrated how perception shaped the different roles of the two girls: "We make jokes about me being born first, meaning that I'm older and I'm the boss. I hear that the firstborn twin is always more outgoing. Dolores plays the baby in the family because she's the sensitive one. I will complain that I'm the one that gets asked to do everything around the house, and my mom will sometimes say, 'You know how sensitive your sister is; just please do this for me.' Oh yeah, I forgot to mention, I also drive all of the time. I have to fight with my sister to get her to drive sometimes because I know she's a nervous driver. Her excuse is that she just doesn't want to. I try to use that excuse, but how many times do you think that works for me? None!"

Charmaine heard somewhere that the firstborn twin is more outgoing, and she fits herself into that stereotype. Her role as the older, more dominant one is reinforced by her mother, who accepts that Dolores is more sensitive and in need of protection. Even if Charmaine tries to fight it, her mother and sister keep nudging her back into the older sister slot.

For some twins, that older-younger perception can make it seem like the difference between them is far more than a matter of minutes. Elaine, in her midtwenties, wrote about what being "younger" sometimes feels like: "I have always been the younger twin. I was born three minutes after my sister, and we have always joked that it felt like I was three years behind her. We still say that I'm the 'Little Sis.'"

Marilyn's role as the little sister was also well established in her mind: "We both perceive my twin as older because she was born ten minutes before me. I was always the 'dependent' twin. I was coddled, the baby of the family, a bit of a Pollyanna, but the peacemaker. My twin was independent; assertive, if not aggressive; and our spokesperson."

The youngest set of twins interviewed for the project was Julie and Elizabeth, five years old. Bouncing around on the sofa as they were being interviewed, they provided an example of a duo in which the spokesperson was very well established. In this case it was Julie, younger by seven minutes, who took the lead, while Elizabeth looked to her for answers to my questions, hardly speaking up at all. Although they looked remarkably similar, their personalities were quite different.

Night and Day

It is commonly known that the extent to which twins look the same has no bearing whatsoever on how similar their personalities are. Although the world expects girls who look alike physically to "be" alike mentally, many women describe their personality vis-à-vis that of their twin as being like "night and day" (in fact, three women used those exact words!). Perhaps this contrast is accentuated by the sisters' need to claim their own identity. Polly, one of the few twins given a name that rhymes with her sister's (Dolly), said, "I was so determined that I have my own personality that I would dress wildly and present myself totally different from her." Not all twins are charmed by being special.

It gets easier to tell identical twins apart when people get to know them because each girl's unique personality becomes obvious. Twenty-six-year-old Jeannie, who is very close to her twin, has a totally different style: "Although we are connected at the hip, our personalities are different. In school, she had a 'cowboy' boyfriend while I had a 'theatre' boyfriend. They didn't get along with each other, which caused conflicts between us. I tried her belly dancing and it wasn't for me—same for her trying my yoga. I'm a vegetarian and she's not. She has leather couches . . . not for me. She keeps bugging me to trade in my ten-year-old car for something new. There's nothing wrong with my car! When people first meet us, they have a hard time telling us apart, but once they get to know us, they find that we're different people and then we no longer look the same."

Daniela described how she and her sister naturally gravitate in opposite directions: "I was always more of the listener and my sister was more of the 'doer.' If a decision needed to be made, she would make it and I would just go along with it, but if anything was going wrong, I was the one who would look after it. I was always more emotional and she's more rational. I'm a physiotherapist and work with stroke victims. My sister finished her degree in engineering and is now working for an architectural firm."

Polly, thirty-four, resents the expectation that she will be like Dolly: "Single kids have an advantage because everyone expects them to have different personalities simply because they don't look alike. Twins are often pushed to behave the same, dress the same, and like it because people think it is so cute. I agree that it's cute, but feeling like you have no personality of your own isn't fun."

Trading Off

I was surprised at a common theme that cropped up in a number of interviews, that of twin sisters being expected to "trade off" characteristics. If one sister was like *this*, then the other had to be like *that*. It's as though the stock of personality traits available is limited, so each girl has to choose which ones she will co-opt for her own. One woman wrote, "We seemed to accept that neither of us could be smart, beautiful, funny, *and* loved, so we traded off those characteristics. I got 'loved' and 'funny'; she got 'beautiful' and 'smart.'" Another said, "When we'd get angry or upset, our parents would say that we'd be 'trading off' because one sister may not have been angry whereas the other one was. If I were upset with my mom, she'd say that it was 'my turn.' This sort of accentuated the idea that there was only 'one anger'—one energy—one person. It infuriated me!"

Thirty-three-year-old Adriana explained how it worked in her family: "It was like we both couldn't like the same things—we had to choose one or the other. Corinne chose art, so I couldn't. She's the 'artist' of the family, so in some way, it was communicated that I was to be something else. We were supported to be different more so than to be alike, but that imposed a limitation on ways that we were alike and wanted the same things. For instance, if we went out to dinner and I ordered the chicken, I could hear my mom saying, 'Corinne, your sister ordered the chicken. Get something else.'"

Identical Versus Fraternal

If there is a distinction between twins in terms of who is seen to be older and more dominant, there is certainly a hierarchy among sets of twins with regard to whether they are identical. Most twins, particularly when they are children, feel that identical trumps fraternal, or, in the words of fifteen-year-old Megan: "What's the point of being a twin if you're not identical?" Megan and her sister Aviva have a deep and close relationship, but you'd never know they were twins by looking at them. That really irked them when they were small children, but Megan says she's come to terms with it and even prefers it at this point in her life: "At times when we were little, I even wished we were Siamese, but my mom had a book about Siamese twins and then I saw how bad it could be, so I scratched that one out. But that's how real twins are. Then I wanted to be identical, because our close friends are identical and you really can't tell them apart. They switched classes and did all of that fun stuff you could do, but sometimes even their mom would get them confused! I don't know; it was a little weird.

"We did a twin festival one year and we had to dress exactly alike. We don't really look alike, so we wore big hats and put on nail polish. We had to take off our hats to do an activity and the person in front of us in line said, "Oh, I guess they're fake twins." It didn't make me feel bad, but it made me feel weird because that's how people see us."

In contrast, nine-year-old Brianna and Ashley both agreed that not only do they wish that they weren't identical (which they are), but they wish that they weren't twins at all. They feel burdened by being expected to do things together all of the time. Brianna said that it would be better if they were just sisters: "If she has homework and I don't and I want to play with my friend, she wants me to wait for her. If she was just my sister, I could leave and go play with my friend." In her completely separate interview, Ashley eerily echoed the identical sentiment: "Sometimes when we're with our friends and we're playing hide-'n-go-seek and I want to be with my friend and she also wants to be with that same friend, I just wish she wasn't there so I can be alone with my friend."

There were lots of stories from women who were so identical growing up that even their parents or siblings had trouble telling them apart. Sometimes they themselves can't quite distinguish who's who when they look at old pictures. Marsha's mom could be forgiven for not keeping it straight—she already had her hands full with four young daughters when the twins came along. Marsha wrote, "We are identical twins and were very hard to tell apart while we were growing up. The only way was that I had a small birthmark on my forehead and Nathalie had a crooked bottom tooth. As babies, our mom kept our hospital bracelets on till they got too tight. Then she painted our big toenail so she could tell us apart. Later, they dressed us alike but in different colors. We even sounded alike. My mom could never tell us apart just by our voices."

Body Inspection

One of the questions I asked twin participants in The Sisters Project was, "How strongly do you think you and your twin sister resemble each other?" They had a field day with that one. From the answers, it was clear that each set of twins had spent an inordinate amount of time standing side by side in front of the mirror in close observation. They would report findings such as:

- "My face is more oval than hers, and her eyes are more open than mine."
- "I'm about a quarter inch or less shorter than she is."
- "She was always a tiny bit bigger."
- "She has a wide face with a squished nose (like my dad), and I have a narrow face with a pointy nose (like my mom)."
- "My shoe size is bigger, but our teeth x-rays are the same."
- "If you look very closely, she has a slightly larger nose, ha ha ha!"

"A quarter inch or *less* shorter," "teeth x-rays are the same," and "eyes . . . more open"! How much time did those girls actually spend in front of that mirror? Of course, there are advantages—you get to really see how your butt looks in those jeans when your identical twin sister is wearing them! Gina wrote, "Once my sister said I had an ugly butt and I just looked at her and said, 'You have the same butt as I do, dork!'" Bianca said, "Since my sister and I have the same physique, it's like looking at myself from a different perspective."

Pia said that she doesn't always see the resemblance to her identical twin, perhaps because they scrutinize their faces so carefully: "Sometimes we really don't see it, when people say, 'Oh, my God, you look so much alike!' Sometimes we do, sometimes we don't. I think that it depends on our moods. This is strange, but if she's angry, she'll look nothing like me. If I'm upset, I'll look nothing like her. We're different in the ways we express emotion."

Weight is often a sore point. In the arena of minute comparison that twin sisters seem to be trapped in, being heavier than a twin is particularly hard to take. Margot, the sister of the reluctant twin, Olivia, struggled with weight all of her life: "I did feel quite jealous about Olivia's weight being less than mine, which was the case for decades. I was always at least one, sometimes two, sizes larger. When I finally did lose weight, three years ago, I remember announcing at a Weight Watchers meeting that it was only the second time in sixty-seven years that I weighed less than my twin sister!" Olivia, for her part, was also very conscious of the competition: "We compared our bodies a lot when we were growing up. I've always been slimmer and pleased about that. Right now, I think I weigh more than she does and that really bothers me!"

Finally, on the topic of resemblance, twenty-three-year-old Sophia poignantly mused: "When people say we look alike, do we look like her or do we look like me?"

Red Keds/Blue Keds

As I noted earlier, the rules are different for twins than for other siblings. Another example involves the whole issue of dressing alike. In general, the only people who dress identically are schoolchildren who wear uniforms, airline and military personnel, priests, workers in fast-food restaurants, and dancers in the corps de ballet! Otherwise, it doesn't typically happen—except with young twins, where, whether or not you agree with the practice, it's somewhat normal and expected. Of course, it usually doesn't go on forever. There seems to be a natural cutoff point at which either the parent feels that the charm has gone out of it or the girls are just so sick of it that they revolt.

Daphne, thirty-two, told the classic twin switcheroo story: "In preschool, we always had matching clothes but I had blue Keds and she had red. It didn't take long for us to figure out that if we each swapped a shoe (so we each had a red and a blue) the teachers wouldn't know which one we were."

The first time twins start dressing differently feels a bit daring—sort of like how a nun might feel if she were to ditch the religious life and venture out in capris. Daniela remembered, "We sort of had this sense that we had to dress the same and look the same, and for years we would decide what we would wear each day. It used to cause incredible fights. One of us would say, 'I don't want to wear that!' It wasn't until just before high school that we realized we didn't have to do this! Dressing differently was fun and different, but it was a bit threatening."

Margot recalled the first time as being a real big event: "We both felt that it was a mistake for my folks to dress us alike until we were about thirteen or fourteen. I distinctly remember feeling absolutely elated the first time we dressed differently and having a new recognition of separate identity." Her sister Olivia also describes that day as having been "*very* liberating."

Balance: Megan and Aviva's Story

I went to interview fifteen-year-old Megan and Aviva in their family's big, artsy house on a sunny October afternoon. It was the kind of place where there's always action going on; I had the feeling that there were unseen people busy in other rooms. It was a couple of days before Halloween, and Megan was downstairs, frantically trying to get her costume ready for some event. Aviva said that normally Megan would have gone first, but because she was busy with her costume, this was Aviva's chance to do something differently. She acknowledged that Megan, who is two minutes older, usually takes the lead and has recently been pushing Aviva a bit to take risks.

The focus of the interview was the passionate desire on the part of both girls for three things: (1) to remain close, (2) to protect each other's feelings, and (3) to ensure that one does not succeed more than the other. But by a stroke of good luck, I had met Aviva and Megan at the exact moment in their lives at which they were struggling through a subconscious process to renegotiate their positions on that alikeness-difference scale from the beginning of this chapter. They told about their efforts to balance having separate friends with their need to avoid either jealousy or guilt. Megan said, "We're really close; we do everything together. It feels strange when we don't. When we started high school, it was really weird if one of us would make friends faster or get invited to different places. For example, Aviva did this project with somebody and they spent all of their time together at school. That girl is now her best friend. I felt a little bad about it, but I worry that Aviva's going to know that I feel bad and start to feel guilty. There's a lot of, 'I don't want to talk about it because I don't want to make her feel guilty that I feel bad, which would make me feel guilty.'"

Megan went on to say, "On the other hand, I was invited to this boy's bar mitzvah and Aviva wasn't. I went and it felt really bizarre that she wasn't there. The whole night, I was worried sick, thinking, 'Oh no, is she going to feel bad? Is she going to be sad?' It didn't end up to be that much fun. It was bad that it happened, but what could we do to change it? She didn't have any classes with that guy, and I had all of my classes with him. It wasn't her fault. But we both felt bad about it anyhow."

I asked Megan if she had a wish for Aviva: "I always want her to be happy 'cause when she's not happy, then it ruins it for me, too. It happens a lot that we come home from school separately and maybe I had a detention and I have another one tomorrow and Aviva is like, 'I had such a great day—I ate lunch with this person and I got a really good mark in this class!' And I'm like, 'I hate my teacher and I'm upset that I'm not doing anything this weekend,' and then she gets all sad and I feel bad that I made her sad, and she feels bad because I feel bad."

Aviva told how impossible it is for them to stay mad when they get into fights: "If we get into fights, we say 'sorry' right away. If I'm mad at Megan and I say something mean and she gets hurt and storms off, then I feel so bad that she is feeling bad that I want to make up right away. That's what makes our fights so annoying."

Megan told how wonderful it is to always have someone back home who will really understand you. "We know everything about each other and we love to talk. Last night, my dad said, 'Don't you guys ever run out of things to talk about?' but we keep on talking because there's always different stuff, even though we know so much about each other. Like if something happens in my class at school, I can't wait to tell Aviva. I'll be on the bus, thinking, 'I can't forget this, I can't forget this.' I'll even think of the words I'm going to say!"

Aviva's wish for the future was, "We wouldn't be better than each other, because then one of us would be jealous, so I hope that if I have a good life, then she will have a good life, too."

At the end of the interview, Megan said, "When we were four, Aviva was really sad about something and that made me feel bad, so I said, 'I feel in my feel what I see in her face.' That about explains it."

The Lack of a Stimulus Barrier

Megan and Aviva's words are so powerful because we are hearing them while the girls are sorting out where they will fall on the alikeness-difference scale. At the age of fifteen, the balance is in flux as close relationships beckon from outside of what Megan called "that little cocoon of Aviva and me." We are catching a glimpse of a twin fusion similar to the one described by Daniela at the start of this chapter. The stimulus barrier that usually separates sister from sister, mother from child, or husband from wife, is thin or nonexistent, so that when something happens to her twin, such as being hit by the bully with the branch, Daniela experiences it as if it were happening to her. The same holds true between Aviva and Megan—they can each *really* feel each other's pain—it's not just a figure of speech. Each one needs the other to feel good so that it's possible to feel good herself. One participant noted, "We're so close, it's almost frightening!"

Daniela explained the sense of fusion further: "We were very, very close as kids; we did everything together. It was almost like we were one—we were always a part of each other. We grew up in the country and went to a small school. We had limited chances to visit other friends because it would be a long drive, so we were always together."

Pia's connection with her sister was similar: "We were each other's security blanket. We never had that one toy or blanky that kids seem to want to carry with them—we had each other. The first day of school wasn't intimidating for us, because we knew who we would sit with on the bus, who we would talk to during recess, and stuff like that. We tended to stick together."

As a young teen, having a twin continues to provide a security blanket. Seventy-year-old Margot remembered, "We both felt a little like 'wallflowers' in early adolescence. We were kind of chubby and wore our hair unattractively, but it wasn't nearly as painful for me as it would have been if I'd had to go through it alone. Twinship protected us from 'the slings and arrows' of being teased, ridiculed, or ostracized, which so often happens to girls in puberty."

Five-year-old Elizabeth and Julie are evidently still wrapped up in their little cocoon together. I asked them whether it was fun to be twins. Julie answered, "Yes! The best part is that we get to play together so we won't be alone. We like to pretend we're animals—cats and dogs and wolves in the wild—sometimes wildcats!" Elizabeth suddenly started tickling Julie, giggling, "The tickle-monster is here!" Then she said, "I felt bad last year when Julie broke her arm, so I made cupcake-land on the cast. I put a lot of cupcake stickers on her cast." Julie didn't want anyone else to decorate her cast—only Elizabeth. Elizabeth felt sad and a little bit jealous and asked their mom, "When am I going to break my arm?" because Julie was getting so much attention. I was struck by the extent to which their connection is so intensely physical. They were hopping and jumping all over each other like playful puppies. They just seemed incredibly absorbed in their twosomeness, as if anyone else would be a distraction.

Being so connected to the other twin's emotional experience puts a lid on the level of jealousy and anger typically found between other sisters. About those strong negative emotions, many twins said that if they're felt at all, they dissolve pretty quickly. Several said things like, "Jealousy is an emotion I don't have a whole lot of experience with," or "Let's say we're jealous about a little thing—well, we forget about it in a minute or so."

With regard to anger, Pia explained, "It sometimes surprises me how fast my anger toward my twin will dissolve. Like I was so angry two minutes ago, I could just . . . I could visualize myself strangling her! And then two seconds later, she's like 'stop' and I'm like 'yeah' and it's just gone. I feel like, 'I want to be still angry at you!' because it's not cool to just forget about it, but, on the other hand, I just can't force that emotion."

Twin Communication

Twins are well known for having private means of communication. The women in The Sisters Project described that special interchange in two ways.

Idioglossia. A large percentage of participants referred to "that twin language," the technical name of which is *idioglossia*. That's the baby talk between twins that seems to be a kind of internal messaging system that others can't understand. Jeannie, who had a "theatre boyfriend" while her sister had a "cowboy boyfriend," was sent with her twin to a speech therapist as a young child because her parents were concerned about their language development: "We had a special language when we were babies. Our mom took us to a specialist because we would talk to each other in 'jibber-jabber.' She would try to figure out what one of us needed, but when it wouldn't work, the other would start talking in the jibber-jabber and come back with a teddy bear."

Another woman told about not using recognizable language until she and her twin were three and a half. Until then, they just babbled together in a direct call-and-response style from separate cribs. Later, the girls were put in a special education class because the school thought they were slow, though they were eventually moved to a class for talented and gifted kids.

As adults, some twins continue using a modified idioglossia. Thirty-three-year-old Darla wrote, "We don't even use full sentences when communicating, but rather a series of invented sounds and code words. We try to be subtle about this when we're in public, but sometimes we forget. At times, we don't need words at all—facial expressions are enough. This afternoon we were walking in a parking lot, and my sister started to wander off in the opposite direction from the car. I guided her back by a series of tongue clicks."

Just Knowing. The second manner of communicating goes beyond language or sound. Like Megan and Aviva, some sisters don't require much in the way of communication; they just know. As one woman wrote, "Our souls are somehow intertwined." Twenty-five-year-old Chase said, "Since we shared a bedroom for seventeen years, not to mention a womb, I think we have ways of understanding each other that don't depend on language. I am able to predict fairly accurately how something will make her feel, how she will explain a memory, and the moments of her past that she will choose to explain her present." That mysterious communication even transcends consciousness: "When we sleep next to each other, we dream of the same elements."

Twins describe a kind of mental telepathy when they're together ("You mean, you didn't just say *out loud* that I should close the window!?"), but some also say that they know what their twin is going through, even when they're apart. Marsha, who lived in a different state from her sister, wrote, "I actually had morning sickness for three months when Nathalie was pregnant. I had gone to a doctor and was going to have tests when the symptoms abruptly stopped at her three-month prenatal visit."

Separation Anxiety

The first time twin sisters experience a lengthy separation can be deeply significant, whether it's an afternoon-long playdate in the second grade or the first year apart in college. It's often a revelation to learn that one can maneuver through the world as an individual. For some girls, it's terrifying; for others, it's elating. Bianca remembered that nervous first time her path diverged from that of her sister: "I remember the first time I experienced separation anxiety. I was six and in grade one, and we were put into separate classes. I kept going over to her classroom to talk to her about nothing really. I just wanted to see her."

From the other end of the educational ladder, twenty-one-year-old Monica told about the relief she experienced when she reunited with her twin after their first long separation: "We always shared a bedroom, from birth through college (same dorm room, then same apartment). I graduated a year ahead of her when she changed her major, and we lived apart for that year. When we finally got back together, around Christmastime, we went shopping with our mother. We all realized at the same time that Darla and I were walking physically flush up against one other, glued from shoulder to knee, unaware of what we were doing or how strange that must have looked. We were just so relieved to be back together that we literally couldn't tear ourselves apart."

Adriana's memory also took place during her college years: "I truly feel I didn't have much of an individual identity until Corinne left for college and I stayed living at home. That was the first time I felt like I was alone and had to cultivate myself as an individual human and not half of a whole."

Lonely Littlest Sister

In their self-absorbed world, five-year-old Elizabeth and Julie don't have much interest in their baby sister, April, who is three years younger. Their mother doesn't know how to help April join in her older daughters' play. When I asked the girls about their little sister, Julie answered first: "It's not so fun having a baby sister, and sometimes she wrecks our games and plays with things we don't want her to play with and she sometimes scribbles on our pictures [switch to Elizabeth talking] and sometimes she bothers us while we're playing and sometimes she loses our favorite stuffed animals . . . and she rips our pictures."

It's pretty hard on a little girl who has twin older sisters. April, in this case, really has to struggle to be included. One day, she may decide to skip the whole thing and go her own way. As was the case with middle sisters, several adult twin participants who treated their younger sister badly felt guilty about it. Twenty-two-year-old Pia was full of regrets: "We picked on her when she was little. We would double-team her all of the time. She'd be doing something and one of us would start picking on her and the other twin would join in, taking her stuff and teasing her. It got so bad that at one point our parents sat us down and said, 'Stop it! You have to stop it. She just wants to play with you guys; she just wants to be in with you guys.' But it had always just been the two of us. There's a six-year age difference. It's been hard for her to get in with us, because when we were together, we never wanted anybody else in our little group; we didn't need them. It's taken us until very recently, the last year or so, to start developing a relationship with our younger sister. I've expressed to her that I'm genuinely sorry for the things that I said or did to her when she was young. I love her very much."

The dynamic is different when the odd woman out is older than the twins. An older sister is already established in the family, and the younger girls may naturally look up to her. Her status is less vulnerable to the exclusivity of the twin bond. Plus, she gets some pride of ownership—her friends may think it's really cool that her little sisters are twins.

The Sister Relationship as Adults

Understandably, the developmental process of becoming an adult puts a strain on the simple bond that exists between many twins as children. They now have to redefine themselves as individuals and try to make room for other adults in their lives.

A Perfect Marriage

The twin sister bond is defined by exclusivity, absorption, devotion, duality, the pleasure of each other's company, and a mutual interest in each other's life. It sounds to me like a terrific marriage. Where else are you free to give so much of yourself with the assurance that the other person will truly accept and understand you? Plus, it's balanced; you're peers. And you can relax into it because it's lifelong—there's very little likelihood of divorce. Your "life partner" knew you from day one, literally! She knew your kindergarten teacher and your dog. Don't they say that couples that have been together for a long time even start to look alike?

Polly described her connection to Dolly in those same terms: "It's the weirdest part of being a twin. We have always balanced each other out. It's like being in a great marriage in which your spouse makes you whole." Margot used a similar term: "It's impossible to describe. She's just like a soul mate and whenever one or the other of us is either jubilant or blue, we share those feelings and get the kind of sustenance that I don't think any other relationship can equal."

However, there's a price to pay for having been in a "great marriage" from day one—it is hard to establish a separate identity. This troubles some women more than others; some appear to value the twin connection above all else. At the age of seventy, Olivia recognized how being a twin delayed her developing an independent sense of self: "I often tell people that I don't feel that I used the word *I* until I was thirty-seven, when I got divorced, because I had been part of 'Margot and me'—we, the twins—and then 'Bob and me'—we, the married couple. I think that's quite sad. I think that nobody should be so wedded, whether it's marriage or not, to another human being that they don't have a sense of their ego. When I got divorced, I felt I could finally be myself. I could do what I wanted to do; I wouldn't have to blend in with my twin sister or accommodate myself to my husband. I could just be in charge of my life. I could develop myself and get a sense of my own personhood."

The Mirror Self

Several women used the word *mirror* in describing their relationship with their twin—an understandable choice. Some commented that seeing their own behavior reflected in their sister's didn't always thrill them. Daphne said, "I know her better than anyone because we are so much alike. I can't stand it sometimes, because I see her do some things that I know I do exactly the same, and I get mad at her because I wish I didn't do it like that. She is my mirror. I look at her and see how people see me." Another participant said, "When we talk, I sometimes get tired of seeing and hearing myself. I ask myself, 'Do I have those mannerisms? Do I sound like that? Do I come across that way?' I know the answer, and it's almost like a course in self-awareness."

Forty-three-year-old Greta from Columbus, Ohio, took the mirror image metaphor to another level: "My twin sister and I had this thing where we never hugged. We said it was like hugging yourself— we were that close. For the same reason, I didn't circle the word *adore* [on the 'Circled Words' part of The Sisters Project questionnaire]. It would be like adoring yourself. We together adored other people. It would have been weird to adore each other." (In the "Circled Words" part of The Sisters Project interview and questionnaire, participants were asked to indicate how they felt about their sisters as children and as adults by circling phrases from a list of feelings—see Appendix D.)

The extent of the closeness means that some women said that they hope that life provides even more good things for their sister than for themselves. As Megan and Aviva explained, their own comfort level requires that their twin be in a good frame of mind. If one twin is troubled, it's impossible for the other to feel okay. Daniela feels as though she can handle disappointment in her own life, but when June is sad, it feels almost intolerable. June, now pregnant, has wanted children for some years but had trouble conceiving. Daniela, who is single, shared her thoughts on the extent to which her sister's happiness is paramount in her life: "Her being pregnant, and the struggle it's been for her to get pregnant, has underlined how close and important she is to me. I would be devastated if I could have a child and she couldn't. I'd feel so guilty. It's almost like, now that she's pregnant, it's okay for me to do it. But, if it were me who couldn't conceive, I'd find that less of a problem than if she couldn't. It's not about my being more able to deal with it; it's just that I want life to turn out so that she can have anything that she wants."

The Anchor

Having a twin keeps a woman grounded. In a sense, most sisters do, but with a twin, the roots are often even deeper because they were wombmates and spent so much time together growing up. Twins go through the same life stages at relatively the same time. I didn't hear from any women in The Sisters Project who said that their twin tore them down. Some felt a bit distant or competitive with a twin, but there was none of the criticism that showed up from time to time in the other TOMY positions.

On the contrary, many said that their twin spurred them to greatness. Elaine wrote, "Having a twin is like having someone to always keep you in check . . . someone who knows you better than you know yourself, someone who keeps you grounded and rooted in the way you grew up. I am positive that my relationship with her and our competitiveness has helped us strive for great things and search out who we are, more so than if we did not have each other." Fifty-one-year-old Ingrid contributed, "My sister was what anchored me. We are very different from our mother, and I think we kept each other focused and supported each other to succeed. It was very difficult to be female in my profession [surgeon], but the fact that there was always someone who loved me for me was a great encouragement."

"He Took My Place!"

Women told about how their relationship with their twin sometimes ebbed and flowed—they could place themselves at various times
at different points on the alikeness-difference scale. A common time
for the wave to recede was when one of the twins got involved with a
lover, turning her attention away from her twin. The word *betrayal*
springs to mind, and I think that some women do feel betrayed, particularly if their twin marries a person they don't like. A rupture may
develop between the sisters that may take years to heal. One woman
wrote, "She is getting married soon, and we might have to 'split up.'
This is so scary that every time the subject comes up, we immediately
repress it." Another said, "She began a long-term relationship, which
took lots of adjustments on my behalf. She started to share all of her
thoughts with her boyfriend, and I was left out." When asked to
describe an unhappy memory, a twenty-one-year-old said, "When she
picks her boyfriend over me. I hate that!"

Again, it is the exclusivity of the twin relationship that gets threatened when one woman looks to someone other than her twin to fulfill her needs for closeness. It becomes hard to juggle two such intimate
relationships, and as we saw with middle sisters, threesomes are unsta-
ble. The woman in the middle feels that she needs to make her primary identification with one or the other—her twin or her lover. That,
of course, engenders a lot of guilt on the part of the twin who has to
make the choice and a lot of resentment on the part of the one who is
left. The sisters may lose their balance for a few years until the dust
settles and one of three things happens: (1) the strength of the twins'
earlier bond reestablishes itself, (2) they water down the closeness and
proceed from there, or (3) the romantic relationship is broken off.

Daniela's outrage said it all: "When June got married, it was
incredibly painful for me and for her as well. Even prior to their marriage, I didn't get along with her husband, and I still don't. He was jealous of our relationship, although he wouldn't admit that. I was
definitely jealous and I was very protective. I didn't like the way he

treated her, and to this day, I still don't at times. I just didn't feel that he was good enough for her. He took my place—she let him take my place—and he made it clear that he didn't want me around very much and she never fought for that. She was ready for him to be the primary person in her life and wasn't ready to say that she still wanted me there, too. We found our way back together very gradually. It's possible that June was looking for another twin in her husband."

Some women may look toward marriage as a legitimate excuse to separate from their twin sister, but others may find that just having a twin interferes with making it to the altar. Polly was conscious that her relationship with her twin may be making it harder for her to find a partner: "I often wonder if the reason I have not found the right man to marry is that I sometimes feel that no one could balance me out better than she. She dated her husband for twelve years before she married him. The strangest thing about him is that he is a male version of me. It's scary how much he's like me. I guess the man I marry will be similar to Dolly! Hmm, very interesting!"

When Polly does find the right man and has children, she may be struck by how close she is to her sister's offspring. Marsha wrote about her sister's kids: "Nathalie and I share an extra closeness with each other's kids. I almost feel like her kids are mine, and it's been like that since they were babies. We could hold and settle each other's kids like they were our own. At times, I don't think the kids would tell the difference." Olivia recalled, "My nieces and nephews feel a special bond with me because I sound so much like my sister. Our voices are exactly the same. They talk about how strange it was when they first got to the age of three or four and they heard another voice like their mother's. I used to say that the children would run up to the wrong pair of knees in the kitchen!"

Heather and Anna's Story

When I was conducting interviews for The Sisters Project, I'd often bring my camera and ask if I could take a photo of the participants.

I did so the day I interviewed Anna and Heather, and I later put their picture in a frame on my desk. In the photo, they are sitting side by side. Anna has her arm protectively around Heather, who is looking straight at the camera with a sweet, shy smile. I was able to capture the items on Heather's bedside table in the background—a bunch of yellow flowers and a Mylar balloon that says "Happy 95th Birthday!" Their birthday was a couple of days before the interview. I love looking at that photo and remembering that poignant interview, the last one of The Sisters Project, when I met these remarkable identical twins.

I began the interview by asking if they had a sense that one was older than the other. Anna said, "I claim to be older because I was born half an hour before her, but she always said, 'Oh no, you couldn't be older because I was there first and kicked you out!' So for her birthday card this year, I wrote on it, 'Happy Birthday to Heather—You claim that you kicked me out, but you only did it because you wanted to be born!'" (We all laughed.) Anna continued, "Our mother died the day after our eighth birthday, so we didn't have her to bring us up, but our older sister looked after us like a mother. She just adored us." Heather said, "Anna used to fight all of my battles." Anna explained, "See, we never played with anybody else but each other. When we went to school for the first time, a girl said, 'C'mon, play with us' and we didn't make a move, so the girl came and gave Heather a shove, so I got up and, boy, did I lambaste her! From then on, if anybody was nasty to Heather, I would stick up for her."

Heather and Anna are both artists. They paint and do handicrafts, often relying on Anna's skill with a sewing machine. They have been close all of their lives, raising their families together. They always lived in the same neighborhood, except for one summer when Heather worked at a big hotel in the mountains. Anna went to visit Heather at the hotel that summer, and although she had never been there, she knew exactly where to go to find her sister.

I asked what it was like having been close for ninety-five years, and Heather's answer was swift and heartfelt: "If anything should happen to me, I'd want to be with her." Heather had had a mild stroke and was no longer able to live in her own home. Our interview took place at the rehab hospital where she was recuperating; the department of social services was looking for a permanent place for her to stay. She very much wanted to move into Anna's house, but Anna had earlier confided to me that she just didn't feel strong enough to take care of her sister. Anna felt terrible anguish about it and just didn't have the heart to tell Heather. After ninety-five years of sticking up for her sister, Anna finally came up against something from which she was unable to protect her.

Anna rarely has someone available who can drive her to visit Heather, so I left the two alone for a while following the interview. When I returned, they were taking care of business—writing checks to pay bills and organizing their affairs. My heart was full as we all said a courageous good-bye and I left with Anna to drive her home.

Twin Pride

I was interested to understand how important it was to adult twins that acquaintances know that they have a twin sister. I wondered how soon after meeting someone a twin would reveal this important truth about herself. Elaine responded, "It is weird, because growing up, it was always 'the twins.' Now, many people don't even know I have a twin unless they get to know me more than as an acquaintance. My twin's so much a part of me, still a special link, someone who I feel is there all of the time, but others don't know that."

Pia's response: "Mostly, it never comes up. I'm not really think-ing about it. Yesterday, I was at school very late working on a project with some friends and I mentioned my twin. One of the girls grabs my arm. She's like, 'This is new!' I'm like, 'Oh, yeah, I have a twin.' She said, 'We've been working together for a month and you never mentioned it!' I'm like, 'What do you want me to say . . . Hello, my name is Pia, and I've got a twin! I mean, did you tell me about your siblings when we first met?' Like, not really! But people seem to feel a little outraged when I don't tell them."

I asked twenty-three of the twins in The Sisters Project whether they would change being a twin if they could. Of the twenty-three, three said "yes," they'd rather not be a twin, and twenty said "no!" very emphatically. Some of their comments included:

- "I wouldn't trade being a twin for all of the money in the world!"
- "Some people search the world for their soul mates and we are so lucky! We came into the world together!"
- "I love talking about my twin. This is really the first time that somebody's been interested to really understand. A lot of people say, 'Oh, you're twins, that's cool!' and then that's it. For me, it's been a lot of fun."
- "I would just like to say that I love being a twin. I don't understand twins that want to look different. It's something special that you were given when you were born. You *are* different than everyone else. Take advantage of it!"

Finally, a giggle spilled out over the Internet when Charmaine e-mailed me her answer to that question: "Heck, no! We love being twins. We laugh when we see identical old twin ladies at the grocery store or somewhere because we know we're definitely going to be just like that!"

The Twin Sister Stamp

As you can imagine, for any woman to grow up believing that her identity is profoundly linked to that of another person would leave an indelible stamp on her self-image as an adult. For 6,570 days from birth to the age of eighteen, the world viewed her as part of a twosome. That internal sense that she is only *part* of a whole entity, formerly known as "the twins," does not evaporate just by her moving to a separate apartment. The consequences of being a twin vary from woman to woman, but certain effects were spoken of time and again by women in The Sisters Project.

Something's Missing

Adult twins talk about having had an unsettling feeling that something's missing when they launched out into the world on their own. They didn't have much practice making decisions without consulting their twin, and many tended to feel insecure going it alone. Perhaps they were looking for someone else to legitimately take the place of their twin sister. Jeannie, who spoke jibber-jabber with her twin as a toddler, wrote, "I might be an individual, but I am not independent. I have my own views and opinions, but it's really hard for me to do something on my own. It's not that I need someone to make my decisions, it's just that I have more strength with my sister around. Since conception, I've never been alone. I don't do well by myself." Chase spoke of the difficulty she has finding "a public identity," and she related that to being a twin.

This feeling of not doing well by themselves leads twins to try to replicate with a boyfriend or girlfriend the level of comfort and intimacy they enjoyed growing up. The problem is that nontwins may feel lost when called upon to fuse to the same extent. This causes the twin to feel disappointed and frustrated. Daniela expressed her thoughts on this: "Mostly with partners or boyfriends, best friends or close friends, I have a tendency to look for a twin. I look for somebody to be as close as I once was with her. I expect someone to be fully there without too much work, to understand completely, to be everything. Intellectually I know that's not what works, but emotionally I get into this trap like, 'You should just know.'"

Monica's e-mail echoed Daniela's wish that someone would just "know": "I find it hard sometimes to communicate verbally with others because I become frustrated when they don't immediately understand where I'm coming from, like my sister would, and sometimes this makes me feel isolated and incompetent."

An offshoot of this wish for closeness is the trouble some women have recognizing how much to give to others because they grew up being close to someone in a world where there are no boundaries. Some twins said that they had to learn not to give so much away. Marsha's difficulty in seeing herself as an independent person leads to her consistently putting others' needs first: "The biggest impact of being a twin is that I don't look after myself like I should. As you grow up, it's never just me, but it's Nathalie and me, so you are always looking out for her. Then, when you're older, you start to look out for others and don't concentrate enough on yourself."

The feeling that there is something missing propels some twins to a greater sense of independence. They don't want to see themselves as only part of a whole, and consequently, they work very hard to develop their own separate identity. One woman said that her parents tried to accentuate the similarities between her and her twin, so in response she became "fiercely independent." Olivia described herself as having this tendency: "What I've realized is that I had this tremendous need to achieve, stronger than my sister's. I think maybe just to make my own mark upon the world. I just had to prove my individuality. I had to get recognition for me as Olivia Dobbs, not just as one of the Dobbs twins."

Polly's parents always encouraged her independent identity. She grew up feeling comfortably separate from her twin and does not have that powerful need to assert her uniqueness: "I think that my personality today is a direct reflection of being a twin. I'm always looking to be different in everything I do, sometimes in an extreme free-spirited mode. My view of myself today is as a person who is confident (my twin is always with me), different/unique (strong personality traits helped me growing up to differentiate myself from my twin), successful (with Dolly there I will always succeed), and free-spirited to this day. Thank you, Mom and Dad! They treated us like two different people with different interests and needs, and this allowed me to be me."

Built-In Best Friend

As we've already heard, just because twins grow up and move to their own places, they don't necessarily move apart emotionally. The twin connection continues to feed them throughout adulthood, in some cases rendering involvement with other people relatively unnecessary. Darla, thirty-three, receives social contact and also the validation that she needs from her sister: "It is hard to make friendships when you already have a built-in best friend. For the most part, social interaction seems unnecessary. I don't even date very frequently. Sometimes I feel odd. Or rather, sometimes I feel that other people view me as odd. . . . Having a person around who is so similar to me gives me validity for the things about myself that might be viewed as strange. If there weren't somebody there who acted exactly the same way, I might see myself as a true oddball!"

I suppose it's hard to find somebody else who enjoys being an oddball in the same way a twin might. Daphne's e-mail had somewhat of the same flavor as Darla's: "I have a hard time relating to other females. I have such a close relationship with Diane that I don't really know how to interact with someone when I can't share, laugh, and yell as much."

Although Margot and Olivia did make friends at college as young adults, Margot felt that she didn't need to work to maintain those friendships over the years, because she relied on their twinship for friendship and support. She now regrets that she let those "good old friends" fall by the wayside.

Peace and Love

Having grown up in a nonhierarchical twosome makes it easy for twins to be good team workers. (Middle sisters also work well in groups, but for very different reasons.) They think of "us" rather than "me" and are very tuned in to what other people feel. Sabine, a twenty-three-year-old graduate student, wrote, "Looking back on the idea of growing up a twin, I realize that great things in life are only important to me when I share them. This really affects my actions and decisions as an adult. I'm very much 'about' sharing both material and emotional things, and I'm even interested in research about human-to-human and human-to-environment/nature connectedness."

Several women talked about having always been very egalitarian, seeing everyone as equal, which led to a worldview that embraces "peace and love"—a philosophical stance that was expressed in The Sisters Project only by twins. Sophia sent in this e-mail: "I wonder about people who are so cruel to others. It's unfathomable to me. I have a connection with my sister that is for life and that is always a loving stream. I can't see how people can behave without compassion."

Corinne expressed the same loving thought: "If everyone had the intimate connection of a twin and developed its positive potential, the earth would be a different place—we wouldn't be killing ourselves and letting ourselves suffer."

On this lyrical note, we will move away from exploring sister relationships based on TOMY positions and take a good look at three different dynamics that characterize the relationships of some sisters—conflicted, bonded, and caretaker.

III

Three Unique Relationship Styles and What It All Means to You

Vikki and Nikki

Star-Crossed Sisters

Sisters in Conflict

"I've felt bad all of my life looking at those nice sisterly birthday cards in the store. I'd always thought—'I can't buy them.' My older sister and I, we really seem to have been 'star-crossed' because I remember once deciding to put the anger aside and buy her a really nice card for her birthday. I sent it to her, but she never received it. I realized after that I had inverted something in her zip code. It seems like we just weren't meant to connect."

—CLARA, fifty-six years old

The Fine Line Between Connection and Chaos

Although the joys of sisterhood are well-known and well docu-mented, there are many women who experience something very different. What about those other women, the ones like Clara, whose description of the hopelessness she feels about her lifetime of conflict with her sister opens this chapter? The ones who have a sister but never enjoy that "sisterly" feeling? Many of those women who participated in The Sisters Project feel that having a sister and not being close is even worse than not having a sister at all. The word *sister* is so synonymous with closeness that if you have a sister and aren't close, it feels like something's wrong—either with her or with you. Some women in this situation have told me with sorrow that the attempt to fashion a sister bond has become a lifelong struggle.

Why do so many star-crossed sisters keep trying? Ten percent of the women in The Sisters Project spoke of relationships that could be defined as conflicted, some describing their sisters with such negative terms as "the demon seed," "Black Mary," "Sybil," "the black sheep," "rain cloud," "kook," "brat," and "certifiably insane"! Yet, even in relationships that continue to be painful, in which women are hurt, time and time again, many doggedly keep trying. Through cutoffs, fights that lead to tearful reconciliations, and more fights, women walk a fine line between connection and chaos and find it very hard just to call it quits.

Through Thick and Thin

Our society seems to give women a lot more leeway to be angry with their mothers than with their sisters; we're much more comfortable accepting that mothers can be deficient in performing their roles. There are plenty of examples in literature, movies, and popular culture of mothers who are self-absorbed, jealous, spiteful, alcoholic, or just plain incompetent. It's okay to put the blame on a mother because it's her job to protect and care for her daughter. If there's a disturbance in their relationship, we expect a mother's love to rise above it all and make it right. The burden of responsibility for the success of the relationship is judged by many in society to be squarely on the mother's shoulders.

It's different with sisters. The sister relationship is more balanced, less hierarchical. Seen from outside the family, the older-younger distinction is blurred. The message comes across loud and clear from the world at large that sisters are supposed to be "sisterly." Under certain circumstances, it's valid to break ties with mothers or fathers. Women can certainly split from their husbands or lovers, but under no circumstances may they break with their children or sisters. This is a powerful, unstated taboo. One must stand by these relatives through "thick and thin" or risk community disapproval.

Part of what defines women in Western culture is our connectedness with each other. We're socialized to value closeness, caretaking, and interdependency. Many women spend their lives struggling to feel good about themselves, and the requirements for feeling like a "good person" are very stringent. Not having a relationship with your sister seems to say something terribly negative about the kind of person you are because it's assumed that a good person rarely gives up on these relationships. If you can't maintain a positive connection with your closest living relative—the person who shares not only the identical gene pool, but the same gender as well—then the implicit message is that there's something seriously wrong.

Marian, forty-three, sounded a bit desperate describing her feeling of being cut off from her sister: "I wouldn't say that there are regrets, but I'm a very, very strong family person—I do believe that blood is thicker than water, and I feel guilt. I know that if my parents were still alive, they wouldn't want this. I feel like I should get back with her, but when I imagine doing it, all I can think about is the pain. I have a lot of pressure from family, particularly my husband's family. My aunt and uncle tried to intervene. One girlfriend comes back every six months or so and insists, 'You're going to make up with your sister!' She puts a lot of pressure on me. People think it's my fault."

Sisters with conflicted relationships often feel that if they could just figure out how to do it differently, they could resolve the problems with their sisters. If only they could rise above all of the bad feelings and not react in their typical fashion, their sisters would finally understand them and respond differently. Women often take responsibility for things that go wrong in relationships—guilt is a deeply ingrained feminine reflex. Thirty-eight-year-old Jean described it this way: "I keep trying to find a way. Sometimes, I try to connect with her and at other times, I try to keep out of her way and keep her out of mine. This hasn't been easy and things aren't really well worked out, but it's not a happy feeling to know that it's probably best for you to have your sister at arm's length."

Years of Struggle: The Nikki-Vikki Story

Like Jean, I have certainly tried to keep my sister at arm's length for much of my life. Many times when I did include her, she would say outrageous things that hurt me or, worse, hurt my children. I would end up boiling inside, vowing never to see her again. But because I was trying to be a "good person" and felt so guilty about shutting her out, I would eventually calm down and reach for the phone again. As soon as the communication was reestablished, Nikki would pick up where she left off, telling me what to do. If I didn't follow her suggestions or if I wanted to get off the phone sooner than she did, she'd often become angry. I could never trust her when she was being loving, because her mood could turn on a dime.

For example, one year my whole family was together sharing a holiday dinner at my parents' house. At one point, Nikki leaned across the table and loudly asked me how much I weighed. I laughingly wriggled out of answering the question. She insisted, "Tell me what you weigh!" I continued to sidestep the question. She got more and more insistent until she finally jumped up from the table and, to everyone's astonishment, bolted from the house. My mother burst into tears, the dinner was ruined, and, feeling miserably guilty, I sat there thinking that it was all my fault—why didn't I just tell her what I weighed?

The on-again, off-again pattern continued until, after yet another counseling session spent talking about my frustration with my sister, my therapist gave me the golden tap on the head and said that I didn't have to keep trying. Then, poof, I just stopped for a while. What a relief!

After my therapist's dispensation, I stayed in distant touch with Nikki. We rarely spoke by phone and would see each other only on occasions involving our parents. At one point, I optimistically invited her to Michele's bat mitzvah, but after ten minutes, Nikki found an excuse to get angry with me and stormed out. I spent the whole ceremony crying; everyone thought it was because I was so proud of Michele. I limited my contact with Nikki, but I could never erase that sense of sadness and disappointment, particularly because my children and I have such a small family. I felt even worse for her. Having alienated her nieces, she had only our elderly mother and me, and I felt bad about that.

The irony is that I honestly believe that, in her fashion, Nikki truly wanted the best for me, but only according to her own definition of what that would be. When I wouldn't do what she wanted me to do, it made her feel unimportant and helpless. Although she often did have good advice to give, she just didn't know when to stop giving it. And when she came rushing in with plans to rearrange the furniture of my life, it was because she believed that that's what older sisters should do. Nikki always wanted to be involved in my life—just not in my husband's and only sporadically in the lives of my daughters. There's a lot I admire about Nikki—her spunkiness, energy, and quirky sense of humor (she spent a year and a half working as a stand-up comic!)—but it's hard to take when her funny outrageousness strays over into vindictive territory.

Just Because You're Sisters . . .

The fundamental question is: Just because you were raised in the same household, and you have the same parents and grandparents and weird Uncle Simon, the same calico cat named Kiwi, the same family kitchen with the same hideous yellow-flowered wallpaper—in other words, just because you are *sisters*—does it mean that you owe something to your sister? If she's the last person on earth that you'd choose as a friend and if being with her always makes you miserable, do you have to keep trying, just because you're sisters?

There is no universal answer to that question, and whatever answer you give today may be different in a few years. Each set of circumstances is unique, and each woman has to make her own decision as to how she can live with the situation and still respect herself. There is no blanket right or wrong. Rebecca, fifty-six, decided to stay in touch with her sister, even though there is nothing in it that brings her pleasure. She said, "I cannot lie to you and tell you that I love her. I'm so tired of hurting. All of the things she's done to my family, to my mother, to the relationship, make it so hard. But I refuse to not speak to her, because then she'll have succeeded in making me feel bad about myself."

Rebecca's choice was to stay connected, but Marian, whose friend keeps pushing her to reconcile, quoted earlier, chose to distance herself. Each choice is equally legitimate and, like most decisions in life, brings with it pluses and minuses. Women need to break free of the limiting idea that there's a prescription to follow that will make you a good person. You need to determine *for yourself* which choice brings you fewer minuses . . . and then decide to go on with your life. There are few emotions more debilitating than indecision and regret. Whatever decision you do make, don't beat yourself up about it. If you can't work it out with your sister, use your positive energy to make meaningful connections with those people in your life who can bring you joy.

Ambivalent Admiration

Few relationships are unidimensional. Even women in conflicted relationships with their sisters report having had some great times together—times that felt so good, they long to replicate them. Here are some of the responses to the "just one sentence to your sister growing up" from women who described their sister relationships as conflicted:

- "I love you. How come you don't love me?"
- "Why do you have to be so wild and unfathomable and uncaring?"
- "I need you to like me and want to spend time with me."
- "I'm lonely. Play with me . . . or just look at me."
- "We're not enemies even though we act like it much of the time."
- "Don't belittle me but help me be more like you."
- "Why can't we just be friends?"
- "I love you and I want to try to help you."
- "Acquire an open mind and try to get to know me. Maybe I'm not as kooky as you think."

These statements reflect a longing to be understood and loved. Whether a woman views herself as the flamboyant one or the reserved one, the family favorite or the black sheep, most wish that their sister could have been along for the ride. I have frequently heard women say that they greatly admire in their sisters the very qualities that make it hard to connect to them. Qualities such as independence, assertiveness, brashness, outspokenness, not caring what others think, and even outrageousness might strain the link between sisters but may also be appealing to the one who lacks them. In the midst of a solemn recitation of her painful adolescence with her older sister, Clara proudly reminisced about her sister's character: "I would describe my sister as the adventurer, the explorer, the courageous one, and the rebel. She definitely had a mind of her own, and she was able to express that without any fear. She didn't really try to please people. You just took her the way she was. And I think all of those qualities are just terrific. She had what I admire most in people—honesty and frankness—even though it cost her a lot of grief. I took the opposite point of view as I was growing up. I wanted to please and I was less adventuresome."

Deprivation and Tragedy: Aileen's Story

Aileen, a school principal in her late forties, told of her continuing struggle to get close to her sister, Dinah, who was three years older. As long as Aileen could remember, Dinah was feisty and combative, giving their parents a run for their money. Aileen recalled, "Dinah would cook up schemes that would push the outside of the envelope, and then there would be scenes—people not speaking for days on end—particularly my mother and she. There was a big clash there, and I've never really figured out what was at the bottom of that—maybe she was too pretty for my mother—the old Oedipal thing—because Dinah was closer with my father." Their mother tried to control her older daughter by force but was constantly thwarted. The conflict between mother and daughter turned the family home into chaos. Aileen's response was to be quiet and well behaved so as not to provoke her already overwhelmed parents. That tactic served to turn Dinah's wrath on Aileen; Dinah did everything she could to make Aileen's life a misery.

The family bumped along from one crisis to the next. Even when things were relatively calm, Aileen always had the feeling that there was something awful brewing: "She would love to take the wind out of your sails—if you were excited about something, it was only a matter of time until—punch!" Dinah would be sure to bring her down.

Dinah seems to have been excluded from the close connection that Aileen had with her mother. The more Dinah acted up, the more family and friends praised Aileen: "I think she was jealous because I had an extremely enviable relationship with my mother. A lot of it is basic personality—Dinah was just a jealous person. Her jealousy became my weapon. I always somehow knew that I was the golden-haired child. I had the so-called brains. I had the right kinds of friends. I always, more or less, did the right thing. I never got into very much trouble, and I had that special position in the extended family, too, just because I had that kind of personality. It extended to all of my friends. Dinah would be as nasty as she could to most of my friends, to my mother's friends, to relatives. I was more popular, better liked, and I think that gave me status."

When asked her feelings about her sister as a child, Aileen said, "Basically, I couldn't stand her. I can remember, when I got out into the world and had friends who actually liked their siblings, I was flabbergasted. I didn't know anything else really."

As an adult, Aileen raised a family and enjoyed a happy marriage. Dinah married, too, but divorced after ten stormy years, and then struggled to raise her three children on her own. The sisters saw a lot of each other at their parents' home when their kids were young, but Aileen felt that plans were always made on Dinah's terms; Aileen would never come up against her sister because she loathed the fighting and the pain it would cause her parents. Summing up their relationship, Aileen said, "She thought I lived a charmed life. I was perfect. I married well, and she was always jealous of that. She always tried to make me pay for the things that I had in life."

In spite of it all, Aileen has spent her life longing to experience a sisterly feeling with Dinah—to have a "true" sister. Although Dinah has done a lot of work on herself and Aileen will no longer tolerate being bossed around, Dinah still keeps her sister at arm's length. They get together occasionally, but the talk centers around superficial things, like gardening, dogs, and the kids. If Aileen brings up anything more intimate, Dinah just steers the topic onto something else. Aileen thinks Dinah stays away from her because "the punch is gone"—she can no longer get the pleasure of upsetting Aileen. When asked what one sentence Aileen would have said to Dinah growing up, she answered, "Why can't we be closer?" Asked the same question as adults, the answer remains the same: "Why can't we be closer?"

Aileen used two powerful words to conclude our interview—*deprivation* and *tragedy*: "I'm stuck with this huge sort of negative ball at the bottom of it all with a lot of possibilities—but it never goes anywhere. I'm always left with this feeling of deprivation about it, and there's nothing I can do about it. She just will not budge. It's sort of a tragedy because it's just kept at such a limited level."

The Seeds of Resentment

The story of Aileen and Dinah highlights several elements that contribute to conflict in many sister relationships:

- Dinah was born with a strong-willed temperament that would have been a challenge for many parents to deal with, while Aileen was naturally more easygoing.
- Their mother was somewhat jealous of Dinah's beauty and of her closeness with her father.
- Aileen was very close to their mother and preferred by friends and family.
- Aileen married a financially secure man and appeared to have an easier life.

As we will see in this section, these issues and more can help sow the seeds of resentment between sisters.

Sibling Rivalry to the Max

Weaving through many of the stories of sisters in conflict were threads of intense sibling rivalry. Competition for a parent's affection was often to be found at the root of a deep disturbance in the sister connection. Sibling rivalry is natural and exists in most families, to one extent or another, but it can corrode a sister relationship when one or both parents fan the flames by comparing the girls or showing favoritism. In Aileen's story, we heard how her mother naturally gravitated toward the younger and easier daughter. Dinah, fearing the loss of her mother's love, resented her sister even more. The harsher Dinah was with Aileen, the more their mother felt that she needed to protect the quieter girl; as time went on, the cycle became more and more entrenched. Marian Sandmaier, in her book about adult sibling relationships, *Original Kin*, referred to the child in Dinah's position as the "unchosen daughter [who] often felt that her mother identified with her sister in some deep, unspoken way that she was powerless to dilute, and which relegated her to the status of perpetual outsider" (1994, p. 94).

Margot, fifty-eight, told about having had a very "caustic" relationship with her mother, who clearly favored Margot's younger sister. Her mother's attitude toward the girls was even reflected in the nicknames they had in the family: "Queeny" for Margot and "Little Princess" for her sister. When asked what roles each girl played in the family, Margot's answer sounds like the bitter poem of an unchosen daughter:

- "I was always in trouble; she never seemed to get into trouble."
- "I was more noticeable; she was quiet and shy."
- "I was told that everything was my fault; she was taught that the strife in our family was my fault."
- "I told my mother everything I did; she kept things to herself."
- "I felt like I had to 'pay my own way'; she kept what she earned for herself."
- "I was abused; she wasn't."

Another "unchosen" daughter, Judy, a middle sister, suffered from her parents' obvious preference for her sisters' slimmer physiques: "My parents were forever comparing us. I was by far the heaviest of the three of us and that this was not acceptable was clear. There was definitely a feeling of favorites being played, and I was always on the losing end. I had to handle a lot of criticism and ridicule, which my sisters didn't get. My older sister supported and reiterated the criticisms about my appearance that I would hear from my mother, aunt, and grandmother."

Twenty-six-year-old Shelby's status as an outsider was made painfully clear to her when she inadvertently learned about her father's tender feelings toward her sister: "I was about thirteen or fourteen when I discovered a note from my father, addressed to my sister. It was dated from when she had gotten accepted at two Ivy League colleges. He referred to her as his favorite child and addressed her as 'dearest.' I think I've successfully blocked from memory all of the gruesomely favoring things he said to her, but I will never forget that note!"

Several women in The Sisters Project described how their sister manipulated their parents into punishing them. Connie spat out these words: "The bitch got me in trouble incessantly throughout my childhood. My sister had it down pat how to manipulate my mother. All she had to do was cry and whine, and my mother would explode into unstoppable fits of rage at me." Tracy had a similar tale to tell: "During disputes with my sister, in order to get her way, she would tell me to give her what she wanted or she would scream and my mother would beat me up." Ariana echoed their experience: "When we were younger, we used to share a bedroom. I remember my sister saying, 'Watch this,' and, for no reason, she'd start screaming. My father would come running in and shout at me, 'Leave your sister alone!' That's when I realized that my sister was using her weakness to manipulate my parents."

Connie's, Tracy's, and Ariana's sisters used their special status with a parent to flaunt their power over their sister. The fault lies less with these conniving instigators, however, than it does with the obliging parent(s) who encouraged and supported that behavior. Sometimes, in a bid to be loved, a child will act in unethical ways, but it is up to the parent to recognize what's going on and to correct her.

Other Ways Parents Contribute to the Conflict

Sometimes parents compare their daughters in a misguided attempt to help the child who seems to be less successful. With statements such as, "Why can't you be more like your sister? She never leaves her homework to the last minute!" the parent hopes the procrastinator will learn from her sister's good example. In reality, the poorer student is actually muttering to herself, "I hate that goody-two-shoes!" and resentment is building up against the "perfect" sister who is being held up as an example. The parents are usually unaware of how their attempt to spur their daughter on to work harder in school contributes to the fighting.

Parents who place the bar very high and demand perfection foster competition as the sisters vie to be the one who best meets their expectations. Thirty-one-year-old Shelby said, "Nothing was ever enough. Our parents incessantly lit fires beneath all three of us, aiming for perfection. School was never my thing, but I felt that I had to 'beat' or 'live up to' my sisters in terms of getting into a good college."

It's often easier for parents to relate to the daughter who is the most like themselves. Marge wrote, "My mother did have favorites, but she didn't bother with me much because I was very unlike her." Veronique, on the other hand, explained how her family saw her closely identified with her mother: "My mother is French Canadian and my father's Irish, but I'm the only one in the family who got the French name, and that indicates something right away. I was sort of my mother's child and was resented quite a lot, particularly by my older sister."

Finally, children may be used as pawns in families where there is conflict between the parents; one girl is perceived to be closer to Mom, as Veronique was, and the other is "Daddy's little girl." Some parents may subconsciously want one of the girls to fail to prove the point to their spouse that their favored child is actually better. Because there's symmetry in this type of configuration, each adult may feel comfortable backing one child while being assured that the other child has her own champion. In divorced families, this kind of splitting up of the kids, although all too common, is particularly destructive of the children's relationship. Children are torn between making an alliance with a parent who may promise them extra love and attention and remaining more neutral, thereby missing out on special treatment. If one girl feels sorry for the father, the other may unconsciously balance things out by promoting the mother's cause. The connection between the sisters is sacrificed to meet the needs of the embattled parents.

Real-Life Events

Real-life events, beyond the control of parents or children, may stress and destabilize families, sometimes resulting in conflict between sisters. Women in The Sisters Project mentioned some of the following circumstances in their early childhoods:

- Death in the family
- Divorce
- Illness—physical or mental
- War
- Poverty
- Being the victim of a crime
- Immigration
- Suicide in the family
- Fires or other catastrophes
- A family member's illegal activities or incarceration

As a therapist working with families who face such challenges, I've noticed that the sibling bond is often strongly influenced by these situations. Either the kids band together into a tight, cohesive team or they scatter to the winds, each one trying desperately to protect him- or herself. Clara, the star-crossed sister from the opening quote of this chapter, spent her early childhood in Germany just after World War II. It was a strange time and place in which to grow up, and she believes that the hardship her family endured contributed to the anger that her sister, Antje, one year older, kept inside. Clara recounts "It was quite safe in postwar Germany; people were too busy surviving to be criminals. So my sister, Antje, at six years of age, would go out and wander about all day with a lunch my mother made for her and not come back 'til suppertime. Sometimes she would take me with her. I would hold her hand, and we would pick over the ruins for scrap metal to rebuild Germany. Sometimes my sister would kind of abandon me, but she always came eventually and got me. She was always there in the background. My sister was the way she was because of the war. She didn't want to be born. My mother was in labor with her for three days. So there she was—not wanting to be born—and I come along and make things worse."

Antje had been scarred by the fear and deprivation that defined her young life. It is not surprising that, as a result, she had to use all of her energy to make sense of her world, leaving very little left to give to her sister.

Kendra told about the death from whooping cough of the eldest of her two older sisters, a tragedy that took place a few months prior to her own birth. Once Kendra was born, her grieving mother clung to her for solace, leaving the surviving sister, Trish, lost and bewildered: "My next older sister, who was about three at the time, was very, very puzzled about her big sister's disappearance, and since those were the '40s, it wasn't explained to her properly. She was just told she was going to have another little sister to play with, and she expected from me the same thing that she was getting from her older sister. So I came along and Trish had this baby to play with, but she didn't know what to do with me. When I was about two months old, she took me out of my crib and propped me up against the wall to play dolls with. I was a tiny little thing, so she got scolded and spanked for doing it. She started disliking me immediately, and that's lasted a lifetime."

Sisters like Trish and Kendra and Clara and Antje, whose childhoods are touched by tragedy, are oblivious that their relationships are distorted by extraordinary events beyond their control. While they're living it, it feels as though their sister's personality is to blame. A child can hardly understand that the anger directed toward her comes from her sister's inability to cope and their parents' incapacity to help her do so. It's only in adulthood that it becomes possible to recognize the powerful forces that served to bend the sibling bond out of shape.

Heredity and Temperament

We all know of families in which Mother Nature appears to have played a cruel joke. One daughter is tall, thin, athletic, clear thinking, easygoing, and funny. The other is awkward, chunky, slow to catch on, introverted, and irritable. One child flits through the social world, lighting up everything she touches, like the steel ball in a pinball machine. The other seems to be condemned to a grim social struggle, like a bowling ball lumbering down the gutter. The eye naturally looks for patterns and the mind naturally looks for similarities, so even if parents don't make an issue of it, the contrast is rarely lost on the sisters themselves. Some examples of the discrepancies related to heredity and temperament that may lead to conflict are:

- A child with a fiery temperament
- A sibling with health problems or developmental delays
- Differences in terms of school performance
- Discrepancies related to athletic or creative ability
- Differing levels of social success
- An adolescent with emotional problems
- Differences related to body type, weight, or attractiveness

When there's a big discrepancy in the natural gifts accorded to sisters, the emotions that the girls feel are often two sides of the same coin—jealousy and guilt. The jealous sister, who feels "less than," may be continually trying to even the score in whatever way she can. As adults, when her sister gets new boots, she buys nicer boots; when her sister loses five pounds, she finally decides to have her nose fixed! The jealous sister may try to hide it, because jealousy is an embarrassing emotion, but she often can't stop herself from constantly weighing and measuring her sister's lot and comparing it with her own.

It's hard to go through life feeling jealous, but the sister who's more gifted also bears a burden. Some girls worry about outshining a less successful sister and, early on, learn to hide their light under a bushel. They downplay their successes and may even limit their achievements to avoid having to deal with their sister's resentment and the guilt that it evokes. Lindsay, who has a much richer social life than her sister, put it this way: "Guilt? Yeah—that's a big thing. All of the time. I always feel guilty. Like when I go with my friends to a movie, I feel guilty if I don't ask my sister to come too, and I'm afraid, if I don't ask her, I'll suffer repercussions."

Tremendous Envy: Camilla's Story. On a rare rainy day in San Diego, I spoke with Camilla, who is three years older than her sister, Nicole. Camilla told me how she had loved the role of the big sister when they were little, relishing how Nicole looked up to and depended on her. She enjoyed teaching Nicole things and could always be counted on to keep her entertained when their mother was busy. Once Nicole reached adolescence, however, their relationship suddenly changed. Camilla had suffered a lot of heartbreak with boys and spent many an evening sitting with her mother at the kitchen table, crying about yet another gut-wrenching breakup. Nicole, on the other hand, seemed to be beating the boys off with a stick. Whereas Camilla had previously been extremely protective of Nicole, once the younger girl's social life blossomed, Camilla found herself awash with jealousy. Camilla explained, "I began to have a horrible self-image because I was overweight, while she was gorgeous and dating the most popular guys in the school. They always fell in love with her, whereas mine would always break up with me."

As adults, that pattern continued. Nicole seemed impervious to problems—everything seemed to go her way—while Camilla found happiness harder to grasp. Now close to forty, Camilla owns a children's bookstore, and, although she likes her quiet life, she can't stop comparing it to Nicole's bon vivant existence as an events planner: "Tremendous envy. I still measure myself against how my sister is doing. That's something that I work on. Our society tends to value strong women who have it all, and I suppose that she has it all. Every time I'm with Nicole, I compare myself. Absurd! But, in my mind, I see Nicole as the epitome of success.

"You take your life in your hands when you call her because you'll be cut off. You may be cut off earlier rather than later—it might be eight minutes, it might be ten—it might be no more than two or three, and then the inevitable 'okay, g'bye!'" Nicole never has time for family engagements, breezing in at the last minute and always running off to some exciting appointment. Camilla's fondest wish would be for Nicole to make time for her, to be interested in her, and, most important, to need her. Camilla says that if you asked Nicole, she would say that they have a good relationship. But from Camilla's point of view, it's always on Nicole's terms.

The Continuum of Conflict

As we've seen, star-crossed sisters don't always have angry, stormy relationships. The level of discord may be located at any point on a continuum that ranges from superficial cordiality through relationships of tense distance to those at the other end of the spectrum— totally cut off. Several women described the struggle to keep their sisters in their lives as an on-again, off-again seesaw, each shift bringing with it a new challenge and requiring a different response. In Letty Cottin Pogrebin's book, *Three Daughters*, the main character, Shoshanna, described exactly that kind of relationship with her sister, Leah: "Where Leah was concerned, Shoshanna measured everything in years. Off years and on years, years when Leah wasn't in her life at all, years when Leah adored her, years when Leah barely tolerated her, and great blocks of time when they made do with the sort of tepid relationship that would shortchange a third cousin" (2002, p. 25).

Suzanne, a woman who maintains a fragile connection with her older sister told me, "It isn't that I wished that I didn't have a sister, but there have been times when the conflict just gets so severe that we don't have much to do with each other. We don't speak very often, we don't see each other, and part of me is like—ahhh!—it's such a relief, but another part of me realizes that it totally sucks that this is the kind of relationship I have with my sister."

Push and Pull

Between sisters in conflict, there is usually one who wants more involvement in her sister's life than the other, as was the case with Camilla and Nicole. The sister looking for more intimacy may be seen as intrusive; the sister needing more distance may be viewed as indifferent. There is a push and pull, with the former always asking for more and the latter trying to establish boundaries.

The intimacy-seeking sister often feels wronged and rejected, jealous of the attention her sibling bestows on others. She's more emotionally involved, critical, and judgmental and always desires a higher level of contact. The distancing sister is just not that interested and may be unconcerned with, or even unaware of, her sister's internal torment. The distancing sister is usually getting her needs met somewhere else, and, whereas her sister feels jealous, she may feel guilty that she can't give what is being asked of her. She tries to avoid contact with her sister as a way of protecting herself from feeling bad. Often, she finds that when she does try to meet her sister's needs, it's never enough. Both women have a different definition of what it means to be sisters. Each is trying to persuade the other to accept her version of how the relationship should be.

Subtext

My friend Meryl is in regular contact with her sister, Joni, but is also aware that Joni is very jealous of her. That jealousy causes Joni to want to knock Meryl down a peg, but Joni would never dare come right out and say something openly critical. Instead, she masks her jealousy-fueled disapproval by using a "subtext"; she finds fault with Meryl's children or husband in the guise of being helpful. It's an indirect way of being critical that appears legitimate. So when Joni is helpfully suggesting that she can find a good accountant for Meryl's husband, Bob, because she knows that he's way too busy to do his own taxes, the subtext is that Bob is not to be trusted with things related to money because everyone knows that he's irresponsible. Joni knows exactly what subtle comment will get to Meryl, but should Meryl get defensive about the tone of her sister's suggestion, Joni can always open her eyes wide and innocently say, "Hey, what are you getting so upset about? I was only trying to help!"

Sisters know which buttons to push to make the other feel guilty. Even between sisters like Joni and Meryl who are not in outright conflict, hidden messages tailored to get a desired effect may be sent. One woman said, "My sister could always twist my words and get away with being mean-spirited. I still feel intimidated by her, and when she decides to throw me the bait, I usually bite!" Biting the bait, having her buttons pushed, being subjected to subtext—these sisters get manipulated into feeling bad. The button-pusher is trying to control the relationship by making her sister feel guilty, an old technique known as "guilt tripping."

The Buttons. When a sister's words pack the punch that gets the emotional response, it becomes hard to think objectively about what is actually going on. Here are some buttons that, when pushed, are guaranteed to make a vulnerable woman feel bad:

- "Mom always loved you more."
- "You never have any time for me."
- "You think you're such a superstar."
- "Dad will probably leave you everything in his will."

- "You always got nicer things when we were kids."
- "If you really loved me, you'd do this thing."

Each woman has her special buttons, and she inevitably responds when they're pressed because she's been conditioned, like one of Pavlov's dogs. Angry, guilty, hurt, frustrated—she reacts with a surge of emotion, making it impossible to think straight. By giving her sister the key to the button cupboard, she enters into the game.

Disconnecting the Circuits. The question is, how can someone learn to disconnect the circuitry so that her sister can push buttons all she likes but she herself no longer responds in the old pattern? The first step is to take the time to think the whole thing through. What exactly does your sister say to get to you? How do you typically respond? Once you have put a name to the game and you can start to step outside the emotion and recognize what's happening, you will be far more likely to be able to short-circuit it.

To be fair, each of us also has the key to our sister's button cupboard and know how to get to her. If we are going to be honest about our relationship, we need to think about what our sister's sore points are and how we take advantage of them. What do *you* do to get a rise out of her? How does she usually respond to *you*? It's a fluid, dynamic interaction that goes both ways.

A Fistful of Hair

Somewhere in the midrange of the continuum of conflict, closer to cutoff than to superficial cordiality, lie relationships characterized by a high level of emotional pain. Women in The Sisters Project who live these relationships told me that it was a relief to be able to talk about it. These sisters are so troubled and, in some cases, feel so much shame, that as much as they need to unload, they find it hard to examine those feelings. Several said that other people just don't understand.

It was with women such as these that the issue of violence came up. As I thought about it, I realized that for many women, myself included, the only person they have physically fought with is a sister. Kicking, "Indian" burns (causing burning friction of the skin), scratching, pinching, wrestling, poking—all are pretty common between sisters, although these girls would never react this way with anyone else. In her book *Psyche's Sisters*, Christine Downing wrote about how the lifelong nature of the sister connection makes room for this way of relating: "Because that permanence helps make it the safest relationship in which to express hostility and aggression . . . the bond between same-sex siblings is very likely the most stressful, volatile, ambivalent one we will ever know" (1988, p. 12).

Kayla, thirty, recollected how, as a child, she once inflicted pain on her little sister, nine years younger: "I remember one time in particular, pulling a fistful of hair from my baby sister's head, because the child would never shut up. I was so angry I just wanted to hurt her. Unfortunately, it felt good." Janet, in her forties now, told how, in their mother's presence, her sister had recently slapped her across the face. Their mother approved, saying that she had had it coming to her. Clara described an extreme example of physical violence: "My sister was violent with me sometimes. Once we got into an argument, and she tried to suffocate me with a pillow until I thought I was going to die. She didn't stop until I stopped screaming."

In the "circled words" part of The Sisters Project interview and questionnaire, participants were asked to indicate how they felt about their sisters as children and as adults by circling phrases from a list of feelings (see Appendix D). Among the variety of positive and negative statements offered, one of the options was "Sometimes wish(ed) she were dead." Very few girls or women circled this option; out of the 165 face-to-face interviews, only seven women chose it. The vignette sent in by Tamar, the second youngest of four, betrayed an unconscious childhood wish to finally be done with her youngest sister: "I remember a rare family vacation to Magnolia Beach. The house we rented was near a tidal pool that formed where a brook entered the sea. The pool would empty at low tide and then fill with one large wave as the tide returned. We all knew of the danger of this, but only my younger sister and I were small enough to be at risk from it. One morning, she and I were playing at the pool as the tide was coming in. I told her more than once to get out of the pool, but the water was warm in there and she didn't want to budge. Finally, *that* wave came and she was sitting in the bottom of the pool, covered up. I went back to the house, and my parents asked where she was; I said I didn't know. They then asked where I'd seen her last, and I said, 'sitting at the bottom of the tidal pool.' My father ran down to the pool and ruined his shoes, pants, and the new watch we had given him for his birthday, just to pull her out. I was very angry that he'd wasted our present."

For many women, it's not a fistful of hair but a metaphorical knife in the heart that characterizes their connection. They are like boxers, hanging on to each other in the clinch, clinging but still trying to get in a last punch. Selma, fifty-six, wrote, "It's as bad as it's ever been. We have never been to such depths and we're only going deeper as time goes on. It's who can hurt the other person more, her or me? We have done so many things to hurt each other that we are at the point of no return." Margot, the grim poet who ended her recitation earlier in this chapter by saying that she was abused but her sister was not, wrote this, addressed to her sister: "It isn't possible for us to have a sister relationship. We just don't understand each other. There is too much water under the bridge. I am very nervous when I'm with you. I've quit wanting to have a sister relationship with you."

I Don't Want to Be a Masochist: The Nikki-Vikki Story

Like Margot, a small percentage of the women in The Sisters Project are cut off from their sisters. For some, it's just for a few months; for others, a number of years; and for a small minority, decades. There is always a heaviness in the voice of these women when they talk about being estranged. It never really ceases to be a stone in their shoe; each step they take along the road of life makes them feel the pinch. They can temporarily forget about their sisters, but pivotal events when families get together, such as weddings, funerals, graduations, confirmations, or bar/bat mitzvahs, remind them of the loss.

Many years ago, I chose not to invite my sister to my wedding. Okay, it wasn't really a formal wedding—just a five-minute "in and out" at City Hall—but she wasn't one of the three guests invited. I made that choice because I couldn't be sure that she wouldn't ruin it for me by upsetting me, and I really wanted to be free to enjoy the day. My mother said she wouldn't come if Nikki weren't invited, so I was relieved when, at the last minute, my mom showed up. My decision not to invite Nikki was the right one at the time, although not easy to make.

I used to have an on-again, off-again, seesaw relationship with my sister. At times, I would try to integrate Nikki into my world but was unable to keep it going for very long. Once the door was opened, she felt she had rights to me that I hadn't accorded her. Time and again, I would erect a very high wall and then, feeling guilty, start to remove the bricks, only to build it up again after another ugly incident.

In recent years, I had felt that I understood more about how to make a healthy boundary for myself, letting Nikki know that I valued her suggestions but without pretending that I'd follow them, simply to get her off my case. I had learned to stop feeling so badly about the times when she got so mad at me. I used to think that if I'd handled things differently, the confrontation could have been avoided, but I now know that those were impossible situations. No matter what I did, she just needed to be mad at me. Not feeling so guilty, I had stopped needing to run away and hide. I could brush incidents off more easily. I started dismantling the wall.

That wall is now higher than ever. The deal breaker came, as so often happens, at my mother's funeral. My mother died last year following an eight-year battle with Alzheimer's, and in the early years, the word *battle* was not just a metaphor. When my mother first got sick, we moved her from New York to Montreal so that I could look after her. A tough-minded, independent woman, she did not "go gentle into that good night." I suffered those long years with her as she raged at her world falling apart and finally succumbed to vacancy, with Nikki looking on disinterestedly from afar. Death finally came, mercifully releasing both my mother and me from her suffering, and I looked forward to giving her the send-off she deserved. I had loved her dearly.

My mother was strangely lovely lying in her coffin. Shrouded in white with a big lace collar, she looked like a wizened schoolgirl. The sun was streaming in the chapel; the atmosphere was calm. But as my sister and I were sitting with the rabbi just before the funeral was about to begin, she described our mother in such hateful terms that it took my breath away. I felt that she had chosen that moment to release her lifetime of bitterness toward our mother and her jealousy toward me. As had happened at so many other pivotal events of my life, rather than feeling free to enjoy the tributes paid to my mother, I sat at her funeral stunned, holding back tears of hurt, fearful that Nikki would publicly repeat her damning epithet. I faked my way through the day and, in the middle of that night, wrote her a letter saying that I wanted to have a relationship with her but needed her assurance that something like that wouldn't ever happen again. She never replied, and I haven't said a word to her since.

This year of cutoff has been a splendid gift from Nikki. Her actions on the day of our mother's funeral were so far over the top that I feel guiltlessly justified in not contacting her. Although to cut myself off from my sister goes against my belief that family members need to help each other, my other belief, the one that says that I shouldn't permit anyone to abuse me, trumps the first. If I were to contact my sister without first receiving her assurance that she understands what she did, I would be opening myself up, yet again, to being hurt, and I don't want to be a masochist.

I know that there are women reading these pages who have also suffered great sadness because of their sisters, a small number of whom have chosen, as I did, to cut the relationship off. This is never easy for a woman to do. But when it's impossible to maintain a productive link, you have no other option. To preserve your sanity, the healthiest move is to separate yourself and get on with life. Because of the importance of this issue, I asked a number of colleagues, other family therapists, whether they thought that there are times in a person's life when it becomes necessary to make a clean break from a family member. Every one of them answered "yes."

Making Changes

I couldn't work as a family therapist if I didn't believe that it is possible for people to change, but I'd also be pretty naive at this point if I thought that *everyone* can change and that all situations can be improved. Even if you can't change a situation, however, you can always change how you react to it—you *can* disconnect the circuitry in the button cupboard. You have the power to alter your perspective and to reduce your own suffering, and often the only way to change someone else's behavior is by changing your response to it. As you start to break the pattern, the other person adjusts as well.

Changing sister relationships is tricky because they develop in childhood, a time when we believe that what we learn about our family members is the gospel truth. It takes an adult perspective to be able to step back and reassess what was really going on. Sometimes it's embarrassing for people to change their behavior because everyone seems to notice it and make comments. People say annoying things like, "If you could do this now, why didn't you do it sooner?" or "I told you you could do it! You should have listened to me!" Change sometimes gives satisfaction to the very person you've been fighting against—the one who kept telling you it was your fault. No matter how miserable you are with the way things stand, changing them requires work. People are often ambivalent about change—there's always something of value that must be given up, even when you improve your situation.

Letting Go of the Anger

If you're carrying a lot of resentment toward your sister, you may ask, "Why should I be the one to try to change things? Why do I have to do all of the work?" Trying to improve the relationship between you and your sister is a hard decision to make and does take some courage. The problem with not trying is that, in many families, the animosity just drags on, with each sister waiting for the other to make the first move. As sixty-nine-year-old Isabella sees it, "There are arguments all of the time; we don't have rapport. It's too bad because I am growing older and so is she. One of us might conk out any minute, and then there would be remorse because it should be better." If you could improve the relationship you have with your sister, even marginally, or at least understand why you can't, you will feel more at peace with yourself. It is hard to feel happy in life when you are distressed about a family member. Some women hesitate to work on the relationship if they have already previously made some efforts to no avail. But I've found that people need to be ready for change. They may not have been able to accept it at an earlier point in their life, whereas a while later, in a different frame of mind, change comes more easily.

When I was talking with one of the family therapists interviewed for The Sisters Project about the effect of family conflict on women, she told me about a maxim that she had heard: "When you hang on to anger, you give your enemy power over you." I don't want to define the struggles you have with your sister in terms of enemies, but I would like to suggest that you can choose to lessen your sister's negative power over you by letting go of some of the anger. It's a choice. She's only one of billions of people on this earth, and she has only as much power over you as you give to her. Reducing her influence over you takes a change in your thinking about yourself. You can choose to let go of the fear, resentment, anger, or avoidance and decide that you're not going to give her the power to hurt you any longer. You can see her for who she is—just another person struggling to get her needs met in life, using whatever means she knows of to do so.

You don't necessarily need to go back and sort out all of the past with her. Sometimes raking up the past can make even more of a mess. The theory that one can minimize damage by leaving a toxic past undisturbed reminds me of a decision recently made in my city about the redevelopment of the Lachine Canal. The Lachine Canal was the center of industry in Montreal in the nineteenth and early twentieth centuries, but it has long been closed to water traffic. The city has decided to reopen the canal to pleasure boats and develop the waterfront banks for recreational use. There is toxic sludge at the bottom of the canal, but because clean water flows on the surface, the city chose to leave the bottom undisturbed. The decision was motivated in part by finances but also by the fear that dredging the canal would likely have contaminated the surface water and surrounding environment for decades to come. So the city decided to leave the polluted part untouched and let people enjoy the canal by just carefully using the surface.

Whatever you may think of that decision environmentally, you can understand the metaphorical use I'm making of it. When there's just too much stuff from the past in your relationship with your sister, clearing it all out might just take too many decades and risk polluting the good things that currently exist, fragile though they may be. It may be better to just enjoy the scenery and sacrifice a deeper connection if you can't be sure that your relationship could survive a thorough cleaning.

Understanding What Led to the Conflict

Before addressing the kinds of things that you can do to improve your relationship with your sister, you need to assess it. What were the underlying causes that led to your particular conflict? By understanding these contributors, it will be easier to know how to change things. Ask yourself the following questions:

- Did your parents play a role in fanning the fire between you and your sister? How?
- Were there real-life events that led to the conflict? Did circumstances beyond anyone's control affect your family?
- Are you very different from your sister in terms of natural abilities, physically, intellectually, or socially? Do you have personality styles or values that clash?

In thinking through what led to the conflict, you may recognize factors that developed separately from your relationship. Once you have identified the underlying causes of conflict in your relationship, it may become easier to empathize with your sister. It's hard to maintain harmony when a family faces serious external pressures. Sometimes the outrageous behavior of a sibling is not her fault—it's the normal outcome of extraordinary circumstances.

Before you can expect your sister to see you in a new light, you must figure out what *you* do that maintains the status quo. What do you do that signals to your sister your readiness to replay the same old video for the trillionth time? If your reputation in the family is that of the bully, what do you do that intimidates her? If your reputation is that of the doormat, how do you act that invites your sister to step on you? You can change your relationship with your sister by making small alterations in your own behavior. You can start to shape a new role and reputation, first with yourself, then with your family.

Leading Toward Healing

The following self-definition exercise will help you establish how you see yourself in relation to your sister and indicate how you can start to make a shift toward a healthier connection with her. Grab a piece of paper and complete the following questions, even if you think that all the responsibility for the problems is on her side of the ledger.

1. What roles do you think you play vis-à-vis your sister? (Options include the bully, the victim, the good daughter, the black sheep, the caretaker, the prima donna, Cinderella, Little Miss Perfect, the competent one.)
2. What advantages come along with those roles?
3. How do those roles limit you?
4. What would you have to give up if you stepped out of those roles?
5. How would you prefer to see yourself in relation to your sister?
6. What one change—something small, concrete, and doable— could you make in your behavior with your sister that would be consistent with your preferred self-image?

Here's how Lonnie responded to the preceding questions. She defined herself as "the black sheep" (in counterpoint to her sister's "Little Miss Perfect"). The advantage of her role was that no one depended on her too much, so she could come and go as she pleased. A limitation of that role was that she felt insignificant and childish around her sister. By giving up the role of the black sheep, she would lose a bit of freedom because she would have to become more accountable to her family. Her preferred self-image was that of a woman who was fiercely proud and independent but worthy of respect. The small step she could make toward her preferred self-image would be to show up on time at the next family gathering.

I once worked in therapy with Lucia, a twenty-two-year-old woman who was deeply angry with her mother, with whom she lived. Lucia wished her mother would stop being so critical of her, but her anger was so intense that she couldn't even look at her mother, let alone talk to her about her feelings. To reduce Lucia's anger so that she could start a conversation with her mother, we instituted a simple, yet highly effective strategy: when her mother came in the room, Lucia would raise her eyes and look at her with a neutral expression. By permitting herself just to look at her mother, an interesting thing happened—

ONE SMALL THING

Figure out the smallest thing you could do or say that is different from the way you usually relate to your sister, and try that the next few times you see her.

Lucia began to feel less angry. From her mother's point of view, seeing her daughter make eye contact made her feel less alienated and led to her becoming less critical. That gesture—raising her eyes—started Lucia on the road toward being able to talk things through with her mother, which she eventually did.

The changes that will lead to healing the conflict with your sister may start with a gesture as simple as raising your eyes. You don't need to deal with every element of the conflict at first. It's often best to start small; begin with a concrete behavioral change on your part that could lead to change on her part as well. When she sees you doing something differently, she may change the way she deals with you, too.

Avoiding Conflict

If part of the structure of your relationship is that your sister is constantly drawing you into a fight, you can learn how to sidestep the argument—not to take the bait that gets you hooked into a pattern of attack and defense—while still being able to keep in touch with her. Just because she needs to express her anger, jealousy, or dominance any chance she gets doesn't mean that you have to accept the role of punching bag.

Many years ago in New York City, I studied tai chi with an eighty-five-year-old Chinese woman who lived on the top floor of my apartment building. Twice a week, I'd take the elevator from the sixth floor to the twelfth, slip out of my shoes, and take my place in her sunlit,

---

TAI CHI TECHNIQUE

You can avoid arguments with your sister by refusing to be drawn into discussions of your perceived failings or mistakes from the past. Instead, stay focused on the topic at issue.

---

sparsely decorated living room. I learned a lot from Mrs. Hsu about tai chi and about life. One of the things that she taught me was that, in self-defense, you never meet force with force. In tai chi, when an opponent is coming to attack you, you step aside at the perfect moment and let him use his own forward momentum to lose his balance. He will fall because he was expecting you to connect with him and fight back.

Arguments often start when sisters try to discuss some topic and one of them feels anxious that she is not getting her point across, so she brings up evidence from the past about a different incident to support her argument. The other one then looks for refuting evidence from the past to prove the opposite argument. Because the past is a huge wastebasket littered with innumerable events that could prove either point, these kinds of discussions tend to be laborious, frustrating, and inconclusive and end up far from resolving the original issue.

Instead, keep returning the conversation to the topic at hand and refuse to veer off into other issues from the past or off the point. In sports terms, it's called "keeping your eye on the ball." By using this Tai Chi Technique, you will be able to stay on the initial topic without mucking about in all of the other stuff, so you can lead the discussion to resolution.

To show you how this works, let's look at a typical interchange, first without the Tai Chi Technique. It starts when you call your sister to discuss something:

You: What are we going to do for Daddy's birthday?

She: Why are you asking me? We always do what you want anyhow. (She uses your question as an opportunity to attack you.)

You: What are you talking about?!? We went to that overpriced Italian restaurant that you chose last time. (Getting angry, you are drawn in to defend yourself.)

She: Carol, you chose that restaurant! And while we're on the subject of money, I don't want you deciding what gift we get him again. You may be married to Mr. Moneybags, but I work for my money. (An hour later, you're still fighting on the phone.)

Outcome? You feel awful and the whole issue of your father's birthday party has become loaded. Now let's replay the tape, with you using the Tai Chi Technique:

You: What are we going to do for Daddy's birthday?

She: Why are you asking me? We always do what you want anyhow.

You: Judy, what do you think he would like? (You sidestep, staying on the topic.)

She: Carol, why do you always have to be in charge of everything? (She persists.)

You: Look, do you think he'd prefer to go to a restaurant or should we make dinner at his house? (You keep ignoring the attacks because you're trying to get something decided.)

She: I don't know . . . well, listen. You know he can't hear so well in restaurants, so why don't we make dinner at his house? (She can't keep on attacking if you won't engage.)

The Tai Chi Technique permits you to stay in touch with your sister but offers you a way to avoid having every interaction become an opportunity to replay the old competition symbolically. You probably fall into the same old patterns just as much as she does and end up mad at yourself for your own behavior. Those old habits die hard, but, with enough practice and determination, you can make the change. Don't expect it to work the first time you try it, but after a few attempts, it will become second nature.

Planning for Contact

Another way to sidestep an argument is to stop yourself from getting swept away by the emotions that well up in you when you're talking to your sister. When you're expecting a tense conversation, prepare yourself mentally by planning how you'd like the conversation to go, so that it's possible for you to maintain your preferred image of yourself.

Using the example of the preceding conversation, you would need to prepare yourself before you make the call to plan your father's birthday dinner, anticipating what the possible sensitive issues might be. That way, when they arise, you won't respond in a way that will end up with you feeling bad about yourself. Thinking through the issues, you may realize that:

1. My sister resents that I'm always organizing everything.
2. She may look for a way to hurt my feelings because she feels bad that I can afford a better restaurant than she can.
3. My doing the planning may make her worry that Daddy will appreciate me more and reinforce her belief that he always liked me better.

Figure out how you want to see yourself in this conversation: "I want to feel like the calm, competent woman that I am at work and not revert to feeling like a helpless ten-year-old again." No matter what your sister throws at you in the conversation, keep your preferred self-image firmly in mind.

STAYING TRUE TO YOURSELF

Before you see or speak to your sister the next time, decide how you would want to act to remain true to your *positive* self-image, and stick with that regardless of what she says or does.

Lowering Expectations

Many of the women in The Sisters Project talked about a lifetime of wishing that their sisters would be different. They measure their real relationship against a mental picture of an ideal one and always find their own lacking. It's much easier to catalog the elements that are missing in a less-than-perfect relationship than it is to value those elements that are actually present. I was struck by one woman who spent her interview enumerating her many disappointments about her sister, but when I asked her the final question, "Is there anything else you would like to tell me?" she responded enthusiastically, "Yes. I'm so glad I have her."

A central principle of Buddhism is the belief that having expectations leads to suffering. If we didn't expect certain outcomes, we wouldn't be angry or disappointed. We would learn to live in the present moment, love and savor it, and accept whatever comes our way in life. Following this line of thought, what brings grief in relationships is the wish that others would behave differently. We are disappointed when they don't. But if we could accept our sisters for who they are without constantly hoping that they would change, it would greatly lessen the tension.

Have you ever thought about lowering your expectations? What if you stopped wishing that she would remember your kids' birthdays, not need to be the center of attention, include you in her social life, stop making comments about your clothes, not have to prove that she's better than you, or any of the innumerable other things she does that disappoint you? What if you just accepted her for who she is? Would that bring you some relief?

Thirty-year-old Farrell told me about her struggle to find some place in which to feel comfortable with her older sister: "I think, where sisters are involved, it's really a matter of going through the absolute worst to come out the best, and some people don't get there. They just go through the worst and they keep on going through the worst. I have so many friends who still hate their sisters. They've never gotten past the point where they move beyond the hurt. I'm just so grateful my sister and I have. We've come to accept each other for the best, for the worst. We complement each other now, and we're two healthier people because of it."

This perspective is not easy to adopt. You probably have thought of yourself as a person with a difficult sister relationship for many years, and it's become part of your identity. Maybe people take your side, and that gives you a bit of cold comfort. By lowering your expectations, you would have to let go of all of the injustices and past hurts without ever having them made right—never getting the apology that you feel is coming to you, nor the acknowledgment of all of the things that you've done for her. But in letting go of the past, you're opening up the path to a better future, however narrow and unscenic it may be.

The Amnesia Technique is a way to trick your mind into thinking differently about your sister, leaving behind all of the junk that's crammed in there—junk that has accumulated over twenty, thirty, or

AMNESIA TECHNIQUE

Imagine how you would relate to your sister if you were meeting her for the first time and had no memory of all of the events of your past.

forty (fifty, seventy, ninety?) years of experience. Try to imagine that you have no preconceptions or expectations as to how your sister will behave. If you woke up today with amnesia only about your history of unhappy events relating to your sister, how would that free you up to be different with her the next time you see or talk to her?

Why Women Keep Trying

Sometimes women keep trying to improve their sister relationship because they recognize that they have contributed their part to the animosity. Although you may obsess about her—what *she* did, what *she* said, what *she* didn't do—your role is also important to understand. Do you participate in maintaining the conflict because of pride, hurt feelings, jealousy, or anger? Do you wish that you and your sister could find your way back to each other? Deep down, do you think that your sister really isn't a bad person and that things just got screwed up somewhere along the way and now it feels too awkward to set them right? If that's the case, you may need some help straightening things out. Let yourself entertain the idea of seeking help. Ask someone to act as mediator between you two—an aunt, an uncle, a cousin, a mutual friend, a religious guide, or a family therapist who is trained in family reconciliation.

Sometimes, however, all of the trying in the world can't improve your relationship with your sister. All of your efforts to do one small thing, to deflect arguments, to plan before you contact her, to try to forget the past and start afresh, or to find someone to act as a mediator end in a stalemate. At that point, you need to shift your focus from trying to improve the relationship with your sister to finding your own balance in your life, regardless. That may mean a promise to yourself that you won't do things to fan the flames with her but that you won't spend your life trying to put out the fire, either. You may not be able to change her actions, but you do have control over your own. You can act in ways that permit you to feel proud of yourself.

One of the most poignant resolutions of the conflict between sisters came with a sister's suicide. Clara, the surviving sister from this chapter's opening vignette, had to admit that, along with the grief, there was a sense of relief that the suffering was finally over. The stormy end to her sister's troubled life, which left her caring for her sister's children, forced her to grow up and seek meaning in her own life. "I've grown closer to my sister over the years, even though she no longer is alive. I've grown closer to the person that she was. When I was younger, I was unable to see these qualities in her because I was too close to the situation. Having had all of this distance from her made me realize what a loyal person she was. In the end, I did really love her, even though it was hard."

Ivah and Iris

I Got You, Babe!

Bonded Sisters

"More than anything, I wanted my daughter, Kylie, to have a sister. When she was three months old, I became pregnant, and because I believed that I was having a boy for some reason, I was so disappointed. I even had my sister, Phoebe, come with me to the ultrasound because I wanted her support in case it wasn't a girl. When my second child turned out to be a girl, Phoebe and I just cried and cried and cried because we knew there was nothing better than having two sisters. All I ever wanted was to have two little girls. If I didn't have two girls, I probably would have had a third, hoping for a girl. I'm just so glad that I had what I had."

—CLAIRE, forty years old

Winning the Sister Lottery

Claire told me this story as I shared a sofa with her and her enormous black lab, Puck, who lay snoring between us throughout the whole interview. Claire candidly described how, from her and her sister's point of view, Kylie had just won "the sister lottery." They envisioned Claire's daughters as having a perfect relationship, just like their own, one that incorporated all of the most positive features associated with the term *sisters*, comprised of an easy connection and an assurance of unconditional love that has more than enough steam to last a lifetime. In their own relationship, commitment to each other supersedes everything; each woman's first priority is the protection of that bond. Phoebe, a forty-two-year-old widow, described it like this: "Claire is the closest person in the world to me. She always has been and she always will be. She's been with me my whole life. We've been through a lot of things together—a lot of good things and a lot of tragedy. She is my rock. She is my life. I've been married, and yes, I was madly in love with my husband, but there's just this intense bond with Claire because of what we've been through together since we were very, very young. I speak to her, minimum, ten times a day. She always knows where I am; I always know where she is."

In the chapter about twins, I described the uncanny connection that often exists between wombmates. That merging of identity is expected between twins, but it seems special when it occurs between sisters of different ages. "Uncanny" is perhaps a good way to describe it among nontwins as well. None of the bonded sisters that I heard from had a bad thing to say about their relationship. It's not an overstatement to say that most were thrilled, and woman after woman used the same word in describing her close relationship with her sister, "lucky"—"I feel so lucky! Lucky I have her in my life, lucky we live so close to each other, lucky she's there when I need her." The word was used so often that I would wait for it, sensing, after five minutes, in which interviews it would eventually appear.

I heard from many bonded twosomes, but I was surprised to find that that seamless connection exists in groups of sisters as large as five or six! Sometimes the intense bond originated in childhood, as was the case with Claire and Phoebe. For other women, it only developed as adults. As one might expect, a good percentage of these women experienced some hardship in their families that led to them relying on each other. Of the twenty-seven women in The Sisters Project who can be clearly defined as having bonded relationships, one-third come from families in which there was some extraordinary strain—a divorce or the illness or death of a parent. Unlike between caretaking sisters, who also often come from high-stress households, the dynamic between bonded sisters is not one of unbalanced intimacy—they rely equally and mutually on each other. Age-related hierarchy is less pronounced in this group; interestingly, the older sister is not necessarily in the more responsible role.

Family Harmony

Sisters Project participants who described their relationships with their sisters as bonded were most likely to say that their parents placed a lot of emphasis on family loyalty and on the sister attachment. Twenty-four-year-old Pam and her twenty-year-old sister, Sunny, are part of a family in which there are bonded sisters in three generations. I was able to interview not only Pam and Sunny, but their mother and grandmother as well. Pam talked about the tradition in her family that encourages sisters to be close: "Family is very important for my parents, so there was always a focus on creating family harmony. There was very little room for Sunny and me not to get along. Whenever we fought, there'd be repercussions. We'd be tossed into our rooms and left to sit and think about it. When we felt we were ready to come out, we would have to kiss and make up. Right from the beginning, my parents were really in love with the idea of having two girls because they thought that two girls would have a very special relationship. My mother and her sister are very close. My paternal grandmother had three sisters. My maternal grandmother and her sister survived the war together. They come from Russia and we call them 'the Russky sisters.' They are the matriarchs of the entire family. Three generations of sisters. And hopefully, there'll be more."

Another example of that parental insistence on sororal harmony came from twenty-nine-year-old Kristin, who wrote: "My parents encouraged cooperativeness between my sister and I, never competitiveness. They would always say, 'You are all you have. Stop fighting!' Whenever we did fight, my parents would get us to make up, right there on the spot. We couldn't walk away upset with each other without hugging and saying 'I'm sorry.'" Kristin attributes the development of a strong bond to the emphasis her parents placed on the sisters getting along. Of course, many parents dream that their children will be close, but that intense connection doesn't occur in all families in which parents nurture closeness. Between sisters who are close, however, the glue that holds them together is made up of not only loyalty, but also a deep affection.

The Friend Who Never Leaves

One of the questions I often asked women I was interviewing was whether they considered their sisters to be a sister first or a friend first. Many women in The Sisters Project replied that although they love their sister, they would never choose her for a friend if they were not related. Bonded sisters, however, usually emphasized that although they value being sisters, they also love being best friends. Claire and Phoebe, from the opening vignette in this chapter, lost their mother suddenly when they were in their early twenties and their friendship became etched in stone. Claire's sadness was evident when she reminisced about that time: "We were and still are best friends. We were very close to our mother, and I'll never forget, as soon as she died,

Phoebe came over to me and said, 'Now, we have to be best friends,' and we really are. We are the friends who never leave. Our friends can come and go, but your sister is always there."

Sunny, although only twenty, had given some thought to the evolution of her relationship with Pam: "When we were little, we were sisters before we were friends, but there was a switchover in adolescence and we became friends before we were sisters. You always love your sister, regardless of what she does and who she is, but at a certain point, you begin to respect her as an individual, as a person, as an entity separate from the family. I gave her a bracelet for her birthday a couple of years ago, and the inscription said, 'Sisters by Birth, Best Friends by Choice,' and that's the way it is. I love having her as a sister. I like her tons. We always have fun together. She's just so much fun to be around. It's hard to imagine not being with her."

The Laughter Factor

Sunny's description highlights an important feature of bonded sisters—they have so much fun. They feel so good hanging out together—even just being in the same room. The connection, although profound, is also quite simple. It brings with it a lot of very good feelings. Karen, twenty-two, who still lives at home, said that she likes to sit in the den with Jane, two years younger, and just watch television. They can sit there all day and not say a word and yet have the best bonding day ever, just being together. Karen continued, "We'd love to move in together. It would be the most ideal situation ever for the simple reason that she doesn't annoy me, and if she does, I tell her and we both laugh about it. I could be with her twenty-four hours a day, seven days a week, and not have to worry about it. We're friends; we like hanging out with each other's friends. I like it when she's there."

Although lots of sisters in The Sisters Project talked about the laughter factor—when sisters get together, they love to laugh—among bonded sisters, it's endemic. In an earlier chapter, I mentioned Jane eavesdropping just outside of the doorway of the room in which Karen and I were talking. Karen was giggling during our interview because she knew her sister was listening: "That's another thing; we can't stop laughing. Don't take it personally—we laugh all of the time. When we're with our boy cousins, we can just look at each other and know what the other one's thinking, even from the other side of the room. We find what's funny and we laugh. They ignore us because they know we're strange. We worked together in our father's store and we would laugh. It's gotten us into trouble sometimes. We start laughing and we can't control it. If something funny happens, I'll be laughing hysterically just thinking about telling her. Just thinking about it is just so funny. Everything's funny."

Talking

What else do women do with their best friends, other than laughing? They talk. Talking is the hallmark of bonded sisters—they talk to each other all of the time. They're in touch day and night; some even talk hourly. One woman said that she talks with her sister fifteen times a day but never on weekends. Why? Her husband would think that she's crazy. Now that so many people have cell phones, it's possible to stay in touch all day long: "Hi, I'm going to pick up Simon from day care—need anything from the drugstore? . . . Hi, I just picked up Simon and he bit another kid again. Could you get me the name of that child psychologist? . . . Hi, I'm waiting at the dentist's. What are you making for dinner? . . . Hi, oh—you're in your therapist's office! I forgot. Call me as soon as you get out!" They talk to each other almost as often as they would if they were in the same room!

I interviewed Julia, the mother of Karen and Jane, and the youngest of five very bonded sisters, all four-and-a-half years apart. I also met with her next older sister, Patty, and received an e-mail questionnaire from a third who lives out of town. These five remarkably devoted sisters make no excuses about how close they are; they celebrate it 365 days a year. There is an arresting photo on Patty's mantel, taken by a professional photographer, which shows all five sisters dressed in white. They look so connected that you can practically sense them breathing in unison. Patty is particularly close with Julia and stays in contact with her throughout the day, very much like in the preceding example. Patty teased me: "Ask me how many times a day I speak to my sisters! I must speak to Julia ten to fifteen times a day. My sister Joyce is in Florida. She calls me five times a day long-distance. My other sister has a job, so she'll call me after work. Our husbands ask, 'What do you possibly have to say to each other?' But it's always something."

Fifty-two-year-old Bethany keeps it up even though her sister lives on the other side of the country: "We talk every day about *everything*, big and little, often several times a day. It isn't unusual *at all* for us to talk for an hour or more. Thank goodness long-distance rates are getting more reasonable—we've been doing this for the past twenty-two years! When my husband complained about the bills, I told him that it was cheaper than therapy!"

Kimberly, thirty-nine, echoed: "We never run out of things to talk about, no matter how many times we talked during the day. We go together like peanut butter and jelly, an ice-cream sundae with fudge sauce; we're like fric and frac. Lucky."

Twinning

In trying to explain the extent to which women feel that their bonded sisters understand them inside out, the word *twin* came up a lot, as in: "We're more like twins with a seven-year age span than sisters." Bethany used a similar metaphor to convey, very enthusiastically, the depth of the connection: "We couldn't be closer! Same soul split into different bodies!" There's no question that Bethany's identity is inextricably linked to her sister. When she thinks about her life—her plans, her hopes for the future, even her feelings about herself—she conceptualizes it all in relation to her sister. In some profound sense, she will always be a "we" and never just a "me." The boundary that delineates where she stops and her sister begins is blurred.

This twinning often gives these women intense pleasure. Perhaps what people yearn for most in any relationship is to be completely understood and, once understood, to be loved for themselves—just the way they are. The satisfaction that comes with being totally accepted for who you are makes a bonded sister relationship so desirable. One woman wrote, "I love my husband and my children infinitely, but my sister remains the soul mate who just 'gets it.'"

Suzanne, forty-one, from Montreal, said that it feels like she and her younger sister, Kerry, are experiencing life side by side, as though their lives were unrolling on the movie screen while they're sitting next to each other in the audience, watching: "We're bonded by a lot of similarities that bring a closeness that I don't identify as a 'love' feeling for some reason. It's more like she's another 'me'—almost a clone or something. The boundaries aren't so clear. It's like your right arm—you wouldn't say 'I love you!' to your right arm.

"Even though our thoughts are distinct, our instincts are similar—like a twinning. We both laugh at the same moment about the same thing; we have the very same flavor to our responses. Kerry will always 'get' things without my having to explain. Other people, you tell them something funny and it falls flat; that doesn't happen with her. It's in those parallel things that make me feel that there's somebody else living in the world the same way as me. I'm imagining a movie theatre, she's in the next seat, and we're both watching the same thing. I'm sitting here and she's sitting here and we're both in the same place together."

She Is My Rock

Bonded sisters feel that they know each other so well that their mutual understanding is beyond conscious thought—they are instinctively tuned in to the other's inner experience. Women talk about a kind of trust that is unbreakable. The metaphor that was used several times was, "She is my rock." Thirty-nine-year-old Lorraine's first impulse in a time of crisis was to call her sister: "When I found out I had diabetes, I called my sister. She dropped what she was doing, came over, and let me wail and cry. Then she made me laugh. I have always been the strong, take-charge one, but the essence of our relationship is the staunch, 'walk through fire' support of each other . . . and unconditional love."

Such is Karen's blanket support of her sister Jane that she doesn't even question whether she approves of Jane's behavior—her belief that she should back Jane up overshadows the validity of the issue at hand: "I'm protective of her just as she is protective of me. If she's upset about something, I'll back her up on it. No matter if she's right or wrong; it's irrelevant. It's just because if she's upset about something, I'll feel it, too. I take it personally." Karen comes by that indiscriminate loyalty naturally—her Aunt Patty, of the five sisters, said something similar: "We all have a tremendous sense of protectiveness and loyalty—major. If somebody would do something to my sister—you don't want to be that person. We don't tolerate that." In a similar vein, another woman warned, "Don't mess with me, or you'll have my sister to deal with!"

Like many other women in this category, Jane is proud of the honesty that goes along with that rock-solid trust: "We're not fake to each other. She'll come downstairs and say, 'Do you like what I'm wearing?' and I'll say 'no.' I won't say, 'Well, ah, you know, eh, it might not be exactly for you.' I'll just say 'no,' and we'll go find something else. We have no problem being 150 percent honest . . . I love it. I love having that one person instead of a few—that one person who is everything—who you could trust, who you could have fun with, there's no little glitch involved in any way. Our nickname for each other is 'Babe,' so the Sonny and Cher song, 'I Got You, Babe!' is our theme song."

Unconditional Love: Colette and Yvette

I found the pure, distilled form of the unconditional love referred to by Lorraine in the relationship of teenagers Colette and Yvette, a year apart—sixteen and fifteen. I interviewed them at their home on a rainy fall evening, talking with each one separately in a small upstairs salon at the front of the house. Their mother had painted a delicate landscape on one wall of the room depicting the countryside around her native village in Morocco. Before we spoke, I admired the artwork, letting myself really take it in so that I wouldn't be distracted once we started talking. I had many experiences that touched me while interviewing sisters for this book, and meeting Colette and Yvette was one of them. There was a tenderness in their description of their feelings for each other that was quite poignant; I suppose it was how mutually protective they were of each other, each passionately wanting the best for the other.

Both girls have long, dark brown hair and dark eyes, which translates into a quiet kind of elegance in Colette, but offsets the spunkiness of Yvette, the younger sister. At the beginning of my interview with Yvette, I asked her to tell me about her feelings for Colette: "She's the person I love the most in this world, and it's very, very hard to describe the relationship I have with her because she completes me totally. She's my right hand; she's my second half. If I take a second to imagine what life would be like without her, I start to cry. We love each other very much. She helps me in a lot of different ways. As long as I can remember, my parents always wanted us to stick together. So we're always, always together. We go to the same parties. At school, we always see each other and go home together. When she's going to need help . . . well, she's stronger than I am, so she gives me a lot of moral support. I couldn't live here without her."

Later, in answer to the same question, the older sister, Colette, said, "I've very rarely seen a relationship like ours. I think we have a very, very unique relationship, and I'm so happy about it and my parents are, too. When we were young, our parents had this little saying they would tell us all of the time, 'Remember to love your sister, forever, whenever, whatever.' I've always been more reserved and my sister's the goofier one; she's very spontaneous, but when we're together, we have a very strong image. We're just much more comfortable being out there in the world when we have each other. My sister is really my role model and I'm hers. We really help each other up! We have so many moments of grace; when she needs me, I'm going to be there, and when I need her, she's just going to come right away. It's just being there for each other."

In every interview, I asked the participant to tell me about a significant memory about her sister, and I was really struck by how many bonded sisters spoke of ordinary times, just being together. Yvette recounted this vignette: "Well, it was last year, after school, and it was windy outside and sort of dark. We had taken the bus home and were just walking from the bus stop together, and I remember she told me, 'I'm so happy that I have you.' We talked about it and she said that if she were alone walking on the street, how sad she would feel, how it was just great to have each other. It was dark out and windy, but we didn't feel that sense of loneliness, because we had each other. I'll always remember that day."

Colette's sentiment echoed Yvette's: "Every time we're together, just walking in the street or doing something unimportant, we tell each other how lucky we are. I'm just blessed by having a sister. Talking about Yvette is always a very sensitive subject—it's emotional. I'm very protective of her. I love her."

Sister Fights Are the Best

We've seen that the protection of the harmonious connection trumps everything else in bonded relationships. There's not a lot of angst involved, not a lot of conflict. All of those negative feelings are sacrificed on the altar of nurturing the bond. To understand how jealousy or anger is dealt with in these relationships, let's revisit Suzanne's statement: "It's like your right arm; you wouldn't say, 'I love you!' to your right arm." Well, you wouldn't say, "I hate you!" to your right arm either. Suzanne's sister is so much a part of her that Suzanne can feel Kerry's feelings, so she naturally wants for her sister what she wants for herself. Therefore, it's very hard to stay angry or jealous. Suzanne's fondest wish is to keep Kerry happy and make her feel good. Fighting with her goes against Suzanne's own aims because it will make her sister feel bad.

Yvette articulated the same dynamic this way: "We've never, ever been jealous of each other. I have to admit Colette always had better grades than I have and she's always been the favorite. People admire her, but I've never been jealous of her and I'm really happy for her because I know what she's like inside." If there were more emotional distance between them, Yvette might well be jealous that her sister gets more attention, but because Yvette always wants Colette to feel good, jealousy can't really get a grip.

Bonded sisters said that serious conflict is incomprehensible to them; it's beyond the realm of their imagination. Jane puzzled about the phenomenon of sisters fighting: "We'll be watching these talk shows and many times there are sisters on who haven't spoken for years, and we'll be saying, 'I can't understand that!' I can't imagine ever getting into an argument with my sister and not talking to her."

For women like Jane, it's more important to be connected than it is to be right. It's not that there's no conflict whatsoever. It's just that it doesn't stick—it gets resolved quickly, ignored, or laughed off. Several women commented specifically how they don't even have to talk things out if there's been a fight. It's like the contentious issue evaporates into thin air, so why bother? Forty-three-year-old Shawanda said, "No matter how much me and Cassie get into it verbally, even if we have the worst scrap, two seconds later, if I call her, she'll be out the door, 'I'm coming over!' All of that stuff will be pushed aside. It doesn't matter what we fought about." Patty commented about fights or the lack thereof: "If we have words, a minute later we'll call back and say, 'Hi! Are you watching Oprah?' We don't have fights."

Wendy, twenty-six, e-mailed this comment: "Sister fights are the best because you don't have to talk out issues and resolve conflict. You just walk back into the room a few minutes later and ask if she wants to go to the pool or go shopping and it's all over."

Their Own Wavelength

Some bonded sisters admitted that they are aware that others tend to feel excluded when they're together. With all of that laughing and intense talking going on, bonded sisters have a comfort level between them that's hard to duplicate in other relationships. They know each other's shorthand; they're each other's in-crowd.

Their friends are sometimes envious, wishing that they could be part of that intimate circle. Because the sisters get their primary needs met with each other, like in the case of twins, friends sometimes feel extraneous. Julia is aware of the effect that she and her four sisters have on the people around them: "When my sisters and I are together, I sometimes feel other people get intimidated. We can make ourselves laugh at the silliest thing and we'll laugh until there are tears running down our faces. We don't intend to be intimidating to other people, but I can see how it could be because we're very close. A lot of our friends say, 'We're the sixth sister!' They want to be in."

Bridget wasn't aware of the effect that her intense focus on her sister had on others until her girlfriend spelled it out for her: "I didn't even realize it. I think we just have a form of communication in which we'll go off on some kind of tangent that no one else will understand. We'll talk about family or memories and it's sort of like we're on the same wavelength. We just get going on these conversations where there's no room for anyone to cut in. If they do cut in, we'll make a quick comment to them and go back to talking to each other. If no one had said this to me, I wouldn't have realized it."

For forty-year-old Shannon, being part of her sister's life softened the loneliness of all of the years she was single: "I have a small number of very close women friends, and I didn't get married until I was thirty-nine. I also didn't date much. I think without my sister, who is my best friend, I would have winced much more at being single for as long as I was and would have felt simply more alone. With her, I have always felt part of a greater whole."

Both Suzanne and her sister, Kerry, are divorced mothers with young children. Suzanne didn't mention whether her intense connection to her sister contributed to her divorce, but she did say that it is certainly a consolation now: "Our sister relationship is more significant than any other relationship that I have. It seems to me that guys are transitory. There's no other relationship in my world that has that enduring, unchanging, comfortable quality to it."

Becoming part of a couple can be tricky when a woman is already getting her needs for intimacy met through her relationship with her sister. If the potential partner is looking for an exclusive relationship defined by a high level of involvement and is not keen to share his or her lover with her sister, making a commitment can be especially hard. A woman who is really close to her sister, however, may not look for an equivalent level of intimacy in her love life. She may purposefully choose a partner who doesn't have a problem with the time and attention she devotes to her sister. Some partners may be perfectly comfortable being in a relationship with a woman who doesn't require them to be her soul mate. Others may accept that she can be deeply connected to two people but in different ways.

The Husband's Point of View

Throughout their interviews, women kept referring to their husband's reaction to the sister bond. Husbands seem to fall into three categories: those who are proud to be part of the clan, those who bemusedly scratch their heads in disbelief, and those who disapprove.

Part of the Clan

Husbands in the first category tended to get along well with their wife's sister and her husband and to buy into the concept of "one big happy family." In some cases, the two husbands are also best friends. Sally, sixty-two, described how smooth it is between the two sisters and their spouses: "They're as involved with each other as we are—they play together. They go curling together, we all used to ski together, the four of us golf. The guys have a very close relationship. They love to take off on their own." Some of Sally's happiest memories are of summers when the two couples rented bungalows near each other and vacationed with all of their kids.

Patty is the only one among the five sisters who has been divorced, and she thinks that her closeness with her sisters had a lot to do with it. Her current husband of ten years, however, is well integrated into the family. Patty explained what it's like for the husbands: "They love to be part of the clan. We belong to the same golf club, most of us belong to the same synagogue; people around us know that we're all part of the same family. They say, 'Look at the sisters! Look at the brothers-in-law!' The guys have gotten the security blanket. They love it. In my first marriage, my ex tried to separate me, and when he started doing that, he pushed me even further away. If my husband loves me so much, he'll know what those girls mean to me. They're my history. I've come a whole long way with them. Fierce loyalty! So that's why our men have to be as 'in it' as we are."

A similar comment was made by Dawn, one of four sisters: "I don't feel bad for our husbands, but it has to be somewhat hard being the husband of one of us because we're always together. Last year, we all went out with the four husbands, and they sat and watched us with smiles on their faces. They were in awe. It's not that they don't like it, but it's not just that you're marrying the girl—you're marrying all of us!"

Bemused

An example of a bemused husband would be the husband of fifty-nine-year-old Kathleen. She described her husband as questioning, but underneath the questions, you can hear a hint of irritation: "My husband keeps saying that he's never seen a relationship like this, 'You're so close, it's insane; you're always calling each other.' He finds it weird.

'Why are you so close?' There are things that you share with your family that you wouldn't even share with your husband; that's just very human and personal."

Disapproving

Thirty-nine-year-old Shelly is very conscious of her husband's disapproval of her closeness with Donna, four years older, but openly admitted that she prefers her sister to her husband: "If it were up to me, I'd spend more time with her. My husband sort of gets in the way. I think he's jealous of my relationship with my sister. He wants to know why I can't do things with him. [I asked Shelly, "Do you feel caught in the middle?" Her answer surprised me.] No, I don't feel caught in the middle; I just want to be with *her*! If that's a sickness, I don't know. Maybe this is terrible to say, but blood is thicker than water. I know she'll always be there for me and I'll always be there for her. She will be there before my husband will. I can go and talk to my sister about my marriage and ask her, 'Am I being ridiculous?' and she'll tell me. I always have her as a sounding board. I don't have him as a sounding board."

Her sister, Donna, told it from the other side: "When her son was born, her husband wouldn't let me near Shelly or the baby; he was very worried about what my influence would be. Her husband probably gets annoyed that we're so close. I can see what happens on the weekend— I won't hear from her from Friday evening to Monday morning."

Weird and Wonderful

Occasionally, during their interviews, women confessed that they worry that others think their level of closeness with their sister is suspect. Shelly wondered if it's a "sickness," Karen said her cousins think that she and her sister are "strange"; Kathleen's husband thinks that she's "weird"; Phoebe said that she spends an awful lot of time with her sister and her family and that people may think it's "unhealthy." Some of the women who describe their sister relationship as bonded display a kind of guilty pleasure. They have a nagging sense that there may be something wrong with it, but it feels so good that they're not willing to consider the possibility of doing anything to change it.

This worry that the closeness is unhealthy is very culturally based. North American society sanctions intimacy between a woman and her husband, first and foremost, and sometimes raises an eyebrow when there is an exclusive bond between a woman and any other member of the family. The field of psychotherapy developed a concept called *enmeshment*. The term is used to describe relationships between family members that are seen to be unhealthily dependent. Therapists have been guilty, at times, of pointing the finger at any woman whose closest ties are with a child, a sister, or a mother instead of with a spouse. Some other cultures, however, do not expect women to develop a deep level of intimacy with their spouses and assume that their primary connection *will* be with their sisters.

The majority of women who describe a strong sister bond, however, are proud of it. They feel special; they're the envy of their friends. Some even enjoy flaunting their uniqueness! Marian Sandmaier, in her book *Original Kin*, wrote about Terry and Marie, two sisters she interviewed. She described the experience of meeting these sisters as "not so much an interview as a piece of sister performance art. I would venture a question and Terry, thirty-two, would fire back a wisecrack answer while Marie, thirty-six, would dissolve in laughter. Or they would simultaneously spout the same one-liner. Then, as often as not, they would turn to each other and intensely debate the question at hand—Whaddya think? No, that's nuts!—and as they did this they frequently touched, smiled, hugged, and hooted. They were clearly crazy about each other, these daughters of working-class Italian American parents, and their bond went deeper than joke-trading and shared hilarity. Each woman felt that a regular 'fix' of sisterly interaction was essential to her emotional well-being, to her sense that somewhere in the world she deeply, unalterably belonged" (1994, p. 103).

I certainly saw that sister pride when I met with Karen and Jane, with Patty and Julia, with Colette and Yvette, and with Shawanda and her three sisters. At those times I felt a twinge of envy that made me think, "Wouldn't it be great if I could have that closeness with a sister?" In this unpredictable world, these women find it hugely comforting to know that they have a walking security blanket. I could understand why women are so fiercely determined to protect and nourish that bond. As Jane said, "Some people say that they're sisters but it means nothing to them. I guess 'sisters' has another definition for us. I can tell her anything and I don't have to say, 'Oh, promise you won't tell anyone.' I'm not worried she's going to say anything; I'm not nervous she's going to sleep with an old boyfriend of mine. There's a lot of that going on between my friends and their sisters. It's mind-boggling to me how they could jeopardize that bond."

I Wish for Her What I Wish for Myself

Women in any kind of sister relationship are usually deeply sad when they see the other struggling in life; for bonded sisters, it's almost unbearable. Like Megan and Aviva, the fifteen-year-old twins who desperately hope that one will not do better than the other when they grow up, bonded sisters also wish for mutual success. Kathleen was embarrassed that she found it so hard to hold back the tears as she talked about her sister's hard life: "I just wish life could have been kinder to her. I feel sad that she didn't marry. She has a good career, but it's not enough of a life. I wish that things were different for her, socially, financially, and in every way. I'd like to see her have a different kind of life—have a wider circle of friends, be more fulfilled—all the things we wish for ourselves."

Phoebe, from the opening vignette of this chapter, suffered greatly when her sister became ill: "Ten years ago, the year Chloe was to be married, she was diagnosed with a tumor. The day she came to tell me was the worst day of my life. I did not believe that it was benign and that she would be okay. It was the worst thing—the possibility that something could happen to my sister. I was beyond neurotic. Four years later, when she became pregnant, I started to believe that she might be okay. I worry about her more than I worry about myself, and she worries about me more than she worries about herself."

For her part, Chloe ached when Phoebe was widowed: "Her husband dying was the hardest thing because it was the first time in our lives that we weren't suffering equally; I was watching her suffer more. I know for her, the hardest time in her life was when I was diagnosed with a tumor. It was harder for her than it was for me. It was benign but it really made her crazy—she thought I was going to die and she was really scared."

In each interview, I always asked how life would be different if the participant didn't have a sister. The answer I usually got was "*boring*," but among bonded sisters, the thought of life without their sister made them shudder. Here's a sample of what they said:

- "That thought is so frightening and horrible, I can't even imagine!"
- "My life would be so much less that the thought of it takes my breath away."
- "Thank God we're sisters because I don't know where I would be without Alice in my life."
- "I would feel empty and alone, like part of me didn't exist."

Bonded sisters who are mothers of only one daughter feel that sense of loss for their child. Many said that they feel very sorry and guilty that they themselves were lucky enough to enjoy a sister's love but they didn't or couldn't provide that experience for their daughter. Bethany said that she worries that her daughter feels "shortchanged" because she doesn't have a sister. Although these mothers may know intellectually that not all sister relationships are so perfect, they tend to assume that their own daughters' connection would be. They take for granted that the idealized vision of the sister bond would be passed on to the next generation.

The super-close connection we've heard about in this chapter is what most women think of as the ideal sister relationship. It's the gold standard that women aspire to and yearn for, particularly if their own connection falls short. Most wish that they could respond as Kimberly did when I asked her what the experience of being interviewed for The Sisters Project was like for her: "I love talking about my sister. I love her. I think she's fantastic. I know how lucky I am. I tell her, 'I love you.' I'm so happy that we're sisters. I'm so happy that we're best friends. I'd talk about her all day long if you'd let me. An hour is way too short!"

Sarah and Dorothy

9

My Sister's Keeper

Caretaker Relationships

"Bunny was like my little project. I was always thinking that I would bring her up differently from the way I was brought up. I would tell her how much I loved her. I was trying to give her self-esteem; I praised her more than I praise my own kids now. I just felt she could do anything. Brooke Shields was in the movie *Pretty Baby* around then, and I used to say, 'You're prettier than Brooke Shields, and you can do anything.' I didn't get any of that encouragement, so I was trying to make up for what I didn't get."

—CHARLOTTE, forty-five years old

Getting Parented by Proxy

Charlotte's childhood was punctuated by the critical voices of parents who rarely had an encouraging word to say to her. The birth of her baby sister, Bunny, when she was twelve, however, gave her a chance to repair the damage that was done to her by their constant criticism. Fashioning a perfect world for her little sister, Charlotte tried to experience, by proxy, the safety and nurturing environment that she craved.

This chapter looks at those overburdened sisters who make sacrifices to tend to their sister's needs, either by requirement or by choice. For these girls, being responsible for their sister can be both a pleasure and a burden. Sometimes the caretaking ends when the girls grow up; sometimes it only begins in adulthood. In families where one sister is ill or truly troubled, that caretaker role may last a lifetime and color the whole of the nurturing sister's life. As for Charlotte and Bunny, the older girl was singularly devoted to helping raise her little sister throughout her own adolescence. The intensity of that role diminished, although it didn't entirely disappear, when Bunny grew up into a healthy and successful woman and made her separate way in the world.

Women in the caregiving role talk about feeling overwhelmed, trapped, and constantly guilty. They are often frustrated and bitter when the caregiving goes on and on, year after year, decade after decade. Providing help and support can become the primary focus in the life of the caregiver. (I'm tempted to say, "in the life of the *older* sister," although it is not *always* the case that the caregiver is older.) There were twenty-nine women in The Sisters Project who, either as children or adults, were clearly in that role. Twenty-five were older sisters and four were younger, but not one was a middle sister!

There are certainly situations in which it is appropriate for one adult sister to look after the needs of another. Women whose sisters are mentally or physically disabled may not be able to divest themselves of that responsibility. Additionally, they may get a sense of satisfaction knowing that they are filling a real need, one that improves their sisters' lives. Some women have made their peace, for very concrete reasons, with needing to keep an eye on their sisters. This chapter, however, will explore those caretaking women who suffer in their role and whose own lives are limited because of it. We will look at the extent to which these women become so bogged down in the daily grind that they lose sight of the fact that their mission in life is not solely to care for a sister. They forget that taking time for themselves doesn't mean that they are bad people or selfish human beings. On the contrary, before they can give to others, they have to be well cared for themselves. As flight attendants always instruct passengers prior to takeoff: "In case of emergency, put your own oxygen mask on first before you assist others!"

The Core of the Problem

It's easy to trace the circumstances that cause one sister to take responsibility for another; just follow the trail back to Mom and Dad—or Mom *or* Dad! Every participant who identified herself as a caretaker described a childhood touched by, at the very least, serious fighting between her parents or, at the very worst, a mentally ill parent or sexual abuse. Alcoholism, violence, depression, "toxic parents," poverty—at least one of these factors always lay at the root of what compelled one sister to give so much to another. In these families, the adults involved were unwilling or unable to nurture the children adequately. As a result, one of the girls stepped in, trying to fill the void.

Consciously or not, some girls attempt to salvage their own miserable childhoods by creating a bubble of safety for their sisters, just as Charlotte tried to do. Charlotte chose to try to experience, vicariously through Bunny, a sense of order and protection that was absent for her. For other girls, choice doesn't enter into it; if they didn't cook and clean, then no one had dinner and clothes for school. Don't bother trying to get Mum up off the sofa—it's not going to happen. Seventy-year-old Erika, the oldest of six, described the dynamics of her household growing up: "My mother was manic-depressive, and at that time, they gave her shock treatments—terrible, terrible. My father couldn't comprehend the whole thing. If you didn't have a broken arm or leg, he couldn't see what was wrong. So he drank. We were always wondering if he was going to come home. Ah, Maritimers! If they bring a bottle of liquor into the house, they finish it—they drink the whole thing. And then he would get quite nasty. He never hit anybody, but he would rant and rave, and I was terrified. Essentially, I became the mother at the age of thirteen or fourteen. When my mother was out of the depressive stage, she was manic, and she was a marvelous cook and everything, but when she was depressive, she couldn't even put a meal on the table. So it was a worrisome childhood. I worried a lot. About everything."

What led Erika to become a caretaker was the general inability of her parents to handle their own lives. In other families, the problem was more specific; several women talked about taking on the protection of a sister because they worried that she was unloved. The unloved girl may even have been made a scapegoat and treated roughly by one of her parents. In a few cases, women said that their other parent entrusted them with the sacred mandate: "Take care of your sister." Peggy was only three when her mother said those exact words to her: "In my family, my father was an alcoholic, and my sister and mother were his victims. He always accepted what I did, but when my sister came in the picture, he didn't love her. If she did little things, like breaking a glass or something, he'd get so mad at her, it was unbelievable. She was so tiny—in my head, she's still this little girl. I was the one who took everything on me. Challenging him all of the time, protecting them, so it was very, very hard." Peggy continues, decades later, to try to fulfill the promise to take care of her sister, Rita, long after her beloved mother and abusive father are dead and gone.

A mental deficit or physical illness on the part of the sister who needs care may also contribute to the development of the caretaking relationship. This factor is usually combined with the inability of one or both of the parents to handle that child's needs. In families where parents can function appropriately, sisters do not need to assume such an exaggerated responsibility for the care of a sibling. Holly, thirty-four years old, comes from a religious fundamentalist background in which both of her parents were exceedingly rigid and remote. They completely missed the developmental delays of the oldest of their trio of daughters, Renee, three years older than Holly. Holly explained: "My mom had a very cold, formal demeanor, and she was raised in a home where there was never any adult-child engagement. She was a woman who was not meant to be a mom. My oldest sister, Renee, didn't get any special attention. She kind of coasted through—she was very quiet. I would spend hours trying to convince her of some logical way of doing something, trying to convince her and trying to convince her, and getting hoarse, but she'd just lapse back. I remember when I was just a kid and she was a young teenager, she'd never scrub her hair with force, so I would help and say, 'Okay, I'll wash your hair and I'll dry your hair.'"

Childhood Sacrifices

These girls had to sacrifice their childhoods in the service of caring for their sister(s) or families. Little Holly was an occasional caretaker for Renee. Peggy was constantly on guard to protect Rita from their abusive father. Erika, at the age of thirteen or fourteen, was saddled with the responsibility for her entire family. To varying degrees, they have spent the rest of their lives coming to terms with fallout from that sacrifice. This is not to say that these girls and others like them didn't also enjoy their sisters and get something back from them. Even in an extreme situation of family disorder and sexual abuse, there can sometimes be positives. Such was the grim reality of forty-five-year-old Taryn, from Albuquerque, who was responsible for her four younger sisters. Although taking care of them was often difficult, in some ways, it also helped: "We had an actively alcoholic, emotionally absent mother; we had a cruel, controlling father. Mom ignored us and Dad criticized us. I was 'the parent' from a little before age eleven. I had to take care of the family, make dinner, and supervise my sisters every day and evening after school. I was jealous that they got to be kids and play and that they learned how to make friends and had many. I had to 'parent' them and daily was angry with them for making me yell at them. My childhood, twenties, and early thirties were 90 percent shaped by my emotional and physical incest with my father and my mother's poor parenting. It harmed me a lot. But my growing up with my sisters saved me from a lot of loneliness and boredom."

Understandably, many caretaker sisters leave home as soon as possible. They move out by the early age of seventeen or eighteen in an effort to make a life for themselves apart from the family. Several talked about fetching their sisters to come live with them and even taking on financial responsibility when they themselves were only teens. Erika, from the Maritimes, moved away at sixteen to live with her grandmother in another province and later, when she found a good office job, brought her three sisters and her brother, one by one, to live with her.

Unbalanced Intimacy

Being the caretaker for your sister when you are a child and still living at home is one thing, but continuing in that role when you are supposed to be separate adults is something else entirely. It may feel like it never ends when one adult sister takes on responsibility for another who is truly unable to care for herself adequately. The caregiving sister is living two lives instead of just one. She not only has her own problems to solve but is dragging along her sister's problems as well. As one woman put it, "It's exhausting to always be the one that's okay." If this describes your reality, it may seem like you are locked in a relationship of "unbalanced intimacy," one in which you are always on the receiving end of your sister's woes but, because you are concerned for her welfare, you're never at liberty to trouble her with yours. The more this dichotomy is reinforced through one-way giving, the more the relationship becomes unbalanced. You become exclusively in the position of caretaker, and she gets strongly identified as the one who couldn't do it without you.

You ask yourself, "Am I my sister's keeper?" And you answer, "Well, I don't have any choice." Or do you? I'm sure that if you asked the next fifty people you met on the street whether they believed that it's a sister's responsibility to take care of a sibling who needs help, the vast majority would answer yes. If kin didn't take care of kin, the burden would fall on a social service system that is already straining at the seams. The social pressure on you to keep on going is enormous, as would be the guilt you'd feel if you stopped.

We've acknowledged the pressure on the caretaker that comes from the family and from society for her to fulfill the mandate of helper. We will now take a look at the pressure on her that comes directly from her needy sister, who will sometimes pull out all of the stops to maintain the status quo. We will also discuss the pressure that the caretaker puts on herself to remain in that role because of beliefs that many women hold about what it means to "be good" and the nobility of sacrifice.

Backing Off a Bit: Sophie's Story

I interviewed thirty-eight-year-old Sophie at her office in Chicago, where she is an art director at a very high-powered public relations firm. She looked put-together in a soft sort of way, very professional, but she had an out-of-character nose stud that suggested another side to her. We sat in a conference room—an odd setting to discuss such an intimate topic—and I think she felt it as well as I. She brought photographs of her sisters that she was keen to show me.

Married with two children, Sophie is the youngest of three sisters. She and Marti, the oldest, were close as kids, but Marti always caused problems in the family. As a child, she was very aggressive. Sophie believes that, growing up, Marti was unloved by their parents. Marti, who does not have kids, is a writer and lives with her boyfriend in Mexico. She suffers from untreated bipolar disorder, compounded by a drinking problem.

Sophie only became the caretaker for Marti after they became adults. For the past fifteen years, the roller-coaster ride that is Marti's existence has had Sophie hanging on for dear life. It's been crisis after crisis, including more than one suicide attempt. Marti tearfully telephones Sophie at her office several times a day; Sophie always takes the calls, even when she's in a meeting, because she fears what might happen if she didn't. Four or five times over the years, Marti has called Sophie to say, "Help me, help me!" Each time, Sophie immediately phoned the airlines and twenty-four hours later, she'd be in Mexico, having left her young family behind. Sophie is so demoralized by the miserable life that her sister is living that she even toyed with the idea of not notifying the police the last time Marti called to say that she'd taken an overdose of pills.

Sophie feels that being locked in this struggle to keep her sister going has "sucked the life" out of her. She was diagnosed with cancer a few years ago and believes that the illness provided her with the only acceptable excuse to take care of herself. I asked her when she thinks she can get away from all of this responsibility? "When Marti dies— which shouldn't be in too long."

Surprisingly, Sophie ended her story on an upbeat note. She has learned something important over the years. Through all of this suffering, she now realizes that she doesn't have to take 100 percent responsibility for improving Marti's life or even for keeping her alive. "I am now a little bit more able to pull away from my sister—from the dominating pain in the neck that she has become in my life. I know that sounds cruel. I've sort of backed off a little bit. What I've been doing is exhausting, emotionally and physically, but most important, it doesn't help Marti. I recently realized, and it's taken me a lifetime, that it isn't my role to make her happy, it isn't my role to save her, 'cause I tried. I'm a nurturer, but I don't nurture myself. That's why I had cancer a few years ago. I had to be in the hospital to allow myself to have cancer. That's when I saw that I'm killing myself."

Sophie has felt, at times, that she has been held hostage by the requirements of her sister's dependency, but recently, she is learning how to take a step back to protect herself. She used to believe that Marti didn't have any resources to keep herself safe or even to keep herself going. When those "Help me, help me!" phone calls came in, Sophie's knee-jerk reaction was to run. She has never said to Marti, "You need to take responsibility for yourself," encouraging Marti to rise to the challenge. Sophie's response of running to Marti's side, and even of leaving her meetings to take the phone calls, transmits the unspoken message that Marti can't do it on her own. By telling Marti, "I'm always here for you, day and night," Sophie is entrenching that dependency, rather than protecting her sister.

Sophie is, of course, afraid that Marti's suffering will lead her to end her own life. In this delicate situation, it's a fine line that Sophie has to walk. But if she were not to leave a meeting to answer the phone, Sophie would be, in a sense, starting the process of rebalancing the intimacy—meaning, letting Marti know that Sophie has needs of her own. Sophie even needs her big sister to take care of *her* sometimes so that she won't get stressed to the point where she gets sick. Not only does Marti need to separate from Sophie, but vice versa. Sophie needs to take the chance to push the boundaries back a bit so that she can start to separate emotionally from Marti. That may mean waiting a little while before returning a phone call, which would change Sophie's unspoken message to her sister from "I'll always be here for you" to "I know you can do it!"

Overcoming the Guilt

Interestingly, fifty-seven-year-old Phyllis, whose sister also suffers from mental illness, has traveled the same path, arriving at a similar destination: "I am definitely the one she leans on, and I sometimes feel like I'm her psychologist and psychiatrist. I am smothered at times and feel I can't escape. She is bipolar and has chronic depression, and she's often told me she could never survive without me. She has tried to commit suicide three times. I recently took a week's vacation, and before I left, she cried and told me she didn't know how she would survive. Needless to say, that made me feel like crap, but I've learned that I need to take a break from her in order to keep my sanity. I still love her very much, but enough is enough. I would do anything to help her, with the exception of risking my own health and well-being."

Phyllis's sister tried to get Phyllis to put her own needs last and cancel her vacation, but was unsuccessful in getting her way. The unspoken message that Phyllis transmitted by going ahead with her vacation plans was, "I have needs too, and you'll survive." It strikes me that, although both of these brave women are trying to change, the guilt still peeks through. Sophie said that talking about pulling away from her sister (because it's killing her) "sounds cruel." Phyllis wrote that her sister is able to make her "feel like crap" for wanting to go on a lousy week's vacation! The next step for both of them is to say to themselves: "No! I refuse to feel guilty! I don't care what anybody thinks. I know how much I've given to my sister over the years. I don't need to give her 100 percent or even 75 percent of my life! Now's my time and I deserve it! I'm not going to permit caring about my sister to eat me up alive!"

Learned Helplessness

In her memoir *Almost There*, the Irish author Nuala O'Faolain wrote about how inflexible family roles can be: "It [family] doesn't allow its members to experiment with themselves. The penalty for being loyally accepted for the whole of your life is that you must stay what you always were. A calm, sardonic family eye rests on the member who tries any little acts or wiles. Reinvention is not possible" (2003, p. 180).

Once some sisters have learned to be dependent and others have learned to be dependable, the pattern is very difficult to break. Each time the dependable sister makes a decision for the needier sister, it's reinforced. Eventually, the needier sister's mind naturally gravitates toward her seemingly infallible resource when she has a problem. The dependent sister is increasingly convinced that her competent sister knows what's right; she becomes less and less likely to have the confidence to think for herself. In a sense, she becomes too scared or emotionally lazy to accept responsibility for her own life choices.

Roxanne, a retired real estate broker, comes from an impoverished family. Like other women described in this chapter, she was loaded down in her childhood with too much responsibility for her sister and two brothers: "Mom didn't work when I was little. She started to work during the summer when I was eleven. My father was unemployed for two or three years; he was fired for playing cards on the job. That summer, we actually didn't have enough to eat. We were kind of stuck out in the country because we didn't have a car, but one day my mother hitchhiked into town and got a job as a saleslady in a dime store. I stayed home with my sister and brothers; the youngest was only about one. When my father found out what she'd done, he said, 'I won't let you keep that job! What will people think of me if they find out you're working?' And this was when we didn't have enough to eat! Anyway, she said, 'Yes, yes,' but she kept the job and she just went. So I took care of the kids. When the summer was over, she had to quit work because I had to go to school."

Roxanne's sister continued to rely on her for everything throughout their childhood. When they were all grown up, however, Roxanne kept waiting for things to change and for her sister to stop depending on her so much. She described her frustration when this didn't happen: "When I was at university, my sister was working in the same city.

She got some kind of rash all over her body, little red dots, and the doctors didn't seem to know what it was. I was helping her out—making sure she had enough food in her apartment and things like that. One night, I was working out of town and got back very late—about midnight. My roommate said there was a message for me: 'Call your sister no matter what time you get in!' I called her, and she was in agony with the rash. It was terrible, and she didn't know what to do. She asked if she should call the doctor, and I said 'Yes!' She did and he came and tried to help her, and I just thought, 'Why did she have to wait for me? She could have called him earlier. She wouldn't have been suffering for so long and he wouldn't have had to come in the middle of the night!' Why did she need my permission? But she seemed to need it!"

Fulfilling a Promise: Peggy's Story

We heard earlier about the sacred mission that Peggy's mother entrusted to her when she was three years old—to take care of her sister, Rita, and protect her from their abusive father. Fifty-two years later, Peggy's day-to-day life is still shaped by her efforts to fulfill that promise. Like a surprising number of other caretaker sisters, Peggy has never married and does not have children. She has recently retired from a thirty-five-year career as a teacher and is dreaming of travel and other retirement activities. She'd even like to sell her house, so she can have less responsibility and relax. Rita, on the other hand, has only ever worked sporadically, going from low-paying job to unemployment to low-paying job. She has neither a pension nor savings and rents a low-cost apartment in Rita's house. She smokes too much and is in poor health. She has few friends; her world revolves around her sister. Peggy said, "I would like to sell here and buy a condo for me—a nice place. I worked for it. I deserve it. But I don't want to see my sister in misery. I know she's always there with her dogs and cats and those monetary problems that she's going to have to face one day." Rita's response to Peggy's suggestion that they move apart was, "You're going to put me in the street with my animals!" about which Peggy said, "She knows how to make me feel very guilty. Oh, yes! But even if she doesn't do it purposefully, I feel guilty anyway." Peggy once saw a psychologist about all this guilt, and he told her that she has an "inner child." He said that she has to take care of the little girl inside of her. She corrected him: "I know I have an inner child, but it's my sister."

Concluding our interview, Peggy said, "For years, I tried everything to please Rita so she could be happy, but nothing worked. She's very negative; I try to see the positive. We're very, very different. In my mind, I always keep the good memories I have of my mother when she was alive. Every night, I talk to my mother. I tell her I'm taking care of my sister."

Peggy retains responsibility for Rita's happiness and isn't yet at the point at which she recognizes that that job belongs to Rita. Peggy's mother may have felt powerless when she entrusted her three-year-old with the protection of her two-year-old sister a long, long time ago, but that desperate act was not meant to endure a lifetime. Peggy is still thinking from a child's perspective. She has not yet challenged the idea that it is noble to take care of her helpless sister. Now that they are adults, that caring has become crippling, to the point that Rita is a middle-aged woman who has little to show for her lifetime of work. In the back of her mind, Rita probably still thinks, "I don't have to worry. Peggy will always take care of me." Although that may be the case, it is far from ideal for either of them.

Wiggle Room

Earlier in this chapter, I raised the question that many caretaker sisters ask themselves: "Am I my sister's keeper?" Now I'll answer it. No, you are not your sister's keeper. You are your sister's sister. Your sister is trying to live her life, but you are entitled to a life, too, and hers is not more important than yours. Together, the two of you may have colluded, over the years, in training her to shut down her discriminatory powers and turn the executive function for her life over to you. But unlike the writer Nuala O'Faolain whom I quoted earlier, I don't believe that reinvention is not possible. I couldn't have spent the past twenty years working as a family therapist if I did! In this section, we will look at ways to create some wiggle room so that your caretaker role can start to change.

Through a painful process, Sophie came to the conclusion that she does not need to sacrifice her own life on the altar of her sister's. Phyllis figured out that she is entitled to a vacation, even though her sister doesn't want her to go. Now that Peggy has retired, she, too, is chafing at the restrictions that caretaking places on her freedom. You may dismiss the possibility of change in your particular case, thinking, "You don't know *my* sister!" but I'm not suggesting that you just cut her loose tomorrow. Right now, we're just looking for ways to make some space for change.

Most things in life have elements of both good and bad. Even things that appear predominantly good usually have some bad imbedded in them—that's why the list of life's ten most stressful events includes marriage, reconciliation with a spouse, and retirement. On the other hand, the burden of being the caretaker for a sister, a situation that may appear predominantly bad, usually has some quantity of good in it. If you were to give up some of that caretaker role, what else of value would you be relinquishing? Here are some possibilities:

- The comfort of not feeling guilty
- The admiration of your family and friends who view your sacrifice as noble
- A perfect excuse for not doing things ("Sorry, I can't come to the party. I have to stay home with my sister.")
- Someone who is always available to keep you company
- A distraction from problems in your own life
- The status of being the person in charge

- A reason why you don't have to challenge yourself socially or professionally
- Someone who provides enough excitement to satisfy your need for drama
- A hedge against feelings of sadness
- The privileged position of "the good daughter"
- Not ever having to risk being called selfish

The following statement of Peggy's is a perfect example: "My relationships with men were a disaster, so after I broke up with someone, I would say to myself, 'My sister is the only person that I can count on. She will always love me no matter what, and I will do the same.'" Rita's dependency is an insurance policy for Peggy, guaranteeing that Peggy will never be lonely. If Peggy encourages her sister to become more independent or to rely on someone else, Rita may not be available the next time Peggy gets her heart broken. That's the chance Peggy would have to take if she truly wants more freedom. That's the negative that's embedded in the positive, and it illustrates how the sister who is the caretaker is a full contributor to the dynamic.

Leading Toward Healing

If you are a caretaker to a sister and are ready to challenge the status quo, you first need to assess what would change if you succeeded. Write down your answers to the following questions:

1. What do I gain by being my sister's caretaker?
2. How would my friends and family view me differently if I gave up some of that role?
3. What would my sister say about me if I reduced the extent to which I'm her caretaker?
4. What would I gain by giving up that role?
5. How would I view myself differently?

Here's how Nell, whose sister, Lois, suffers from depression, answered these questions. What she gains by being Lois's caretaker is a sense of control—she feels that she is keeping the lid on things so that she won't have to go in to clean up a mess later. If Nell gave up some of that role, however, her husband would be happy—he is always saying that she is overfunctioning and doing too much for her sister. But Lois might accuse her of not caring. The risk that Nell would have to take would be that her sister might take even less care of herself in an effort to get Nell back into playing her role. Lois might be secretly insulted that Nell is unilaterally changing things, and she might fight very hard to reestablish the usual dependent pattern of their relationship. Lois may start to miss work so that Nell will come over, cook dinner, and take care of her as usual.

Nell would have to be prepared for a rocky ride for a while, but to actually change the relationship, she would have to be determined to stay the course, regardless of the pressure her sister exerted on her. Nell would have to be tough and not susceptible to Lois's trying to make her feel guilty by saying things such as, "You care more about your husband than you do about me. That's why you're not coming over." Nell would have to believe that fostering Lois's independence is as essential for Lois as it is for Nell. This is not to say that Nell would stop caring entirely, but just that she would learn to put limits on the amount of responsibility she takes on so that Lois can start to learn to exercise that self-care muscle.

How Much Does She Really Need You?

There's no question that some women do need help making their way through the difficulties of life. Some women are legitimately dependent because their lives are restricted by a disability; others, however, are emotionally fragile but function relatively well. Sometimes a woman with a disability is far more independent than another woman who appears to have it all. Instrumental caretaking—accompanying a sister to a doctor's appointment or cooking dinner for her family when she is feeling ill—may be far less burdensome than the emotional care-taking described by Sophie, who felt that she had to be available at any moment to jump into her sister's troubled world and advise her.

Think objectively about how much your sister actually needs your help to get through life. Don't rush to answer that question—really think about it. Have there been times in her life when she was more independent? What was going on that made those times possible? When you go away or are unable to assist her, who else does she rely upon? Do others see her as more competent than you do? Does she express ambivalence about leaning on you? Would she feel better about herself if she could stand on her own two feet?

When you accept that your sister may be a more well-rounded, multidimensional person than you see her to be, you will discover strengths in her personality that may get expressed occasionally but that you tend to minimize. Sometimes it's just easier to take care of someone else than it is to step back and have to worry about whether she is taking care of herself. No matter to what extent you believe that your sister actually needs help, there is always some area in which you can encourage her independence without putting her at risk.

Paula, for example, told how her family had been having Christmas dinner at her house for twenty-five years, every single year. This past Christmas, she was tired and told them she couldn't handle it. Surprisingly, her purportedly incompetent sister, Josie, volunteered to take over. Josie's apartment was too small to fit the whole family, so she offered to bring the food and host the dinner at their elderly parents' home. Paula wrote, "It was a lesson to me because when you're very competent, there's no room for other people to show that they can be competent, too."

Encouraging Independence

When I teach parenting classes, one of the suggestions I make to parents who want to foster independence in their children is that once a child becomes capable of doing something for herself, the parents shouldn't do it for her anymore. When a four-year-old has learned to tie her shoes, for example, she should be in charge of shoe-tying from then on. It will probably take a whole lot longer than when the parent does it, and the bow may become untied in five minutes, but by being allowed to add that skill to her repertoire, little by little she will master it and be proud that she did.

The same holds true in caretaking relationships. You may need to be a little less competent to foster independence in your sister. She may do things less carefully than you, but, at the end of the day, she will feel better about herself. She needs to be in charge of her life, not you! When it starts to dawn on her that you are not going to help her with everything, she'll have no choice but to get motivated to do things for herself.

When a caretaker relationship has been long established, both parties stop challenging its assumptions. It is expected that the caretaker is more able to handle problems. By highlighting the things your sister can do for herself, you are challenging that assumption. Each time you turn the tables and expect her to manage something on her own, you chip away at her self-image as an incompetent person. It's also important not to feel guilty if she tells you that the reason you are not spending as much time on her problems is that you don't care. On the contrary, it's because you do care that you are encouraging her strengths, whether she sees it that way or not.

Turn conversations away from a constant discussion of her problems. Try to spend as little time as you politely can on her complaints

MAGNIFY HER STRENGTHS

Highlight the things that your sister *can* do for herself, and minimize the focus on those things that she needs help with.

and focus on the topics that she raises that are more positive. By high-lighting the positives, you will be indicating to her that she is more than a bunch of problems and that you are interested in other sides of her. It is basically a technique that makes use of positive reinforce-ment—people will naturally do more of behavior that is approved of by others. I am reminded of a story my husband told about his Psy-chology 101 class at college. The professor had the habit of walking back and forth across the front of the room as he lectured. The stu-dents didn't like the professor much, so they decided to play a trick on him and shape his behavior using the very technique he was lecturing on—positive reinforcement. They planned that whenever he was on the right side of the classroom, they would look very interested, take copious notes, and nod at whatever he was saying. Whenever he was on the left side of the room, they would look bored and distracted, play with their pens, and stare up at the ceiling. After a few classes, the students had succeeded in corralling the professor, 90 percent of the time, into the right side of the room. In the same way, if you consis-tently spike your interest when your sister is talking about her accom-plishments, however rarely that occurs, she will slowly become more likely to talk about the positives in her life.

You will need to stop feeling so sorry for her. Feeling sorry for her puts the focus on her deficits. When you pity someone, they feel piti-ful and learn to feel sorry for themselves. Although she may have expe-rienced real suffering, there is probably another side to her story that doesn't require your pity. At the very least, she does have you in her life!

You will also have to stop feeling sorry for yourself! Having a sis-ter who worries you is the deck you've been dealt. Now, how are you going to extract meaning from that fact and challenge yourself to cre-ate balance in your own life? You may feel trapped, but the truth is that most people do have options—they just don't like them. Dependence is a pas de deux you do together. It can't exist, or persist, if one of you stops dancing.

Empowerment

When you talk to your sister about her problems, your words and attitude serve to either empower or discourage her. If you sound very worried or anxious, if you jump to solve problems for her, if you get easily irritated, by the end of the conversation, she will probably feel more anxious, helpless, and frustrated. If, however, you are able to step back and look at the big picture, remain calm, and encourage her to think of options for herself, she will leave the conversation feeling more hopeful. For example, when my kids were little, they would often come to me with their problems or with decisions they had to make. I would often adopt a "dummy" stance—as though I had no idea what the right answer would be—and encourage them to talk through their thinking on the issue. I could easily have said "do this" or "do that," but that wouldn't have taught *them* how to think. Instead, I would say, "Hmm, that's a hard decision. What have you been thinking about it?" and then gave them space to talk it through. By the end of the conversation, they would have figured out what they wanted to do, with me listening carefully and just clarifying their thoughts.

Discouraging

Look at the following example of a discouraging interchange between Mary-Lou (in the caretaker role) and Abby:

ABBY: I hate my boss and I think I'm going to quit that job. The guy is always on my case. It wasn't my fault that I was late again. If I hadn't stopped for gas on the way, I would have run out!

MARY-LOU: I don't understand why you didn't get gas yesterday. Anyway, you can't quit your job. You've only been there three months and you're not covered by unemployment insurance.

In this exchange, Abby is blowing off steam about her boss giving her a hard time. She's trying to get Mary-Lou's agreement that it wasn't her fault that she was late. She probably knows full well that her sister would not want her to quit her job and expects that her sister will put the brakes on her plans. Mary-Lou is playing her expected part and entering into the drama with Abby. She's thinking through the issue for Abby and both admonishing her (*You should have gotten gas yesterday*) and instructing her (*Don't quit your job*) as though it were her problem, too. By the end of the interchange, Abby probably feels annoyed that her sister doesn't see it her way and Mary-Lou probably feels irritated that Abby would be so irresponsible as to think about quitting, and they both feel disempowered.

Encouraging

Now, let's play the scene again with Mary-Lou taking a different position—one in which she takes that step back and lets Abby solve her own problem—an empowering conversation.

ABBY: I hate my boss and I think I'm going to quit that job. The guy is always on my case. It wasn't my fault that I was late again. If I hadn't stopped for gas on the way, I would have run out!

MARY-LOU: Sounds like that guy is really hard to take. That must have been a dilemma, deciding whether to get gas when you knew it could have made you late.

Does that feel different to you? In this case, Mary-Lou is not telling her what to do. She's acknowledging Abby's feeling (*That guy is hard to take*) and restating the situation (*You had a dilemma about whether to stop for gas*). By not telling her what to do, she is indicating that she has confidence in Abby's ability to problem-solve. She may not like the thought that Abby is tempted to quit, but she doesn't sound

---

EMPOWERING CONVERSATIONS

- Acknowledge her feelings.
- Restate the problem in a neutral way.
- Let her know that you have confidence that she will come up with a good solution.

---

very invested in Abby's decision, one way or the other. At the end of this interchange, Abby may feel that her sister understands her anger and can see the dilemma about whether to stop for gas. Abby may feel a bit up in the air because Mary-Lou avoided her usual responsible role. Eventually, however, that will lead Abby to learn that she has to figure things out for herself. And throughout, it feels like Mary-Lou is dealing with this as if it's Abby's problem to sort out, not her own.

In telling her story, Abby is clearly inviting her sister to get involved. What Mary-Lou chooses to do with that invitation is what makes the difference. If Mary-Lou had wanted to try to influence the decision, the two sisters may have got into an arm-wrestle about whether Abby should leave her job. Taking that step back requires that Mary-Lou not be too invested in the outcome. Of course, there may be implications if Abby quits, but really, in the final analysis, it's Abby's choice and Abby's life. That's a hard, but necessary, pill for her sister to swallow. If Mary-Lou could stop taking responsibility for Abby's decisions, even if it means that Abby will make mistakes, then the relationship between them would become more equal and mature.

Taking a Step Back

I want to focus for a moment on the concept of taking a step back. In typical caretaking relationships, some issues act as triggers, causing both sisters to slip into their old roles. For example, when the needier sister talks about dropping out of school, not paying her parking ticket, or fighting with her neighbor, the caretaking sister becomes nervous. The caretaking sister grabs hold of each of those scenarios and projects them into the future. "If my sister drops out of school, then she will be stuck in a minimum-wage job, and who is going to have to pay for her health insurance?" Or, "If she doesn't pay that parking ticket, she will get in trouble with the law and probably end up with a huge fine to pay." Or, "If she gets into another fight with her neighbor, she's going to get kicked out of her apartment and then where is she going to live?" The fears don't come out of nothing—there is probably enough history there to warrant worrying—but by projecting the scenario to its disastrous conclusion, the caretaking sister justifies jumping in and taking over. Doing so, even just giving advice, helps lessen *her* anxiety—at least she feels more in control. But by getting involved, the situation may become more complex for the sister with the problem. That sister has both the problem (*I'm fighting with my neighbor*) as well as her caretaking sister's reaction to the problem to contend with. She may get more confused, trying to do what her sister wants her to do even if it doesn't jibe with her own assessment of the situation.

The situation gets simplified when the caretaker sister takes a step back, permitting her sister to solve her own problem. The caretaker would have to learn to talk herself down from the anxiety of not being in control. She would have to learn how to stay in the present moment (*No, she's not getting kicked out of her apartment; she's just having a fight with a neighbor*). If she can keep her perspective, she can avoid the knee-jerk reaction to help. What the caretaking sister needs to learn to do is similar to what nervous flyers should do when they encounter turbulence. They need to stay in the present moment and talk themselves down from the fear (*No, the plane is not crashing, it's just a bumpy ride*). Learning the trick of staying in the present moment makes living a whole lot more comfortable.

Caring for the Caretaker

People often ask me how therapists cope with listening to clients' problems all day long—don't we feel overwhelmed by the amount of suffering that we come in contact with daily? After all, we are all professional caretakers. Learning how to remain separate yet empathetic to our clients' pain is one of the first skills that people in the helping professions need to develop. After all, we wouldn't be very effective if we were sobbing along with the people who consult with us.

During the years of my practice, however, there certainly have been times when I was profoundly troubled by a client's story. I have learned that the best way to regain my balance is by immersing myself in peace and beauty. For me, that might mean a trip to the botanical gardens, a walk in the park, or a visit to the museum. In good weather, I might take a hike in the country. In the winter, a long walk on a snowy afternoon helps bring me back. I'll listen to some beautiful music or go to a funny movie. It's so easy to get caught up in the problems of day-to-day life that it's sometimes an effort to remember that I need to nurture myself. However, anyone who is a caretaker for any reason must remember that it's absolutely essential to care for herself.

You need to think about ways to protect your own energy, especially if your sister does concretely require your help. Another way for caretakers to maintain balance is to put limits on giving. I often suggest to families that are caught up with illness or other troubles that it helps to put an artificial limit on how much of their lives will be consumed by worry. Everyone's entitled to be "off-duty" for some part of the day. For example, you can make a rule—no obsessing about your sister after 7:00 P.M. and on Sundays. Confine your worrying to daylight hours. Don't pay attention to those disturbed thoughts that come to you in the night between midnight and 6 A.M.—those witching hours tend to distort reality. Haven't there been times when you've woken up in the morning after a disturbed night and said to yourself, "What *was* I thinking!"

Make sure to take vacations! Your sister may not like it, but you need to get away from it all from time to time. If she actually needs care, let someone else do the job for a while. Give yourself permission to completely forget about her while you are away. By getting away, you refresh your mind and gain some perspective. Things often look less dire when you're away from them for a while.

Remember to delegate! Other relatives can help out. You may have trained your family to assume that looking after your sister's needs is your job and yours alone. Start to change that by asking for help. Be creative. Is there an old friend or neighbor who can pick up a small part? You may hate to ask, but sometimes others like to feel needed, too. You don't have to keep it all for yourself. If your sister is disabled, have you explored all of the community resources that may offer her some variety and you some respite?

Women are often susceptible to feeling guilty when they put themselves first. We females have been taught that the worst thing we can be accused of is being selfish. Think about that word—*selfish*. If you take the emotion out of it and just register the meaning, doesn't it sound like you are being blamed for taking care of your "self"? Is that really so bad? Where is it written that women must always take care of others *before* themselves?

Finally, be sure not to be a caretaker in all of your relationships. When you have strengthened the muscle that makes it possible for you to look after your sister, it may be hard for you to relax it with other people. Let your friends and family look after you sometimes. Permit yourself to put your feet up and ease into their loving arms. You deserve it!

10

Lily and Peggy

That Sister Stamp

Recognizing Its Influence on You

"Being part of this study got me thinking about all of my good friends and their places in the family makeup. I realize now that my four closest friends are all youngest sisters like myself (the youngest of four sisters). Do I look for a certain similar trait in these friends, perhaps that they are more deferring or flexible, less judgmental?"

—LUCY, twenty-four years old

Hidden Dimensions

Before she was sensitized to the effect of her TOMY position on her adult choices, Lucy was oblivious to how she naturally seeks out younger sisters like herself as friends. After she'd done some thinking about it, however, that preference became clear to her. Those hidden dimensions that shape our lives sometimes require a bit of sleuthing to reveal. Here's a recent example from my own life.

As part of my work of teaching beginning family therapists, I supervise a small group of students at an institute. I usually work with a coteacher. This year, a supervisor-in-training named Melissa was assigned to work with me; this was to be the first time she was supervising family therapists. By the end of our initial two-hour session, I became aware that I was feeling intimidated by Melissa. Although I am a seasoned supervisor, I still found myself seeking her approval. In the days following that first class, I was preoccupied with trying to understand my reaction. Then the penny dropped. Had I subconsciously been relating to her as if she were my domineering sister whom I felt that I could never come up against? Was Melissa unwittingly playing out a hardwired overfunctioning role, feeling that *she* had to be responsible for the group? I guessed that Melissa must be an older sister!

As soon as that realization filtered its way into my consciousness, I relaxed. I could see that I had probably sniffed out Melissa's natural alpha position and assumed my own little sister stance without the slightest awareness of doing so. Regardless of our assigned roles in the classroom, in our heart of hearts, she was still a big sister and I was a little one. Anxiously looking forward to the next class so that I could check out my theory, I wrote, "Melissa is an older sister," on a slip of paper and stuck it in my wallet. I really hoped that the statement would turn out to be true, not only because it would explain my weird reaction but also because it would further confirm the premise of this book. As it turns out, Melissa *is* an older sister *and . . .* she's the oldest of four!

In the arena of our classroom, she and I were reenacting some deeply imbedded internal script that really had nothing to do with each other as individuals—we hardly even knew each other. When I understood this hidden dynamic between Melissa and myself, it was easy to stop feeling intimidated. I was able to remember that, although I'm a little sister, I'm also an experienced supervisor. I made a choice to downplay the "little sister" identity in my own mind and strengthen that of the "competent professional." Deciding to do so liberated me. Our next class was the best I've ever participated in.

How strong the stamps of those TOMY positions are! It doesn't matter how old we are or how much insight we have—even if we've just spent two years thinking and writing about sister relationships. Those hidden dynamics are so powerful that, in our current relationships, we may be unconsciously reading from an old script. We assume that our reactions to people are based solely on our response to their personalities, but as we become ever more aware of the stamp that being a sister makes, we can recognize another dimension at work.

My Party Trick

I now find that I can often recognize a woman's TOMY position without her telling me, as I did with Melissa. The personality traits that stem from each role have become so sharply defined that I seem to be able to call it, even based on some pretty flimsy evidence. For example, I was shopping at a boutique a while ago, and in the course of chatting with the saleswomen, I mentioned that I was writing this book. The woman who had been helping me was very interested and told how happy she was that she didn't have any sisters; she loved being the only girl because it meant that she didn't have to compete with another female for attention. Another saleswoman surprised me by echoing the same sentiment—she also loved being the only girl among brothers. The cashier, who hadn't said anything up to that point, countered that *she*, on the other hand, loved having three sisters. I glanced at her. The way she was standing triggered something in my mind, and, without thinking, I said, "I'll bet you're the third out of the four girls." Everyone stopped and stared at me. I really don't know how I knew, but I did. I must have been using that sixth sense that Malcolm Gladwell described in his book, *Blink*, the one that permits you to know something even though you can't put your finger on the steps that brought you there—you go straight from *A* to *Z*, without stopping at *B*, *C*, *D*, and *E*. I've learned so many subtle signs about sister roles that I can now use my sixth sense to identify a woman's TOMY position, and I don't even know how I do it!

I'm now finding my party trick easy to do in my therapy work with new clients. Last week, I met with a young couple for their first session of marriage counseling. Like so many couples, they came in to talk about their problems communicating, and as they were talking, something about the way the wife insisted on being in the spotlight rang a bell. I was thinking about them after they left and realized that the wife had a "younger sister" quality to her. When I checked this out the next week, it turned out to be the case.

What is the point of this intriguing but useless party trick? It's not that I've become a psychic, but that women's smallest gestures unknowingly broadcast their TOMY position to an informed observer. The roles women played in their families growing up affect their personalities so profoundly that although the clues may not be obvious all of the time, they are certainly evident a good portion of the time. Once our eyes are opened to what's going on, it becomes possible to soften the influence and to do things differently.

Being able to recognize that sister stamp in yourself makes it easier to decipher why you respond to others as you do. If you're a younger sister, are you hypersensitive about being belittled? Do you hear yourself regularly saying, "S'not fair!"? Do you get insulted if things don't go your way? If you're a middle sister, is your first impulse to walk away from problems? Do you find yourself always ready to be accommodating? Do you tend to see things as black and white? If you're an older sister, are you overly critical? Do you take on responsibility for making sure everything works out? Do you find it hard to let others take care of you? If you're a twin, do you seek out ultraclose relationships? Are you sensitive to issues of inequality? Do you find that you easily feel lonely?

If you recognize yourself in these TOMY position archetypes, you can cut yourself some slack for falling into those patterns. You react that way not because of some quirk of your personality but because your TOMY position programs you to do so. You can now appreciate how your imprinted but unconscious sister stamp influences your relationships and start to identify why you get along well with some people and have problems with others.

Identifying Your Sister Factor

Get a blank piece of paper, and take a minute to write down your answers to the following questions. They will help you put into words the ways in which being a sister shaped who you are:

1. What particular stamp has being an older, middle, younger, twin, conflicted, caretaker, or bonded sister made on your personality?
2. What features of that stamp do you value and want to keep?
3. What features of that stamp do you want to change?
4. What would you have to do differently to soften the effect of that stamp?

Now that you have identified how your TOMY position has imprinted your personality and have determined which features of that imprint you want to keep and which you want to discard, you're probably going to be hyperaware of your reactions to people over the next days and weeks. You'll be able to say, "That's my sister stamp at work!" when you see yourself falling into those old patterns with people, as I did with my cosupervisor, Melissa. You'll probably have more clarity about why you have chosen certain friends, why you are uncomfortable with particular people at work, or why you always seem to be competing with your partner for dominance.

As an older sister, you may become conscious of the teacherly tone of voice you use when explaining things to people. As a middle sister, you may find yourself tempted to show how competent you are and take a more dominant role. As a younger sister, you may think twice about asking for help or, conversely, let someone help you without feeling diminished by it. As a twin, you may think about widening your circle of friends. Although these may not be your particular issues, your awareness of how being a sister shaped your identity will come into sharper focus as time goes on.

In the course of thinking about how my TOMY position affected me, for example, like Lucy from the opening quote of this chapter, I realized that ten of my twelve closest women friends are older than me. I'm comfortable in the role of the ingenue and, therefore, seem unconsciously to seek out older friends! The strange part is, however, that nine of those ten friends, although older than me, are themselves also younger sisters. I suppose that I also best understand women whose role in their own family was the same as mine.

Sisters and Their Mothers

The effect of the sister stamp in relationships even crosses generations. At times, it is at the root of mother-daughter conflict. For example, a woman who was a younger sister in her family growing up may have learned to expect others to take care of her. She may have incorporated that expectation into her personality so much so that as a mother, she leans a bit too heavily on her oldest daughter for support.

One of my clients, twenty-five-year-old Felicia, the oldest of four sisters, often fumes about how her mother is so helpless and dependent. The woman had never learned to drive, and because they live in the country, she counts on her daughter to transport her everywhere. However, when Felicia mentioned in passing that her mother was the youngest of eight children, I was able to understand an important reason why her mother was so dependent. Felicia's mother had grown up being doted on by her parents and seven brothers and sisters; when she had her own children, she unconsciously tried to recreate this pattern. Through identifying the role her mother's TOMY position played, Felicia accepted that this dependency was not due solely to a flaw in her mother's personality. It was at least partly the result of an unconscious effort to resume the position she had enjoyed in her family growing up—one that provided her with a familiar sense of safety and comfort. Felicia also became aware of how her own hyperresponsible character as the eldest caused her to try to solve her mother's problems while, at the same time, resenting being asked to do so. As this all became clear, Felicia's level of frustration dropped dramatically.

Sisters and Their Daughters

TOMY position patterning also affects women in their relationships with their own daughters. Several older sisters in The Sisters Project commented that they find the job of being a parent very familiar. Those older sisters, who were given a lot of praise and status in the surrogate mother role growing up, tend to find raising their own children a pleasure. Those who were burdened with too much responsibility and not given adequate support by their parents when they were kids sometimes experience parenting as an unwelcome chore. Several older sisters said that by the time they reached adulthood, they felt like they'd already raised a bunch of kids.

I have often worked with mothers who have a hard time being appropriately parental with their own daughters. It always amazes me how a three-year-old can push a grown woman's buttons and make her cry! I've noticed that mothers who have trouble controlling their little girls are often women who didn't have very much power in their own childhood families.

Several years ago, Cindy, the mother of twelve-year-old Natasha, came to see me, pleading for help in dealing with her daughter. Cindy was completely unable to set limits for Natasha, who would fly into a rage if she didn't get what she wanted. They were constantly fighting. Things had got so bad that the girl had no compunction telling her horrified mother, "Shut up! I hope you die!"—and far worse. Cindy felt completely helpless.

When I helped Cindy trace the trail back to her own childhood family, it became clear that the helpless feeling she experienced with Natasha was reminiscent of how she had felt during her own childhood. Her older sister tormented and belittled her, and her younger sister, the family princess, bossed her around mercilessly. As a child, Cindy had never learned how to stand up to overbearing females, and she wasn't much better at it as an adult. Although Natasha was *her* child, in the heat of a fight, Cindy relived the chaotic feelings she'd experienced as a little girl. Her daughter seemed to have the upper hand, which made it very hard for Cindy to really act like a mother with Natasha.

Hidden dynamics can shape mother-daughter relationships in more benign ways as well. I often see it at work in my own family. Prior to meeting with my editor for the first time, I consulted my older daughter about what I should wear. Later, we laughed about how I had slipped into the little sister role, letting her boss me around. I'll easily defer to her suggestions about restaurants or movies—I'm always impressed that she seems to know exactly what she wants. My younger daughter, however, is less invested in the choice of restaurant or movie. And she and I are both younger sisters, so we tend to defer to each other!

White Elephants

Remember the old adage, "When someone says, 'Don't think of a white elephant,' then all you can think about is white elephants!"? Well, it's become like that for me since learning about the importance of TOMY positions on women's identities. I see the effects of a woman's sister position in everything we do. I worry about becoming a terrible bore because I find it both fascinating and suddenly very obvious—I'm always drawing attention to it. I'm reminded of one of those puzzles that, at first glance, looks like a random pattern of dots. When you stare at it long enough, however, the picture camouflaged within takes shape, and once it does, you can't imagine how you didn't see it before.

The stories from the lives of the four hundred women, teens, and girls who contributed to The Sisters Project have brought to us a new understanding of the power of that sister stamp. In your childhood home, being a sister influenced how you thought about yourself and helped shape your identity. To this very day, it continues to influence how you relate to people in all facets of your world. Whether your sister's role in your life has been to clear the path, follow in your footsteps, walk by your side, or any of the myriad other possibilities, you were fashioned by the type of sister relationship you experienced. Now that you know that it's possible to soften that sister influence, as well as celebrate it, you can take charge of the hidden dynamics that have shaped your life and make them work for you.

APPENDIX A

The Sisters Project Questionnaire

1. What city or town, state or province, and country do you live in?
2. How did you hear about this study?
3. What is your occupation and that of your sister(s)?
4. What is your current age and that of your sister(s) and brother(s)?
5. How would you describe your relationship with your sister(s) growing up?
6. What roles did you and your sister(s) play in the family?
7. How did your parent(s) contribute to competitiveness or cooperativeness between you?
8. What kinds of things made you or your sister(s) jealous?
9. Could you describe a happy memory having to do with your sister(s)?
10. How about an unhappy or angry memory?
11. If you could have said just one sentence to your sister(s) growing up that expressed your true feelings about her, what would it be?

12. Did your relationship with your sister(s) have an effect on how you feel about your body and, if so, how?
13. How would you describe your relationship as adults?
14. If you could say just one sentence to your sister(s) now, what would it be?
15. How do you think being a younger, middle, or older sister has shaped your view of yourself as an adult, apart from the family?
16. How do you think being a younger, older, or middle sister has affected you in terms of your self-confidence?
17. Do you see yourself acting like a younger, middle, or older sister with other people and, if so, how?
18. If you had a choice, would you rather have been a younger, middle, or older sister?
19. How do you think your life would be different if you were the older sister instead of younger or vice versa? The older or younger sister instead of the middle?
20. Could you say how your life would be different if you didn't have a sister?
21. Anything else you would like to tell about your relationship with your sister(s)?

(Followed by Circled Words—Appendix D)

APPENDIX B

Twins' Questionnaire

1. What city or town, state or province, and country do you live in?
2. How did you hear about this study?
3. What is your occupation and that of your sister(s)?
4. What is your current age and that of your (nontwin) sister(s) and brother(s)?
5. Do you and your twin sister have a perception of each other as older and younger?
6. How would you describe your relationship with your sister(s) growing up?
7. What roles did you and your sister(s) play in the family?
8. How did your parent(s) contribute to competitiveness or cooperativeness between you?
9. How strongly do you think you and your twin sister resemble each other physically and personality-wise?
10. Do you think that your parents accentuated your similarities or differences? How so?

11. Did you and your twin sister accentuate your similarities or differences? How so?
12. What kinds of things made you or your sister(s) jealous?
13. Do you feel that you and your twin sister have a special understanding of each other, beyond just being sisters, like a private language or means of communicating?
14. Could you describe a happy memory having to do with your sister(s)?
15. How about an unhappy or angry memory?
16. If you could have said just one sentence to your sister(s) growing up that expressed your true feelings about her, what would it be?
17. Did your relationship with your sister(s) have an effect on how you feel about your body and, if so, how?
18. How would you describe your relationship as adults?
19. If you could say just one sentence to your sister(s) now, what would it be?
20. How do you think being a twin has shaped your view of yourself as an adult, apart from the family?
21. If you had a choice, would you rather not have been a twin?
22. Could you say how your life would be different if you didn't have a sister?
23. Anything else you would like to tell about your relationship with your sister(s)?

(Followed by Circled Words—Appendix D)

Kids' Questionnaire

1. What is your age and the age of your sister(s) and brother(s)?
2. If you are older, do you remember your sister(s) being born or early days with your sister(s)? What was that like?
3. If you are older, did it feel like your relationship with your parents changed when your sister was born?
4. What do people in the family call each of you, like "the baby of the family," "the big kid," "the responsible one"? Do you have those kinds of nicknames or reputations in the family?
5. What things make you most jealous of your sister(s)?
6. Are there things that you are proud of your sister(s) about?
7. Does it feel like people compare you to your sister(s)? About what?
8. Are you in the same school with your sister(s)? What is that like?
9. How much do you feel responsible for your sister(s), and how much do you think your sister(s) feels responsible for you?
10. Do you have a wish about your sister(s)? What is it?
11. How would your life be different if you were the older or younger sister?

12. What's the best and worst part about being an older, younger, or middle sister?
13. Can you think of three words that describe what you feel about your sister(s)?
14. Can you think of a particular memory about your sister(s) that feels important?
15. Anything else about your relationship with your sister(s) that you want to share?

Kids' Questionnaire Circled Words

Circle or underline all the words that describe how you usually feel toward your sister(s). (If you have more than one sister, please copy the words and repeat the procedure for each.)

scared of her	hate her
devoted to her	love her a lot
resent her	friends with her
want to be like her	wish she would act nicer
want attention from her	proud of her
protective of her	wish she'd be nicer to parents
angry with her	sometimes wish she were dead
like her	wish she liked me
wish she'd leave me alone	wish she understood me
can't talk to her	love having her as my sister
don't care	feel sorry for her
have fun with her	adore her
jealous of her	wish we had a better relationship
other _____	other _____

Circled Words

Please indicate which words describe how you usually felt toward your sister(s) when you were growing up, by circling or underlining them. (If you have more than one sister, please copy the words and repeat the procedure for each.)

scared of her

hated her

loved her

friends with her

she hurt my feelings

wanted attention from her

sad

wished she'd be nicer to parent(s)

sometimes wished she were dead

wished she liked me

guilty

couldn't talk to her

indifferent

in awe of her

devoted to her

resented her

admired her

wished she'd behave

proud of her

protective of her

angry with her

liked her

wished she'd go away

wished she understood me

loved having her as my sister

felt sorry for her

had fun with her
jealous of her
adored her
other _____

wished we had a better
relationship
other _____

Please indicate which words describe how you usually feel about her now.

scared of her
hate her
love her
friends with her
she hurts my feelings
want attention from her
sad
wish she'd be nicer to parent(s)
sometimes wish she were dead
wish she liked me
guilty
can't talk to her
indifferent
have fun with her
jealous of her
other _____

in awe of her
devoted to her
resent her
admire her
wish she would act nicer
proud of her
protective of her
angry with her like her
wish she'd move away
wish she understood me
love having her as my sister
feel sorry for her
adore her
wish we had a better
relationship
other _____

Bibliography

Davis, Laura. *I Thought We'd Never Speak Again: The Road from Estrangement to Reconciliation*. New York: Quill, 2003.

Downing, Christine. *Psyche's Sisters: Reimagining the Meaning of Sisterhood*. San Francisco: Harper & Row Publishers, 1988.

Faber, Adele, and Elaine Mazlish. *Between Brothers and Sisters: A Celebration of Life's Most Enduring Relationship*. New York: Avon Books, 1989.

—————. *Siblings Without Rivalry: How to Help Your Children Live Together So You Can Live Too*, 10th anniversary ed. New York: HarperCollins Publishers, Inc., 1998.

Fishel, Elizabeth. *Sisters*. New York: Bantam Books, 1980.

Foster, Patricia, ed. *Sister to Sister: Women Write About the Unbreakable Bond*. New York: Anchor Books, 1995.

Ginsberg, Debra. *About My Sisters*. New York: HarperCollins Publishers, Inc., 2004.

Gladwell, Malcolm. *Blink: The Power of Thinking Without Thinking*. New York: Little, Brown and Company, 2005.

Isaacson, Cliff, and Kris Radish. *The Birth Order Effect: How to Better Understand Yourself and Others*. Avon, MA: Adams Media, 2002.

Leder, Jane Mersky. *Brothers & Sisters: How They Shape Our Lives*. New York: Ballantine Books, 1991.

Mackay, Shena, ed. *The Virago Book of Such Devoted Sisters*. London: Virago Press, 1993.

Mathias, Barbara. *Between Sisters: Secret Rivals, Intimate Friends*. New York: Delta Books, 1992.

Mauthner, Melanie L. *Sistering: Power and Change in Female Relationships*. Hampshire, England, and New York: Palgrave Macmillan, 2005.

McNaron, Toni A. H., ed. *The Sister Bond: A Feminist View of a Timeless Connection*. Oxford, England: Pergamon Press, Inc., 1985.

Messud, Claire. *When the World Was Steady*. New York: Granta Books, 1994.

Neale, Jenny. *No Friend Like a Sister: Exploring the Relationships Between Sisters*. Wellington, Australia: Victoria University Press, 2004.

O'Faolain, Nuala. *Almost There: The Onward Journey of a Dublin Woman*. New York: Riverhead Books, 2003.

Pogrebin, Letty Cottin. *Three Daughters*. New York: Farrar, Straus and Giroux, 2002.

Richardson, Dr. Ronald W., and Lois A. Richardson. *Birth Order & You*, 2nd ed. North Vancouver, BC: Self-Counsel Press, 2000.

Ripps, Susan. *Sisters: Devoted or Divided*. New York: Kensington Books, 1994.

Rueschmann, Eva. *Sisters on Screen: Siblings in Contemporary Cinema*. Philadelphia: Temple University Press, 2000.

Saline, Carol, and Sharon J. Wohlmuth. *Sisters*, 10th anniversary ed. Philadelphia: Running Press Book Publishers, 2004.

Sandmaier, Marian. *Original Kin: The Search for Connection Among Adult Sisters and Brothers*. New York: Dutton, 1994.

Index

Join the Community
of Sisters

Now you can be part of The Sisters Project! Visit my website at www.MySister-MySelf.com—the meeting place for women to share their sister stories. You can read what other women have to say about their relationships with their sisters, whether they are close or conflicted or somewhere in between, and add your own unique point of view.

I look forward to hearing from you!

www.MySister-MySelf.com